Routledge Author Guides
William Cobbett

Routledge Author Guides

GENERAL EDITOR B. C. SOUTHAM, M.A., B. LITT. (OXON.)
Formerly Department of English, Westfield College, University of London

Titles in the series

Browning by Roy E. Gridley

Byron by J. D. Jump

William Cobbett by J. Sambrook

Nietzsche by R. J. Hollingdale

Tolstoy by Ernest J. Simmons

Routledge Author Guides

William Cobbett

by

James Sambrook

Department of English
University of Southampton

Routledge & Kegan Paul
London and Boston

First published in 1973
by Routledge & Kegan Paul Ltd,
Broadway House, 68–74 Carter Lane,
London EC4V 5EL and
9 Park Street,
Boston, Mass. 02108, U.S.A.
Printed in Great Britain by
Cox and Wyman Ltd,
London, Fakenham and Reading

ISBN 0 7100 7560 X (c)
ISBN 0 7100 7561 8 (p)

Library of Congress Catalog Card No. 73–79113

For Patience

General Editor's Preface

Nowadays there is a growing awareness that the specialist areas have much to offer and much to learn from one another. The student of history, for example, is becoming increasingly aware of the value that literature can have in the understanding of the past; equally, the student of literature is turning more and more to the historians for illumination of his area of special interest, and of course philosophy, political science, sociology, and other disciplines have much to give him.

What we are trying to do in the *Routledge Author Guides* is to offer this illumination and communication by providing for non-specialist readers, whether students or the interested general public, a clear and systematic account of the life and times and works of the major writers and thinkers across a wide range of disciplines. Where the *Author Guides* may be seen to differ from other, apparently similar, series, is in its historical emphasis, which will be particularly evident in the treatment of the great literary writers, where we are trying to establish, in so far as this can be done, the social and historical context of the writer's life and times, and the cultural and intellectual tradition in which he stands, always remembering that critical and interpretative principles are implicit to any sound historical approach.

BCS

Contents

Acknowledgments

I am grateful to the Warden and Fellows of Nuffield College, Oxford for permission to quote from Cobbett manuscripts in their Library, and I wish to thank Professor J. S. Bromley, who offered me much sound advice, but is not responsible for the Cobbett-like generalizations – not to speak of errors – which remain.

I

Merry England?

Throughout his adult life Cobbett believed that he had been born in 1766, a freeman of Merry England. In fact he was born in 1763 into a civilized, pre-industrial, stable, prosperous society where most wealth, virtually all political power and many of the most cherished cultural values were attached to the land itself, a land which had just reached a fullness of cultivated beauty that it never would see again.

Cobbett himself would have been the first to agree that figures, even when accurate, are not always facts; nevertheless, the statistics, even of eighteenth-century political arithmeticians, give us some rough idea of the shape of society in Cobbett's youth. Estimates of population and income distribution were made by Gregory King (1688), Joseph Massie (1760) and Patrick Colquhoun (1803),[1] and, though Massie and Colquhoun reveal the growth of manufacturing industry, all three sketch essentially a society of the same shape.

The shape is a pyramid, of course. At its summit stood a small landed aristocracy consisting of about one-seventieth of the population and receiving about one-seventh of the entire national income; within this aristocracy were gradations of wealth from the great lords, such as the Duke of Devonshire whose gross annual rental in the year of Cobbett's birth was £35,000, to the sixth-rate gentlemen with less than two-hundred a year who lived less comfortably than some working farmers and who resembled the Duke only in the fact that they had no need to earn a living. Below the aristocracy lay the middle ranks and below these again the lower orders. Most remarkably there were, at the time of Cobbett's birth, roughly two million people (that is, nearly one-third of the population) in the middle ranks as they were then defined; they received about three-fifths of the national income, while the lower orders (who made up two-thirds of the population) received about a quarter. The middle ranks included merchants, shopkeepers, manufacturers and craftsmen who 'employed capital', clerks, civil officers, lawyers, clergymen, teachers, naval and army officers, and the numerous body of farmers both tenants and freeholders. Gradations of wealth in the middle ranks were as great as among the aristocracy. Some great overseas merchants, financiers, public officers and judges were as wealthy as some peers: they bought estates, married their daughters into the aristocracy and founded new landed families. On the other hand, there were the many curates who were not passing-rich on forty pounds a year, or the little farmers who rented thirty or forty pounds a year and worked and fared harder and were, in effect, poorer than the day-labourers they employed.[2] 'The middle ranks were distinguished at the top from the gentry and nobility not so much by lower incomes as by the necessity of earning their living, and at the bottom from the labouring poor not so much by higher incomes as by the property, however small, represented by stock-in-trade, livestock and tools, or the educational investment of skill or expertise.'[3] The lower orders included artisans, labourers, servants, soldiers, sailors, paupers and vagrants, that is, all those who had no property other than their labour. The fact that productive labour is the foundation of society and creates the wealth that the higher ranks consume had already been recognized: Arthur Young wrote in 1767 that 'the chief support of a nation ever lies in the lower ranks of its people . . . . It is agreed, by the most sensible politicians, that the true riches of any state consist in the employment of the labouring poor'.[4] Though they might make the state rich, the lower orders were, indeed, commonly called 'the poor'. Adam Smith acknowledged that poverty is 'the state of every one who must labour for subsistence',[5] but this was something very different from indigence, the miserable state of the pauper who lacked the regular means of subsistence. The English labouring poor in 1763 lived a hard, precarious life, but they probably lived more comfortably than their counterparts in every other part of the world except the North American colonies.

The gap in living standards between rich and poor was enormous, but the hierarchy of ranks was not a caste-system. Cobbett's own (admittedly remarkable) career shows that it was possible to move upon the social ladder. His life was spent partly among the lower orders as ploughboy, gardener and soldier, and partly among the middle ranks as clerk, tutor, journalist, farmer, seed-importer, publisher and news-paper-proprietor, but when he was buying land and receiving rents at Botley, and when he became a Member of Parliament, he moved into

the ranks of the lower gentry. He was not the only man of his generation to rise socially by authorship, though the more spectacular eleva-
tions came by way of trade (especially in the East and West Indies),
banking and the law. At lower levels, advancement was possible for the
industrious apprentice and even the day-labourer. In the other direction, landed families might fail through competitive expenditure,
merchants and manufacturers go bankrupt, and farmers sink to become
labourers.

The lower orders were not a 'working class' in the modern political
sense. When there was widespread industrial unemployment or when
food prices were unduly high, mobs might riot and force government
action; in 1766, for instance, in many parts of England the poor were
'driven to desperation and madness, by the exorbitant prices of all
manner of provisions' (the effect of a poor agricultural summer), and
rioted[6] until Chatham's administration was compelled to forbid the
exportation of corn; the London mob could be called out in particular
political causes, such as those of Wilkes or Gordon, but its influence on
Parliament was only marginal and intermittent. The lower orders had
no place of their own in politics; they existed to be ruled, and most of
them were scarcely aware of any agent of government other than their
local magistrates. According to Burke in 1796:[7]

> Those who, in any *political* view, are to be called the people are of
> adult age, not declining in life, of tolerable leisure for such
> discussions, and of some means of information, above menial
> dependence; i.e. about 400,000. This is the British public; and it
> is a public very numerous. The rest, when feeble, are the objects
> of protection; when strong, the means of force.

There were fewer than 400,000 Parliamentary electors at this date,
many of whom were not 'above menial dependence': so Burke's
'people' or 'public' evidently embraces all fairly well-propertied,
educated men.

The 'people' constituted certain functional interests – landed,
moneyed, commercial and manufacturing – which were the dominant
political and economic divisions within society, and it was claimed that
the principal interests were directly represented in Parliament or could
make their influence felt there. According to Arthur Young in 1794:[8]

> The principle of our constitution is the representation of property,
> imperfectly in theory, but effectively in practice ... the great

mass of property, both landed, monied and commercial, finds itself represented . . . virtual representation takes place even where the real seems most remote.

The propertyless labourers were assumed to have interests identical with 'the general interest of society' and so could also enjoy the benefits of virtual representation. Adam Smith wrote:[9]

Though the interest of the labourer is strictly connected with that of the society, he is incapable either of comprehending that interest, or of understanding its connexion with his own. His condition leaves him no time to receive the necessary information, and his education and habits are commonly such as to render him unfit to judge even though he was fully informed. In the public deliberations, therefore, his voice is little heard and less regarded.

'The general interest of society', Smith demonstrated, was 'strictly and inseparably connected' with the interest of the landed order: 'Whatever either promotes or obstructs the one, necessarily promotes or obstructs the other. When the public deliberates concerning any regulation of commerce or policy the proprietors of land never can mislead it.'[10] So it was right and proper that most Members of Parliament and most of the men whose 'influence' elected them should be landed gentlemen. Nevertheless, there was a long-standing fear that a Parliament, even when it consisted largely of landed men, might fail to serve the general interest of society if it were corrupted by the ministers of the Crown, or by unduly powerful commercial and moneyed interests, or by a combination of both. Opposition spokesmen claimed that such a hellish combination occurred during the long period of Walpole's power, and in the union of King's Friends, East India Company nominees and other moneyed men which brought the younger Pitt no less securely to power in 1784. In the face of some traditional habits of thought it was of little significance that one of these men was a Whig, and the other a Tory, since any strong Prime Minister with a secure, long-standing majority in Parliament spelt danger.

Blackstone, writing in 1766 and summarizing over a century of English political thought, declared that the independence of Parliament from the Crown, the separation of the legislative and the executive powers, was the cornerstone of political liberty. Any tendency to unite in one man or one body of men the right both of making and of enforcing the laws spelt tyranny.[11] Cobbett often referred to Blackstone; and to Bolingbroke, too:[12]

In a constitution like ours, the safety of the whole depends on the balance of the parts, and the balance of the parts on their mutual independency of each other, for this reason Mr. Rapin observes very justly 'that there are but two ways of depriving the English of their liberties; either by laying aside parliaments, or bribing them.' And in another place he says, 'that the English freedom will be at an end whenever the court invades the free election of parliaments.'

The 'Court', that is the King's ministers, had, seemingly, made a move towards the 'laying aside' of parliaments, when the Septennial Act was passed at the beginning of the reign of George I. Bolingbroke claimed that the seven-year interval between elections made it easier for the Ministry to bribe and corrupt Members of Parliament, so he advocated annual parliaments. Swift – Cobbett's greatest literary hero – agreed, believing that annual parliaments were part of the medieval constitution of England and an example of Gothic wisdom.[13]

The Court could corrupt Parliament and influence its decisions by giving offices, pensions and contracts to Members and their dependants. From time to time, independent country gentlemen and other 'patriots' cried out against the presence of such 'placemen'; and there was even a clause in the Act of Settlement (1701), enacting that after the Hanoverian succession 'no person who has an office or place of profit under the King, or receives a pension from the Crown shall be capable of serving as a member of the House of Commons'. Nevertheless, under Walpole's and his successors' well-oiled apparatus of 'influence', the Court invaded both the workings of, and the elections to, Parliament, and perhaps it was as well for the efficient and continuous working of government that they did so. Instead of political parties in the modern sense there were, as Sir Lewis Namier has shown,[14] only shifting alliances between various 'connexions'; but any administration that was to be stable had to gather to itself a well-disciplined 'Court and Treasury Party', consisting of such 'placemen and pensioners' as civil, judicial, military and naval officers, court officials, government contractors and others who were obliged to it for their employments and seats. This was the jobbery and bribery much complained of by 'patriots'; but it never became a wholesale corruption of Parliament. Any successful administration had to obtain the confidence of a substantial body of relatively independent members who wished to see the King's government carried on effectively, but who sought the patronage of the Crown to only a small degree. Parliamentary opposition consisted of a less stable alliance between various groups of 'outs' who longed for the spoils of office and a core of Tory country gentlemen who were truly 'independent' in that they desired no offices or pensions and maintained in all its purity the constitutional theory of separated powers – under which the King chose his 'servants', or his ministers, and the House of Commons existed as a kind of watch-dog, guarding the 'public interest' and acting as a check and balance against the King's servants. These independent country gentlemen constituted, in effect, an old-fashioned, backward-looking 'Country Party' which was a serious political force largely on account of its nuisance value. Such a party, by its very nature, could never form an administration, and, just as naturally, it saw political questions in relatively simple terms. In or about the very year of Cobbett's birth that staunch old High Tory Member of Parliament for the University of Oxford, Sir Roger Newdigate, sketched the political scene during the previous half-century, and summed up the Country Party attitude which was to be Cobbett's inheritance:[15]

> Tories were the friends of liberty, watchful against every
> encroachment of prerogative, enemies of oppression and
> corruption and every ministerial art or abuse. From the Whigs,
> the boasted advocates for liberty, proceeded septennial parliaments,
> standing armies, revenue officers without number, riot act,
> martial law. These were the fruits of a 50 year Whig administration.
> To restrain prerogative within due bounds, and to punish
> corrupt and abandoned ministers, has been the Sisyphean labour
> of a party ridiculously called Tories, unjustly called Jacobites, but
> who deserve civic crowns as the genuine friends of their country.
> From their hands they have derived a nobler name – the Country
> party, as opposed to administration, to watch the encroachments
> which power, the great corrupter of the human mind, is always
> at work to make. No other names or distinction as a party will
> they acknowledge. They equally disdain the names of Tory and
> Jacobite, they abhor the principles of both. They are the
> disinterested friends of their country, unmoved by all the
> discouragements of power, or opprobrium of the vulgar who

follow or admire it; declared enemies to bad men and bad measures.

In the 1760s the old rhetoric against placemen and pensioners was still heard constantly. A month after Cobbett's birth there appeared the famous Number 45 of the *North Briton* in which Wilkes attacked the King's servants and government corruption, and began that intermittent popular agitation which grew eventually into the Radical movements to which Cobbett would attach himself. Placemen and pensioners were a prominent issue in the first general election to take place after Cobbett was born. Even the cautious and respectable *Gentleman's Magazine* complained (on the score of expense rather than corruption) of superfluous pensioners and placemen supported in luxury out of taxes levied upon hungry day-labourers,[16] while a more ranging and damning attack was made at this time in the *Political Register* – a periodical which anticipates in more than its title Cobbett's famous journal. The *Political Register* ran from 1767 to 1772 and was written by John Almon, friend of Wilkes and publisher of 'Junius'. During the 1768 election, he denounced placemen, pensioners, boroughmongers, standing armies, the power of the House of Lords, the unequal and irregular representation of the people in the House of Commons, and called for equal Parliamentary constituencies, wider suffrage, annual elections and a militia or 'citizen-army'. This was a form of conservative hostility to 'Court' very different from the Toryism of Bolingbroke and Swift, for where they placed the defence of the constitution in the hands of independent landed men, Almon, and other men of his day who called themselves 'Commonwealthmen' or 'Real Whigs' and believed they were the heirs of Algernon Sidney, Hampden and Harrington, placed it in the hands of the vaguely defined 'people'. Of course, for Almon, as for nearly all eighteenth- and many nineteenth-century reformers, 'the people' expressly excluded 'the illiterate rabble, who have neither capacity for judging of matters of government, nor property to be concerned for'.[17] However, Wilkes in 1776 guardedly suggested that 'Some share . . . in the power of making those laws which deeply interest them . . . should be reserved even to this inferior but most useful set of men' [the day-labourers and mechanics];[18] and, in the same year, Major John Cartwright asserted the principle of universal adult male suffrage according to his notion of a mythical 'Gothick' constitution.[19]

Since everyone paid indirect taxes, the right of universal suffrage might appear to be implicit in the principle of 'no taxation without representation', revived at this time by the rebellious American colonists and their many English sympathizers; but it was a right that could easily be rejected, if one accepted the notion of 'virtual representation' expounded so plausibly by Burke.

In 1780, when the government was blundering through its expensive and disastrous war against the American colonists, reform movements were begun by several groups of upper-class 'patriots' who wanted to reduce the influence in Parliament of the Crown and of certain aristocratic factions. Burke, as spokesman for the aristocratic Rockingham Whigs, introduced a parliamentary motion for 'economical reform' intended to eliminate certain sinecures in the gift of the Crown, while, outside Westminster, the 'Yorkshire Association' of country gentlemen and freeholders had begun their county meetings and petitions to Parliament calling for short (i.e. triennial) parliaments, a redistribution of parliamentary seats to abolish rotten boroughs and provide more equal representation, and calling, too, for the reduction of corrupt influence and profligate expenditure by the government. From such activity inside and outside Westminster stemmed the Whigs' concern for limited parliamentary reform which Cobbett would share for a while.

Cobbett was a great organizer of county meetings and petitions, and never (or hardly ever) lost his faith in their efficacy as political tools, despite the fact that the government of the day generally looked upon them with the cynicism that Johnson displays in his *The False Alarm* (1770):[20]

> The progress of a petition is well known. An ejected placeman goes down to his county or his borough, tells his friends of his inability to serve them, and his constituents of the corruption of the government. His friends readily understand that he who can get nothing, will have nothing to give. They agree to proclaim a meeting, meat and drink are plentifully provided, a crowd is easily brought together, and those who think they know the reason of their meeting, undertake to tell those who know it not. Ale and clamour unite their powers, the crowd, condensed and heated, begins to ferment with the leaven of sedition. All see a thousand evils, though they cannot shew them, and grow impatient for a remedy, though they know not what.
>
> A speech is made by the Cicero of the day, he says much, and

suppresses more, and credit is equally given to what he tells, and what he conceals. The petition is read and universally approved. Those who are sober enough to write, add their names, and the rest would sign it if they could. . . .

The petition is then handed from town to town, and from house to house, and wherever it comes the inhabitants flock together that they may see that which must be sent to the king. Names are easily collected. One man signs because he hates the papists; another because he has vowed destruction to the turnpikes; one because it will vex the parson; another because he owes his landlord nothing; one because he is rich; another because he is poor; one to shew that he is not afraid, and another to shew that he can write.

If the 'Court' was one threat to liberty and the general welfare of society, as 'independent' landed men understood them, the 'City' was another. The years following the foundation of the Bank of England in 1694 saw the rapid growth of banks, stock-markets and other elaborate financial institutions. Government was no longer to be financed only by current revenue but by loans from wealthy subjects to whom it would return perpetual interest on a perpetual National Debt. People of many kinds – trustees of charitable bodies, spinsters, widows, professional men and foreigners (especially the Dutch) – lent money to the government by purchasing stock issued by the Bank of England and the great chartered companies. The most prominent individual lenders, however, were City of London merchants and financiers, and it was these men, together with all who worked in the Stock Exchange as factors, jobbers or brokers, and anyone else closely involved in the complicated new machinery of public credit, who constituted the moneyed interest. While financiers always formed only a tiny minority in Parliament itself, they exercised a disproportionately large influence because any administration needed the confidence of the moneyed interest to maintain the system of public credit without which national finances would collapse. This dependence seemed to grow as the National Debt swelled from three million to one hundred and fifty million pounds in the seventy years before Cobbett was born.

It seemed to many men that the moneyed interest, working in-sidiously behind government, had devised a mysterious machine for enriching itself and impoverishing the rest of the nation. Swift's papers in the *Examiner* (1711) worked upon the suspicions many of the 'people' shared, that 'through the contrivance and cunning of stock-jobbers there hath been brought in such a complication of knavery and cozenage, such a mystery of iniquity, and such an unintelligible jargon of terms to involve it in, as were never known in any other age or country of the world';[21] and Pope, in the *Epistle to Bathurst* (1733) created a frightening comic fantasy of the diabolical workings of 'blest paper-credit'. Men's worst suspicions about the iniquity of paper-credit were confirmed by the South Sea Bubble of 1720, but the Treasury and the City learned the lessons of that affair, so that for the rest of the eighteenth century English public finance was more honest and efficient than that of any other European country. Had it not been so, England could not have fought its many expensive wars so success-fully. Nevertheless, prejudice against stock-jobbers in particular and moneyed men in general persisted – and not only among Tories. In 1723 those Commonwealthmen, Trenchard and Gordon, who wrote under the virtuous pseudonym of 'Cato' exclaimed:[22]

> What Briton, blessed with any sense of virtue, or with common sense; what Englishman, animated with a public spirit, or with any spirit, but must burn with rage and shame, to behold the nobles and gentry of a great Kingdom, men of magnanimity, men of breeding, men of understanding, and of letters; to see such men bowing down, like Joseph's sheaves, before the face of a dirty stock-jobber, and receiving laws from men bred behind counters, and the decision of their fortunes from hands still dirty with sweeping shops!

Such hostility was reinforced by racial prejudice, for, as many stock-jobbers were Jews, it was readily assumed that all were. The extra-ordinary rise of Sampson Gideon as financial adviser to the government in the 1740s and 1750s shocked many contemporaries.

The growing power of the moneyed interest seemed to pervert the natural order of government. Swift wrote in 1721: 'I ever abominated that scheme of politics (now about thirty years old) of setting up a money'd interest in opposition to the landed. For, I conceived, there could not be a truer maxim in our government than this, that the possessors of the soil are the best judges of what is for the advantage of the kingdom.'[23] Moneyed men whose property was liquid could have little real care for the kingdom since no tangible part of it belonged to them. As John Toland declared in 1701, government should be in the hands only of men with considerable landed estate who 'have a firm pledge in England to answer for their behaviour'; moneyed men could 'remove their effects into another country in four-and-twenty hours, and follow themselves the next night'.[24] So, in order to check the moneyed interest, the Tory majority in 1711 passed Bolingbroke's Landed Property Qualification Act which was intended 'to preserve the constitution and freedom of Parliament' by excluding from the House of Commons all except substantial landed men. In so far as it was not a dead letter, this Act merely encouraged more men of wealth to buy country estates, in many cases displacing old landed families who truly represented the 'landed interest'. The King of Brobdingnag asked Gulliver whether the English Commons chose as their representatives strangers with fat purses of money, or landed men from the neighbourhood; in the election of 1768, John Almon cautioned voters against 'fund-mongers, stock-jobbers, directors of incorporated companies, government contractors, court-jobbers, and such other sorts of people as may be rather styled instruments of power and preyers upon the people';[25] but the moneyed men inside and outside Parliament continued to exercise their influence upon government.

In Cobbett's youth the most celebrated denunciations of the moneyed men, the 'muck worms', came from the great Lord Chatham. The following passage from a speech in the House of Lords on 22 November 1770 was used as a motto in Cobbett's *Political Register* (25 January 1806):

> There is a set of men, my Lords, in the city of London, who are known to live in riot and luxury upon the plunder of the ignorant, the innocent, the helpless; upon that part of the community, which stands most in need of, and that best deserves, the care and protection of the legislature. To me, my Lords, whether they be miserable jobbers of Change Alley, or the lofty Asiatic plunderers of Leadenhall Street, they are all equally detestable. I care but little whether a man walks on foot, or is drawn by eight horses, or six horses; if his luxury be supported by the plunder of his country, I despise and detest him. My Lords, while I had the honour of serving his Majesty, I never ventured to look at the Treasury but at a distance: it is a business I am unfit for, and to which I could never have submitted. The little I know of it has not served to raise my opinion of what is vulgarly called the 'Monied Interest'; I mean, that blood-sucker, that muckworm, that calls itself 'the friend of

government'; that pretends to serve this or that administration, and may be purchased, on the same terms, by any administration; advances money to government and takes special care of its emoluments. Under this description, I include the whole race of commissaries, jobbers, contractors, clothiers, and remitters. Yet, I do not deny, that, even with those creatures, some management may be necessary; and, I hope, my Lords, that nothing I have said will be understood to extend to the honest industrious tradesman, who holds the middle rank, and has given repeated proofs, that he prefers law and liberty to gold. Much less would I be thought to reflect upon the fair merchant, whose liberal commerce is the prime source of national wealth. I esteem his occupation, and respect his character.

The manufacturing interest counted for little when Cobbett was born, but its importance and influence would grow in his lifetime. The commercial interest was important but aroused far less resentment than the moneyed, except in the case of the 'Nabobs' who had made enormous and rapid fortunes on the side of the activities of the East India Company and had returned home to use their wealth to buy landed estates and seats in the House of Commons. Poor Lord Chesterfield attempted to buy a seat for his son at the 1768 election, but his offer of £2,500 was contemptuously refused by a boroughmonger, who said:[26]

that there was no such thing as a borough to be had now; for the rich East and West Indians had secured them all, at the rate of three thousand pounds at the least; but many at four thousand; and two or three, that he knew, at five thousand.

Lord Chatham complained:[27]

The riches of Asia have been poured in upon us, and have brought with them not only Asiatic luxury, but, I fear, Asiatic principles of government. Without connections, without any natural interest in the soil, the importers of foreign gold have forced their way into Parliament by such a torrent of private corruption as no private hereditary fortune could resist.

In attacking the Nabobs, Chatham makes the customary link between luxury, corruption and tyranny. Most politicians and moralists of the century regarded luxury much as the preacher regarded sin.

Chatham's objection is against men who have no 'natural interest in the soil'. Mere possession of a landed estate might, *pace* Toland (p. 10 above), not be a sufficient pledge of good behaviour and a proper sense of responsibility for the general welfare of society. A natural interest in the soil implied an awareness of the prime importance of the land itself in the creation of national wealth. Farming supplied not only nearly all England's food (barring 'luxuries' and spices) but the greater part of its industrial raw materials. At the time of Cobbett's birth most machines were still built largely of wood, and horses were a principal source of industrial power – the others being wind and falling water. Husbandry was still what Socrates had called it, 'the mother of arts'. Even that inveterate and vehement town-lover Johnson wrote two essays in 1756 elaborating the self-evident truth that agriculture was 'the most necessary and most indispensable of all professions', and that it alone was the support of society.[28] He even went on, following a tradition stretching back beyond Virgil's *Georgics*, to praise the virtue of rural life:[29]

> Luxury, avarice, injustice, violence, and ambition, take up their ordinary residence in populous cities; while the hard and laborious life of the husbandmen will not admit of these vices. The honest farmer lives in a wise and happy state, which inclines him to justice, temperance, sobriety, sincerity, and every virtue that can dignify human nature.

About this time the French 'Physiocrats' restated old commonplaces in new jargon by demonstrating that the farmer produces his own subsistence and a surplus, and that it is this surplus which maintains the rest of society. Forty years later Malthus commented on the superiority of English farming over French, and observed:[30]

> It is this great surplus produce in England, arising from her agriculture, which enables her to support such a vast body of manufactures, such formidable fleets and armies, such a crowd of persons engaged in the liberal professions, and a proportion of the society living on money rents, very far beyond what has ever been known in any other country of the world.

Though he hated Malthus's inferences, Cobbett would not have disagreed with this observation.

At the time Cobbett was born, English agriculture produced a large surplus because it was technically advanced and well organized for the market. There was hardly any 'peasantry' as that word was understood in most European countries. Farmers, both freeholders and leaseholders, great and small, produced for the market a great variety of cash crops – flax, hops, dairy produce, root vegetables, meat and much else, besides the staples of cereals and wool. When we read Defoe's *Tour through the Whole Island of Great Britain* (1724–6) we feel the pull that the London market in particular exercised upon farming in many parts of England. He writes of black dray and coach horses coming from Leicestershire, turkeys and geese being marched to London from Essex and Suffolk, Hampshire hogs and honey, Surrey fowl, Tewkesbury mustard and Cheshire cheese all finding their way to London. In all areas of the country there were cottagers and small-holders who lived off their own small patch of land together with their earnings from agricultural or industrial labour or both, and the vaguely defined 'yeoman' and the forty-shilling freeholder survived, but by the time Cobbett was born the ownership and cultivation of a great part of the land formed a three-tier structure where a few thousand landowners, large and small, leased out their land to some tens of thousands of tenant-farmers who worked it with the labour of some hundreds of thousands of day-labourers, servants 'living in' the farmhouse and small-holders who hired themselves out for much of their time. The first tier lived on rent, the second on profit and the third on wages. Agriculture was 'commercialized'; the three tiers formed an economic structure, but economic relationships reflected a social order and, ideally, what was thought to be a moral order, where each rank in rural society had both duties and obligations.

In accordance with natural, Heaven-ordained order the leader and head of rural society was the landed gentleman. He is described in ideal perfection by Steele in *Tatler* 169 (1710):

> There is no character more deservedly esteemed than that of a country gentleman, who understands the situation in which Heaven and Nature have placed him. He is father to his tenants, and patron to his neighbours, and is more superior to those of lower fortune by his benevolence than his possessions. . . . His counsel and knowledge are a guard to the simplicity and innocence of those of lower talents, and the entertainment and happiness of those of equal. When a man of country life has this turn, as it is hoped thousands have, he lives in a more happy condition than any that is described in the pastoral descriptions of poets, or the vainglorious solitudes recorded by philosophers.

In this same paper, though, Steele gives a character of the oafish landed gentleman, and in other *Tatler* papers he ridicules or admonishes the fox-hunting, gluttonous boors in this rank of society – men who 'commit immodesties upon haycocks, wear shirts half a week, and are drunk twice a day'.[31] It was not unknown for country gentlemen to share both the coarse pleasures of the lower orders and the refined amusements of their own rank. Thus Thomas Coke of Holkham in Norfolk, the great patron, art-collector and wide-acred agricultural improver, never missed a chance to see a boxing-match or a cock-fight; Sir Thomas Parkyns, squire of Bunny in Nottinghamshire, the Latin grammarian and notable architect, was also a celebrated wrestler in the Cornish style. The 'manly sports', such as pugilism, cock-fighting, wrestling and singlestick, united the ranks of society. So did fox-hunting and hare-coursing, particularly the latter; but not the socially exclusive sport of shooting. Everyone could turn out, as Cobbett did at eight years old, to follow the hounds.

The many eighteenth-century literary representations of squires benevolent or tyrannical – de Coverley, Allworthy or Bramble, Western or Mr B. – reflected accurately enough the country gentleman's power for good or ill. In that century the administrative and judicial powers of the Justices of the Peace reached their zenith, and the principal resident landowner of a village if he was a magistrate, as he often was, effectively had control of the wages, dwellings and morals of his cottage tenantry. He could temper the severity of the parish overseer towards people he regarded as the 'deserving poor', or he could show the utmost rigour in enforcing those Game Laws which prohibited all but certain categories of substantial propertied men from killing game. In the course of Cobbett's lifetime the increasing severity of the Game Laws would perhaps cause more friction in rural society than anything else. The Justices who heard poaching cases were interested parties often unable to maintain judicial impartiality, while the offence itself was condoned by nearly all common folk. Poachers, in fear of whipping, imprisonment, transportation or the gallows, operated more and more in armed gangs and resisted arrest. In many districts there was an intermittent rural war between gamekeepers and poachers, which only rarely had what, even in that 'manly' age, might have seemed a lighter side:[32]

In 1780 there was a great battle between keepers and poachers on Chettle Common [in Dorset]. One keeper was killed, another had his knee broken by a swindgel. A poacher whose hand was cut off by a keeper's hanger turned out to be a sergeant of dragoons. He was lucky, perhaps because he was popular: his sentence of seven years' transportation was commuted to a short prison sentence. . . . His regiment buried his hand, with full honours of war, in Pimperne Churchyard.

Such events undoubtedly upset the ideal harmony between the squire and the lower orders, but the squire would argue that poachers, like vagrants, were especially vicious cases (even though by the end of the century hunger might tempt more of the honest, industrious poor to join their number). A landlord's concern for his own popularity and self-respect, might be sufficient to ensure that he was charitable to the poor, while these considerations, buttressed by his long-term economic interest and sometimes by his need to maintain 'influence' at elections, might affect his dealings with his tenants. A not untypical paternalism towards the poor is illustrated in the correspondence of the First Earl Harcourt with his steward in Oxfordshire, while away from his estate on public business. The steward, who knew what his Lordship's wishes would be, wrote in December 1766:[33]

I don't know my Lord, what will be done with the poor people here. There is not a labouring man in the whole village that is able to do a day's work; and there are more than forty men, women, and children that have now the ague. I got a parcell of barks, salts of wormwood, and snake-root, together with some vomits, and have given it to some of them; but I can't yeat bost of the success, and what to do farther I don't know. I have like-wise kill'd an ordinary sheep this week, and distributed a bit to a house, to make a little broth for the sick.

(An 'ordinary' sheep was a sound one, not one that had died and had to be disposed of.)

If Harcourt kept what were thought to be traditional obligations to the poor, some other landlords did not. The decay of 'old-fashioned housekeeping' had been an urgent social theme in Tudor and Stuart sermon, tract, drama and ballad,[34] and continued to be a source of complaint in the eighteenth century, though by then this decay might be attributed to new causes. Thus John Byng on his travels through England in 1790:[35]

An hundred years ago, every village afforded two good gentlemens' houses; and within these sixty years, the hall, or the court still remained. These were the supporters of the poor, and of their rights; and their wives were the Lady Bountifuls of the parish; there was then a good country neighbourhood, whose families intermarried with each other. But since the increase of luxury, and turnpike roads, and that all gentlemen have the gout, and all ladies the bile, it has been found necessary to fly to the bath, and to sea-bathing for relief; there the gaiety, and neat houses make them resolve upon fixing on these spots; whilst the old mansion being deserted, and no longer the seat of hospitality, and the resort of sportsmen, is left to tumble down.

Desertion and dereliction of duty were not as widespread as Byng implies. Other travellers were prepared to find landlords who had avoided the more baneful effects of modern luxury, and still had a lively sense of the moral and social obligations attached to what Steele had called the 'situation in which Heaven and Nature' had placed them. Approaching Holkham, the Norfolk estate of Thomas Coke, in 1784, Arthur Young noted the trim farms and cottages:[36]

This is the diffusion of happiness; an overflow of wealth that gilds the whole country, and tells the traveller, in a language too expressive to be misunderstood, *we approach the residence of a man, who feels for others as well as for himself.* . . . The fault of modern luxury is the selfish concentration of wealth: praise is, therefore, justly due when it flows in a liberal stream that connects the ease and comforts of the tenants with the taste and pleasure of his landlord.

Coke seemed to be a type of the 'fine old country gentleman' benevolently presiding over a healthful, prosperous, well-knit community, but his importance for Young was that he was also an enlightened modern improver of his estate. At the time Cobbett was born, many parts of England were being 'gilded' as they were at Holkham by intensive, advanced farming, and the reclamation and cultivation of waste-land. The lead in such improvement might come first from the landlord or from his tenants, but the process usually benefited both because it could greatly increase both rents and profits. What Young called 'the agricultural spirit' was moving over the face of the land and diffusing more and more widely the advanced techniques of husbandry which had been first introduced from the Low Countries in the previous century. Most important was the cultivation of certain fodder crops, such as clovers, sainfoin, lucerne and turnips, which could be sown in rotation with the usual cereals to provide winter feed for the animals; thus more beasts could be stocked while the increased quantity of dung improved the yield of the cereals. This was the famous 'Norfolk System' of convertible husbandry which increased the produce but maintained the fertility of the soil without wasteful fallows.

Agricultural improvement was possible where the medieval 'open-field' system of landholding survived, as it did in many parts of the country in 1763, but the opinion of most writers on agriculture and, increasingly, of landlords was that improvement was synonymous with enclosure in either or both of its forms. Enclosure might entail the consolidation and redistribution of the scattered, variously owned strips in the arable fields and the partition of common meadows and pastures among the open-field farmers, thus creating compact farms on which drainage schemes, selective stock-breeding, convertible husbandry and other improvements were possible, or it might entail the reclamation and division of the wastes where the soil was potentially good enough, thus expanding the area of land under full cultivation. Both kinds of enclosure, carried out by agreement among several landowners or as a result of a monopoly of landownership, had been proceeding since medieval times, though very unevenly in different periods and localities. In the eighteenth century the movement continued through the new process of private Bills in Parliament, moved on the petition of the largest owners in a parish. Enclosure might eventually bring higher rents and profits but it was expensive, and the expense bore most heavily upon the very smallest owners, people who had 'little parcels of land in the [open] field with a right of common for a cow or three or four sheep, by the assistance of which, with the profits of a little trade or their daily labour they procure a very competent living'.[37] These had little monetary capital and many had to sell their land on what was, locally, a buyer's market. So we find Earl Harcourt writing to his agent in 1773 about the enclosure of Stanton Harcourt, Oxfordshire:[38]

> The gravelly ground will make good turnip land, or will bear clover, or sainfoin, and the deeper or richer land will be greatly benefited, so as to make the improvement very considerable. If

the charge of the enclosure should make any of the people willing to part with their estates, rather than embark in an undertaking that some of them may have been averse to, as well from an apprehension of the trouble, as for fear of the charge, I should be willing to purchase them.

'Engrossing', or the amalgamation of small-holdings into large farms, had not been in the past and was not in the eighteenth century necessarily linked with enclosure, but often the two processes went together, and commonly the arguments in favour of enclosure were employed also in favour of engrossing. Arthur Young, in *The Farmer's Letters* (1767), after claiming 'the universal benefit of inclosures' went on to argue that only the large farmer with plenty of working capital, good horses and good tackle could farm efficiently and prosper. Most eighteenth-century large landlords preferred, where they could, to let their acres to few large tenants rather than many small ones. By doing this they found that their rents were more secure and their expenditure in poor-rates and maintenance of buildings was lower. However, tenants with enough working capital and practical ability to rent a large farm were not always easy to find. There was, too, a traditional social objection to an agricultural system consisting wholly of large farms.

Some men claimed that it was possible for any ambitious young day-labourer who lived in a cottage with common rights attached to it to run a few beasts on the village common, rent a few acres (which he could do particularly cheaply if the village still had open-fields where rents were so much lower than for enclosed farms), work this holding part-time, then, while relying on labouring for part of his income, rent a few more acres and so work his way up until he obtained a farm that could be worked full-time. Such a process depended upon the existence of an unbroken social and economic ladder between the poor labourer and the well-to-do farmer. A system of large farms, by contrast, tended to polarize rural society. The political economist Nathaniel Forster wrote in 1767 of farmers as 'a body on all occasions of the utmost importance to the security and welfare of the public . . . a spirit of equality is the very life and soul of this body; and can alone diffuse health, and vigour, and enjoyment through every part of it'. But in districts where small farms had been swallowed up by large:[39]

Instead of an hardy, free, and intrepid race of men, contentedly enjoying the sweets of labour and alternate ease, the state's most useful subjects in peace, and its best soldiers in war, we are presented with the horrible picture of a few tyrant planters amidst a crowd of wretched slaves.

Tyrants or not, some of these large farmers, as they became wealthy, assumed the dress and manners of the gentry; and so, inevitably, became the objects of satire. Smollett wrote of them in *Sir Lancelot Greaves* (1760–2):[40]

> They kept their footmen, their saddle horses, and chaises; their wives and daughters appeared in their jewels, their silks, and their satins, their negligees and trollopees; their clumsy shanks, like so many shins of beef, were cased in silk hose and embroidered slippers; their raw red fingers, gross as the pipes of a chamber organ, which had been employed in milking the cows, in twirling the mop or churn-staff, being adorned with diamonds, were taught to thrum the pandola, and even to touch the keys of the harpsichord.

Cobbett one day would write in similar vein about large farmers enriched by the high agricultural prices of the Napoleonic Wars.

The small farmer did not disappear. A modern historian has reckoned that in 1831 nearly half the farmers in England employed no labour other than that of their own families, and so must, on any reckoning, have been 'small'.[41] Nevertheless, in Cobbett's lifetime and in Cobbett's country (the mainly arable South and East), many observers claimed that they could see small farms rapidly becoming fewer, and many pamphleteers were prepared to predict national decline if the process continued. They saw this as part of a general problem of rural depopulation where such of the 'hardy, free, and intrepid race of men' as did not become 'slaves' (that is, day-labourers) were compelled to seek employment in sordid, unhealthy towns, or, worse, to emigrate. Rural idealization and a rough-and-ready demography came to the assistance of one another in these writings, as they would later in Cobbett's. Thus Nathaniel Kent in 1775:[42]

> Cottagers are indisputably the most beneficial race of people we have; they are bred up in greater simplicity, live more primitive lives, more free from vice and debauchery, than any other set of men in the lower class; and are best formed, and enabled to sustain the hardships of war, and other laborious services. Great towns are destructive both to morals, and health, and . . .
> must cause a diminution, or waste of people. . . . The country

must be the place; and cottages, and small farms the chief
nurseries, which support population.

Goldsmith's *The Deserted Village* (1770) perfectly crystallizes in pastoral-historical-pathetical vein the emotions underlying many such socio-politico-economic pamphlets of this period.

As in pastoral poetry, so in economics and morals the town threatened the countryside, and did so at all social levels. Where luxury, gaiety and good roads according to Byng sucked away the resident gentry, according to Young they drew away the lower orders:[43]

> Young men and women in the country fix their eye on London
> as the last stage of their hope; they enter into service in the
> country for little else but to raise money enough to go to London,
> which was no such easy matter when a stage-coach was four or
> five days creeping an hundred miles; and the fare and the expenses
> ran high. But now! a country fellow one hundred miles from
> London jumps on to a coach-box in the morning, and for eight
> or ten shillings gets to town by night, which makes a material
> difference; besides rendering the going up and down so easy, that
> the numbers who have seen London are increased tenfold and of
> course ten times the boasts are sounded in the ears of country
> fools, to induce them to quit their healthy clean fields for a region
> of dirt, stink, and noise. And the number of young women that
> fly thither is almost incredible.

Not many years after this was written Cobbett would be just such a young country fellow jumping on the box of a London coach.

Depopulation was a bogey. Cobbett and many others railed against the unnatural concentration of people and wealth in debilitating cities, but the facts were that the total population of England increased greatly in Cobbett's lifetime and that rural population did not fall. Cobbett may have taken the high road to London, but most farmer's boys remained in their native villages, subject to the chances and circumstances of a material existence which varied greatly as between, say, open-field and enclosed parishes or woodland and champaign, and varied according to the extent and availability of commons or cottage gardens, according to the temper of squires, parsons and large farmers, according to the closeness of large town markets or industries which might compete for labour, and a hundred other variables.

At the time of Cobbett's birth, labourers' food varied from region to region – as Johnson's witty definition of 'oats' in his *Dictionary* (1755) indicates – but for most in the South and East the main diet was bread and cheese. Milk and ale were available to most labourers and so was bacon; other kinds of meat, including 'the roast beef of Old England' were probably more rarely seen in labourers' cottages, but could hardly have been unknown in view of the fact that in the 1760s some work-house diets allowed for meat (beef, mutton, pork, veal or lamb) three days a week.[44] Cottage gardens supplied vegetables, while the wastes provided brambles, herbs and nuts, and forage if the labourer possessed poultry or animals. Labourers in the North of England ate less meat and white bread, but consumed more oatmeal, potatoes and milk than they did in the South, so that they fared better when the prices of meat and wheaten bread rose enormously towards the end of the century. Detailed evidence of diet is scanty before the 1790s, and by that decade most observers agreed that living standards for the landless farm labourer had declined from the mid-century level.

Two articles of labourers' diet, tea and potatoes, aroused con-troversy. In the eighteenth century the 'luxurious' habit of tea-drinking spread to the lowest orders of society, and thereupon became the object of furious denunciation by moralists, physicians and economists. Tea and sugar drained our national reserves of gold and silver, profited Nabobs and West Indian planters, involved the country in expensive foreign wars, and took the bread out of the mouths of English brewers and growers of barley and hops. Labouring families cut down on necessaries and neglected useful employments in order to devote time and money to the 'tea-tackle' and to firing and preparing a drink which caused scurvy and bad teeth, irritated the nerves and fibres, convulsed the bowels, robbed women of beauty and shortened life! Nevertheless, as the century wore on, labouring families turned more and more from ale to tea as their staple drink. By contrast, labourers – in the South at least – were slow to adopt the potato, though it had been one of the main foods of the Irish since the end of the seventeenth century. In Cobbett's youth, Arthur Young recommended it as a staple food for the English poor, but the terms of his advocacy would have confirmed Cobbett's, or any proud southern cottager's prejudices against the 'lazy root' and the 'barbarians' who ate it:[45]

> If any one doubts the comparative plenty which attends the board of the poor natives of England and Ireland, let him attend to their meals; the sparingness with which our labourer eats his bread and

cheese is well known; mark the Irishman's potatoe bowl placed on the floor, the whole family upon their hams around it, devouring a quantity almost incredible, the beggar seating himself to it with a hearty welcome, the pig taking his share as readily as the wife, the cocks, hens, turkies, geese, the cur, the cat, and perhaps the cow – and all partaking of the same dish. No man can often have been a witness of it without being convinced of the plenty, and I will add the chearfulness, that attends it.

According to Young's observations, the average day-labourer's wage in lowland counties of England in the late 1760s was six to eight shillings a week, representing a slight advance in real terms from the time of King's estimate (1688). But Young's detailed figures reveal considerable variations in farm wages and the cost of provisions in places only a few miles apart. Wages were dictated not only by the local supply of labour and the availability of alternative work, but also by the weather; in rain or frost day-labourers might be stood off, while the busy days of harvest brought higher wages. The price of food, too, depended much upon the weather. The annual grain harvest produced the greatest part of the labouring families' food and drink, so the weather was of vital importance. There might be considerable regional differences in yields, and so of prices. It was a common eighteenth-century observation that harvests in the clay vales and on the light-soiled downlands varied inversely, since the moisture-retentive soils of the vales were less able to resist a wet season but better able to withstand a drought than the free-draining soils of the downs; but as communications were improved during the century price differences between regions became smaller. There was an enormous increase in food prices in the 1790s, continuing through the Napoleonic Wars.

In many cases the labourer's family did not depend wholly upon his agricultural wage. At the time of Cobbett's birth, industry was still fairly widely dispersed about the rural areas, especially in the well-wooded regions which provided fuel and raw materials. In tiling, potting, charcoal-burning and brick-making some labourers found part-time employment. Others spent their spare days, particularly in winter, felling, cleaving, carting and sawing timber. In the Home Counties labourers' wives and children supplemented family income with straw-plaiting – an industry very prosperous for a while after a change of fashion brought in the huge Leghorn hats so often depicted by Gainsborough. In some places lace-making was important, but the most widespread by-employment in the countryside as a whole was the spinning and weaving of wool, flax or hemp. Defoe, whose writing always takes on a rosy glow at the spectacle of human industry, commented in 1728:[46]

> a poor labouring man that goes abroad to his day work and husbandry, hedging, ditching, threshing, carting, etc., and brings home his week's wages, suppose at eightpence to twelvepence a day or in some counties less, if he has a wife and three or four children to feed, and who get little or nothing for themselves, must fare hard and live poorly. . . .
>
> But if this man's wife and children can at the same time get employment, if at next door, or at the next village, there lives a clothier or a bay maker or a stuff or drugget weaver, the manufacturer sends the poor woman combed wool or carded wool every week to spin, and she gets eightpence or ninepence a day at home; the weaver sends for her two little children, and they work by the loom, winding, filling quills, etc., and the two bigger girls spin at home with their mother, and there earn threepence or fourpence a day each: so that put it together, the family at home gets as much as the father gets abroad and generally more. This alters the case, the family feels it . . . and as they grow they do not run away to be footmen and soldiers, thieves and beggars, or sell themselves to the plantations to avoid the gaol and the gallows, but have a trade at their hands and everyone can get their bread.

With industrialization such opportunities of cottage-employment were to decrease during Cobbett's lifetime.

Another resource was the waste, owned by the local Lord of the Manor, but over the surface of which in many parishes various classes of people had rights of common to graze their cows, pigs or geese, cut turf for fuel, catch fish, or gather wood for fuel and building materials. Thus the tenant or owner of a cottage with common rights attached to it could manage a little stock or poultry farming to supplement his labourer's wage, and conceivably even raise his status. By the time of Cobbett's birth, in many thickly populated lowland parishes with good soil (and so the stongest motives for enclosure), there was little left of the waste, whereas ample unappropriated wasteland remained in heathy, woodland or upland districts. It was these areas that attracted 'squatters' or 'borderers' who exploited all that the waste could provide in the way of rough grazing, nuts, rabbits, wildfowl, firewood, gravel and much else for the greater part of the year, and who migrated for a few weeks to the corn lands for harvest work. It was partly against such people that the Act of Settlement, 1662, had been directed, whose Preamble reads:

> By reason of some defect in the law, poor people are not restrained from going from one parish to another, and therefore do endeavour to settle themselves in those parishes where there is best stock, the largest commons or wastes to build cottages, and the most woods for them to burn and destroy; and when they have consumed it, then to another parish, and at last become rogues and vagabonds.

So the Act sought to restrict the movement of all who were not freeholders or able to rent a tenement of ten pounds a year. The inhabitants of heath and woodland areas lived far from the shadows of the manor house and parsonage, and it was often remarked in the eighteenth century that they were more 'insubordinate' towards the upper ranks and less amenable to law and order than were the regular wage-labourers in the vales and plains.

The Act of Settlement might be a threat to the squatter, but for the labourer living in his rude forefather's hamlet it could be a source of security, since, if he became unemployed or too ill or old to work, a settlement entitled him to a share of the poor relief administered, under the Act of 1601, by the parish overseer and paid for by a parish rate levied upon householders and occupiers of land. There was a seventeenth-century ballad with the refrain 'Hang care, the parish is bound to find us' which popularly expressed this sense of security. Such an attitude, though, disquieted some of the poor man's betters. John Shebbeare wrote in 1755: 'The poor claim the revenue arising from this tax as their proper right, they receive it without thankfulness, the giver does not bequeath it from the principle of charity, nor the receiver take it with the sensation of gratitude.'[47] A man obtained a settlement by various means, such as being born in a parish, paying parish taxes or being hired for a year's service (hence the custom among some rate-paying employers of hiring servants for fifty-one weeks at a time), and if he became sick or unemployed thereafter the parish overseer had to assist him by out-relief in the form of a weekly pension or indoor relief in the poor-house or workhouse. By the standards of the time such relief was not ungenerous, but it is clear that much of the overseers' concern was to prevent men, women and children who might one day be a charge on the parish from becoming settled, for they had powers forcibly to remove such people within forty days of their arrival. The law of settlement was not enforced in the expanding, crowded, labour-hungry, new manufacturing towns, but rural parish accounts contain frequent references to the forcible removal of potential paupers. Sir William Meredith said in a Parliamentary speech in 1773:[48]

> Coming up to town last Sunday I met with an instance shocking to humanity: a miserable object in the agonies of death crammed into a cart to be removed lest the parish should be at the expense of its funeral. Other instances every day met with are the removal of women with child and in labour, to the danger of both their lives, lest the child should be born in the parish.

Meredith spoke amid that swell of humanitarian feeling in the 1770s which led to Gilbert's Act of 1782, making the Poor Law kinder; but for the earlier part of the century the well-to-do seem to have been fairly content with the existing situation. They could always comfort themselves with the words of Dr Snape's sermon, as quoted by Steele in *Spectator* 294 (1712): 'The wise Providence has amply compensated the disadvantages of the poor and indigent, in wanting many of the conveniences of this life, by a more abundant provision for their happiness in the next.'

Later in the century more enlightened men, no less comfortably, could counter any tendency to excessive indulgence in organized or private charity by their new knowledge of the economic laws laid down by Divine Providence. Burke was one of the new economists who saw the labour of the poor as a commodity or article of trade:[49]

> When any commodity is carried to market, it is not the necessity of the vender, but the necessity of the purchaser that raises the price. . . . The impossibility of the subsistence of a man, who carries his labour to the market, is totally beside the question in this way of viewing it. The only question is, what is it worth to the buyer? . . .
>
> [We must] resist the very first idea, speculative or practical, that it is within the competence of government, taken as government, or even of the rich, as rich, to supply to the poor those necessaries which it has pleased the Divine Providence for a while to withhold from them. We, the people, ought to be made

sensible that it is not in breaking the laws of commerce, which are the laws of nature, and consequently the laws of God, that we are to place our hope of softening the Divine displeasure to remove any calamity under which we suffer, or which hangs over us.

Though Dr Snape trusted that the poor would have more abundant provision for their happiness in the next world, there remained some provision for happiness in this one. The country labourer, for instance, still enjoyed his old games and holidays: 'The common people will endure long and hard labour in so much that after twelve hours hard work they will go in the evening to football, stock-ball, cricket, prison-base, wrestling, cudgel throwing, or some such like vehement exercise for their recreation.'[50] Country fairs, with their tumblers, mounte-banks and 'Jack-puddings', or clowns, and their stalls glittering with all the wares of Autolycus were an occasional diversion, while the rural entertainments, songs, morris-dances, jigs and May-games of Robin Hood and Maid Marian, that figured so prominently in Eliza-bethan pastoral poetry were continued into the eighteenth century. Country mummers performed their plays at Christmas, Easter or Plough Monday – the day on which work was resumed after Christmas. The earliest surviving texts of such plays come from the 1770s and the earliest surviving reference is in Parson Woodforde's *Diary* for January 1769, but the plays are linked to old customs and superstitions. With their references to Wolfe at Quebec, to Admiral Vernon at Porto Bello and to other heroes, they are often vehicles, too, for the noisy, bellicose, Francophobe patriotism of the eighteenth-century English common man. The famous maypole in the Strand was taken down in 1717 and – in a triumph of the Enlightenment over superstition – was used by Sir Isaac Newton to raise a great telescope at Wanstead, but rural maypoles continued in their proper use. At regular fairs and occasional impromptu revels, gold-laced hats or legs of mutton were offered as prizes in wrestling, bowls, cudgelling and foot-racing. Some-times a pound of tobacco was 'to be grinned for, by old women, through a horse-collar as usual'.[51] By custom the great farmers and squires provided a welcome, well-laden board for their labourers at such working festivals as sheep-shearing and harvest-home, even if sometimes the food was not always of the best; a farm account from Ditchley in Oxfordshire reads 'Provisions for the Harvest home – N.B. a giddy sheep and some unwarrantable venison used for supper'.[52]

These events provided only rare relief from long, back-breaking labour, but even this labour might have its intangible rewards. Adam Smith observed that:[53]

> the man who ploughs the ground with a team of horses or oxen, works with instruments of which the health, strength, and temper are very different on different occasions. The condition of the materials which he works upon too is as variable as that of the instruments which he works with, and both require to be managed with much judgment and discretion. ... His understanding ... being accustomed to consider a greater variety of objects, is generally much superior to that of [the town mechanic] whose whole attention from morning to night is commonly occupied in performing one or two very simple operations.

There was a kind of freedom working in the open air to the tempo of the seasons which this ploughman's grandson in the town, bound by the logic of the division of labour and the tyranny of the factory bell, could not experience.

In 1763 the material conditions of the agricultural labouring poor in Cobbett's countryside were probably somewhat better than they had been fifty years earlier (and than they would be fifty years later), and they were quite probably better than those of the same class of people in every part of the world except North America. Contemporary observers would have called this a certainty rather than a probability, particularly if they were comparing the English with their rivals, the French. Smollett travelling through France in 1765 was one of the more prejudiced of many travellers who contrasted the miserable, beggarly French peasants in their wretched fields – men and beasts alike the images of famine – with the men and landscape of the country he had left:[54]

> the country of England smiling with cultivation; the grounds exhibiting all the perfection of agriculture, parcelled out into beautiful inclosures, cornfields, hay and pasture, woodland and common ... her meadows well stocked with black cattle, her downs covered with sheep ... her teams of horses and oxen, large and strong, fat and sleek ... her farm-houses the habitations of plenty, cleanliness, and convenience; and her peasants well fed, well lodged, well clothed, tall and stout, and hale and jolly.

Arthur Young, a more reliable witness, gave his sober, impartial account of the state of England after he had travelled through many parts of it in the 1760s:[55]

> From this review of the agriculture, etc., of this kingdom I apprehend there is no slight reason to conclude that England is, at present, in a most rich and flourishing situation ... that her industrious poor are well fed, clothed and lodged, and at reasonable rates of expense; the prices of all the necessaries of life being moderate; that our population is consequently increasing; that the price of labour is in general high, of itself one of the strongest symptoms of political health.

Twenty years later, after commenting on the wretched condition of the French peasantry, he spoke of the English agricultural labourers as 'well nourished, tolerably drunken from superfluity, well lodged and at their ease'.[56] More significantly, foreign visitors to England shared these impressions. Voltaire in his *Letters on the English* (1734), observed that English 'peasants' ate white bread, were well clothed, and their feet were not bruised by wooden shoes. Another French visitor, whose account was published in 1747 was struck by 'the air of plenty and cleanliness that reigns in the smallest villages', and found a touch of Arcadia in the inhabitants of the countryside: 'A young country girl in other countries is a mere peasant, here by the neatness of her dress and the genteelness of her person you would take her for a shepherdess in one of our romances.'[57] A Swedish visitor in 1748 offered similar evidence of well-being, while at the same time he wondered at the amount of time and money that common labouring men could afford to spend in the inn: 'But the custom of the country that friends and neighbours come together, sit, and converse, the abundance of money in this country, the ease with which a man could in every case have his food if only he was somewhat industrious seem to have conduced to this result.'[58]

At the time of Cobbett's birth, the myth of an English rural golden age, a 'blessed Eden', a 'pudding-time', was already shaping the part played in the nation's consciousness by the countryside and the men who lived and worked in it. In his letter (p. 28 above), Smollett told of beauty-in-prosperity, a free and favoured race tilling a fertile land, in terms that were as familiar as they were welcome to his readers. Such a patriotic blend as this of idyllic reverie and accurate observation grew out of a long literary tradition descending from Virgil and other Romans, and was the material of much of the eighteenth century's formal art (especially the georgic, the local poem and landscape painting) as it was the inevitable theme of travellers' tales and politicians' harangues. Even in the short extracts quoted above (pp. 13, 19–21) from Johnson, Forster and Kent, there are distinct echoes of Virgil's *Georgics*. The legendary Roast Beef of Old England which provided subject-matter for Fielding and Hogarth, and the English adaptations by Gay, Thomson, Dyer and innumerable other poets of that canonical closing passage of Virgil's *Georgics* Book II, praising the frugal, pious, virtuous, healthy, happy husbandman, together with the dancing peasants in ballad operas, and the luminous *genre*-paintings of Gains- borough, all testify in their different ways to the pervasive and persua- sive qualities of this myth of England as a smiling landscape peopled by free, well-fed rustics. While it was certainly not an accurate or complete image of reality, this myth (like most myths) was not wholly false, but even if the 'Merry England' of the eighteenth-century countryside were as fictitious as the Land of Cockayne, the idea of it was potent. This myth, a controlling, unifying image of the land and its workers, so effectively embodied widely held values and hopes that it affected men's way of perceiving the reality, and no man of the next age was more profoundly affected by it than Cobbett.

2

Ploughboy, Soldier and
'Peter Porcupine': 1763–1800

Almost the only authority for the early biography of Cobbett is
Cobbett himself – in *The Life and Adventures of Peter Porcupine* (1796)
and in many short passages of autobiography scattered through his
later writings. He has selected the significant reminiscences which will
indicate the stages in his own growth, and point the contrast between a
golden past and an iron present. There is, however, some independent
corroboration that Cobbett's birthplace was as prosperous and lovely
as he claimed it to be.

The town of Farnham is in west Surrey, close to the Hampshire
border at a point where the North Downs are cut by the Riber Wey.
Through this gap lay the main Neolithic route across southern England,
the medieval Pilgrim's Way, and, in Cobbett's time, the busy road
(turnpiked in 1758) from London to the naval base at Portsmouth; by
the time he was twenty Cobbett had travelled impulsively to both ends
of this road. Farnham was not a sleepy rustic village but a neat well-
built town and a busy centre. In Defoe's day it had been, after London,
the greatest corn-market in England, with 'on a market day, eleven
hundred teams of horses, all drawing wagons or carts loaden with
wheat'.[1] By the 1760s the corn-market had declined, but Farnham
was hardly less busy now that it had become a great centre of hop-
growing; Gilbert White reckoned that about eight thousand people,
besides the natives, were employed in the Farnham hop-picking of
1770.[2]

The most prominent natural feature near by was Crooksbury Hill to
the east, whose conical profile was accentuated in the 1760s by a
plantation of a newly introduced exotic fir. Beyond lay the Hog's
Back and a region of poor sandy heath running away to the north in
the direction of Windsor. This waste-land provided fuel for, and helped
to support the pigs, geese, poultry and bees of the poor 'borderer'

families whose cottages skirted it; Cobbett recalled 'I have seen not less than ten thousand geese in one tract of common, in about six miles, going from Chobham towards Farnham ... raised entirely by care and by the common'.[3]

The town's main street was dominated by Farnham Castle, one of the residences of the Bishop of Winchester, John Thomas, who was Lord of the Manor and the principal landowner in the parish. There were two other great houses. Just over a mile downstream on the banks of the Wey was Moor Park, once the seat of Sir William Temple and home of Swift, near which the celebrated grotto, 'Mother Ludlam's Cave', was hollowed in a sandy cliff. A mile downstream again lay the ruins of Waverley Abbey, set, like other Cistercian houses, upon fertile land in surroundings of great beauty. John Byng on his visit in 1782 was charmed:[4]

> Many of the cloisters yet remain; and a large kind of chapter-house has been repaired for a retreat in a summer day. The ruins are not only well clothed with ivy, but in many places with fig-trees, vines and jessamine. In the aisle of the church I could touch the pavement with my stick which surely any man of taste would wish to discover.

However, Byng detested the great staring house rebuilt near by in the 1760s and owned in the seventies by Sir Robert Rich. According to Cobbett, Sir Robert grew very fine fruit – for the kitchen-garden at Waverley:[5]

> was the spot where I first began to learn to work, or, rather, where I first began to eat fine fruit. ... Ten families, large as they might be, including troops of servants (who are no churls in this way), could not have consumed the fruit produced in that garden. The peaches, nectarines, apricots, fine plums, never failed; and, if the workmen had not lent a hand, a fourth part of the produce never could have been got rid of.

Up the Wey valley, going south-west towards the town of Alton in Hampshire, lay some land of exceptional fertility and beauty. Byng found it enchanting.[6] Arthur Young praised its 'hazel-coloured' loamy soil and claimed that this vale was the finest ten miles in England. His description in 1767 shows that the land was cultivated intensively according to modern methods of convertible husbandry, that farms were of middling size and that labourers were reasonably well paid.[7]

The labourers' loaf was wheaten, and Surrey was a populous county with the London market exercising a beneficial effect upon agriculture. According to the Board of Agriculture's Report on Surrey, in 1794,[8]

> there are perhaps few counties where the land is possessed in a fairer proportion. Neither are the farms occupied in an extreme, as to extent. Perhaps it may be said that a great many are too small, being from thirty to forty pounds a year, and very few exceed from three to four hundred pounds.

These reporters, like most of their kind, despised small farmers who not only practised poor husbandry but in many cases had 'so little business capacity that they preferred to sell their corn cheap to old customers than to accept better offers from persons with whom they were unaccustomed to deal'.

If some small farmers valued old habits more than modern economics, so did many cottagers. Between Farnham and the small Alice Holt Forest to the south, on heathy land beside the Bourne Brook where Cobbett used to play as a child, many encroachments had been made on the waste and little enclosures made, not all of which had earned the subsequent approval of the Bishop's manorial court. The site of Cobbett's father's house suggests that it was possibly built on such an encroachment made by some 'independent' borderer intent on carving out a living for himself from the waste of Farnham manor. Cobbett once wrote approvingly of 'the labourers who spudddle about the ground in the little *dips*' between the 'heath-covered sand hills of Surrey amongst which I was born'.[9] Alice Holt Forest itself was a valuable amenity for those Farnham cottagers and landholders who possessed common rights, 'by furnishing them with peat and turf for their firing; with fuel for the burning of their lime; and with ashes for their grasses; and by maintaining their geese and their stock of young cattle at little or no expense'. These words were Gilbert White's, who also observed that the Forest provided an irresistible temptation to poachers: 'Neither fines nor imprisonments can deter them; so impossible is it to extinguish the spirit of sporting which seems to be inherent in human nature.' There was further evidence of a spirit of insubordination when in 1784 Lord Stawell, who held part of the Forest on a grant from the Crown, felled timber and laid claim to the 'lop and top' (i.e. the small branches suitable for fuel). The poor from several places on the edge of the Forest, wrote White, 'assert that it belongs to them, and assembling in a riotous manner, have actually

33

taken it all away. One man, who keeps a team, has carried home for his share forty stacks of wood. Fifty-five of these people his lordship has served with actions.'[10]

In Farnham town itself the common folk had taken the opportunity given by the long absences of Bishop John Thomas to make use of his park:[11]

It was cut with unlicensed paths, the trees were mangled to browse the deer, and a cricket ground had so long been suffered, that the people conceived they had now a right to it. This last was a great nuisance. Such a scene of riot and disorder, with stands for selling liquor, just under the castle windows, could not easily be endured.

Bishop Brownlow North (later one of Cobbett's targets), when he succeeded to the see in 1781, had great difficulty in expelling the Farnham cricketers, ale-sellers and other folk who imagined they had a right to share his park.

Such insubordination could be maintained only on a full belly. Travellers' accounts of Farnham in the years of Cobbett's youth all point to a general prosperity shared, to some extent, even by the lower orders. This prosperity depended primarily upon hops. Hops were the most important specialized crop in eighteenth-century farming, and Farnham had the reputation of growing the finest hops in England. Mostly sold at the great Weyhill Fair near Andover in Hampshire, they fetched far more than those from any other district and frequently twice as much as Kentish hops. Rents for Farnham hop-gardens were therefore very high; so were expenses because hops required careful and assiduous cultivation. The land was ploughed or spade-dug deep and fed very richly, the bines had to be carefully trained around ten-foot poles, frequent hoeing by hand was called for 'as in the most elegant garden', and picking, drying and bagging all called for much labour. Hardly had the picking ended (celebrated by frolics with the pickers parading the streets of Farnham, a fiddler at their head) when manuring of the ground for next season began. Though this labour-intensive cultivation was expensive, small acreages could yield great profits to the grower, and, of course, offer frequent work to all active members of many labouring families. Conditions of life for these families were probably not very different from those described by Gilbert White in near-by Selborne in the 1780s:[12]

We abound with poor; many of whom are sober and industrious, and live comfortably in good stone or brick cottages, which are glazed, and have chambers above stairs; mud buildings we have none. Besides the employment from husbandry, the men work in hop-gardens, of which we have many; and fell and bark timber. In the spring and summer the women weed the corn; and enjoy a second harvest in September by hop-picking. . . . The inhabitants enjoy a good share of health and longevity; and the parish swarms with children.

The hop-gardens gave a prosperous appearance to Farnham, not only by the beauty of the hops themselves, but by the fact that they required quickset hedges for shelter against the wind. Young, seeing these hedges, so neat and well-kept and giving the whole countryside the appearance of a garden, declared: 'I never beheld anything equal to them.'[13]

Independent evidence of the beauty and prosperity of Farnham in the 1760s and seventies thus lends colour to Cobbett's proud and sweeping claim that his native place was 'the neatest in England, and, I believe, in the whole world. All there is a garden'.[14]

Cobbett was proud of his own plebeian ancestry:[15]

With respect to my ancestors, I shall go no further back than my grandfather, and for this plain reason, that I never heard talk of any prior to him. He was a day-labourer; and I have heard my father say, that he worked for one farmer from the day of his marriage to that of his death, upwards of forty years. He died [1760] before I was born, but I have often slept beneath the same roof that had sheltered him, and where his widow dwelt for several years after his death. It was a little thatched cottage, with a garden before the door. It had but two windows; a damson tree shaded one, and a clump of filberts the other. Here I and my brothers went every Christmas and Whitsuntide to spend a week or two, and torment the poor old woman with our noise and dilapidations. She used to give us milk and bread for breakfast, an apple pudding for our dinner, and a piece of bread and cheese for supper. Her fire was made of turf, cut from the neighbouring heath, and her evening light was a rush dipped in grease. . . .

My father, when I was born, was a farmer. . . . When a little boy, he drove plough for two pence a-day; and these earnings were appropriated to the expenses of an evening school. What a village school-master could be expected to teach, he had learnt; and had, besides, considerably improved himself, in several branches of the mathematics. He understood land-surveying well, and was often chosen to draw the plans of disputed territory; in short, he had the reputation of possessing experience and understanding, which never fails, in England, to give a man in a country place, some little weight with his neighbours. He was honest, industrious, and frugal.

Cobbett's father was also violent-tempered, to an extent that may partly have accounted for his son's flights from home in youth, and his determination, when a father himself, never to beat his own children. Cobbett was, as he said, bred at the plough-tail:[16]

I do not remember the time, when I did not earn my living. My first occupation was, driving the small birds from the turnip-seed, and the rooks from the peas. When I first trudged a-field, with my wooden bottle and my satchel swung over my shoulders, I was hardly able to climb the gates and stiles; and, at the close of the day, to reach home, was a task of infinite difficulty. My next employment was weeding wheat, and leading a single horse at harrowing barley. Hoeing peas followed, and hence, I arrived at the honour of joining the reapers in harvest, driving the team, and holding plough.

In spare moments, Cobbett's father taught his sons (William was the third of four boys) how to read, write and cipher. There were holidays, too, and cricket (perhaps in the Bishop's park), singlestick and coursing, and the fairs with their mountebanks and Jack-puddings. At thirteen or fourteen years of age, Cobbett was a strong, unruly, inquisitive, intelligent boy, already feeling that hunger of the imagination that would drive him so far. One episode of his life, about this time, witnesses to that hunger. He was then a gardener's boy clipping box-edgings and weeding flowerbeds at Farnham Castle:[17]

I had always been fond of beautiful gardens; and a gardener, who had just come from the King's gardens at Kew, gave such a description of them as made me instantly resolve to work in these gardens. The next morning, without saying a word to any one, off I set, with no clothes, except those upon my back, and with thirteen halfpence in my pocket. ... A long day (it was in June) brought me to Richmond in the afternoon. Two-pennyworth of bread and cheese and a penny-worth of small beer, which I had on the road, and one halfpenny that I had lost somehow or other, left threepence in my pocket. With this for my whole fortune, I was trudging through Richmond, in my blue smock-frock and my red garters tied under my knees, when, staring about me, my eye fell upon a little book in a bookseller's window, on the outside of which was written: '*Tale of a Tub*, price 3*d*.' The title was so odd, that my curiosity was excited. I had the three pence, but, then, I could have no *supper*. In I went, and got the little book, which I was so impatient to read, that I got over into a field, at the upper corner of Kew Gardens, where there stood a *hay-stack*. On the shady side of this, I sat down to read. The book was so different from any thing that I had ever read before: it was something so *new* to my mind, that, though I could not at all understand some of it, it delighted me beyond description; and it produced what I have always considered a sort of birth of intellect. I read on till it was dark, without any thought about supper or bed. When I could see no longer, I put my little book in my pocket, and tumbled down by the side of the stack, where I slept till the birds in Kew Gardens awaked me in the morning; when I started to Kew, reading my little book. The singularity of my dress, the simplicity of my manner, my confident and lively air, and, doubtless, his own compassion besides, induced the gardener, who was a Scotchman, I remember, to give me victuals, find me lodging, and set me to work. And it was during the period when I was at Kew, that the present king [George IV] and two of his brothers laughed at the oddness of my dress, while I was sweeping the grass-plat round the foot of the Pagoda. The gardener, seeing me fond of books, lent me some gardening books to read; but these I could not relish after my *Tale of a Tub*, which I carried about with me wherever I went; and when I, at about [twenty-two] years old, lost it in a box that fell overboard in the Bay of Fundy, in North America, the loss gave me greater pain than I have ever felt at losing thousands of pounds.

After this impulsive move to Kew, Cobbett spent little time in Farnham. For a while he lived in Guildford at the house of the Reverend James Barclay, author of *A Complete and Universal English Dictionary* (1774). It is not known in what capacity Cobbett was

employed, or whether it was here that he first came to despise that
other lexicographer of the day, Samuel Johnson, but he certainly made
use of the library, for it was here that he wrote his first little book, now
lost, *A History of the Kings and Queens of England*.[18]

But this unusual farmer's, gardener's boy was not yet ready to turn
author. His next impulse took an altogether different direction. In
autumn 1782 he went on foot to visit an uncle near Portsmouth; from
the top of Portsdown Hill he saw for the first time the sea and at once
wished to be a sailor:[19]

> But it was not the sea alone that I saw: the grand fleet was riding
> at anchor at Spithead. I had heard of the wooden walls of Old
> England: I had formed my ideas of a ship, and of a fleet; but,
> what I now beheld, so far surpassed what I had ever been able to
> form a conception of, that I stood lost between astonishment and
> admiration. I had heard talk of the glorious deeds of our admirals
> and sailors, of the defeat of the Spanish Armada, and of all those
> memorable combats, that good and true Englishmen never fail to
> relate to their children about a hundred times a year. The brave
> Rodney's victories over our natural enemies, the French and
> Spaniards, had long been the theme of our praise, and the burden
> of our songs. The sight of the fleet brought all these into my mind
> in confused order, it is true, but with irresistible force. My heart
> was inflated with national pride. The sailors were my countrymen;
> the fleet belonged to my country, and surely I had my part in it,
> and in all its honours: yet, these honours I had not earned; I took
> to myself a sort of reproach, for possessing what I had no right to,
> and resolved to have a just claim by sharing in the hardships and
> dangers.

Next morning he got a boatman to take him out to the man-of-war,
the *Pegasus*, but:

> The Captain had more compassion than is generally met with in
> men of his profession: he represented to me the toils I must
> undergo, and the punishment that the least disobedience or
> neglect would subject me to. He persuaded me to return home,
> and I remember he concluded his advice, with telling me, that it
> was better to be led to church in a halter, to be tied to a girl that
> I did not like, than to be tied to the gang-way, or, as the sailors
> call it, married to *miss roper*. From the conclusion of this whole-

some counsel, I perceived that the captain thought I had eloped on account of a bastard. . . . I returned once more to the plough, but I was spoiled for a farmer. I had, before my Portsmouth adventure, never known any other ambition than that of surpassing my brothers in the different labours of the field; but it was quite otherwise now; I sighed for a sight of the world; the little island of Britain, seemed too small a compass for me. The things in which I had taken the most delight were neglected; the singing of the birds grew insipid, and even the heart-cheering cry of the hounds, after which I formerly used to fly from my work, bound o'er the fields, and dash through the brakes and coppices, was heard with the most torpid indifference.

The next winter was the last that Cobbett would spend in the English countryside for more than twenty years. In that period conditions of life for agricultural labourers would change, while in Cobbett's memory Farnham would gather to itself the golden haze that lies on childhood scenes.

On 6 May 1783, dressed in holiday clothes and with a pocketful of money, he set out to collect two or three lasses he was to accompany to Guildford Fair:

but, unfortunately for me, I had to cross the London turnpike road. The stage-coach had just turned the summit of a hill, and was rattling down towards me at a merry rate. The notion of going to London, never entered my mind, till this very moment, yet the step was completely determined on, before the coach came to the spot where I stood. Up I got, and was in London about nine o'clock in the evening.

By now he had only half-a-crown left, but by good luck a London hop-merchant travelling with him on the coach knew his father, having dealt with him often at Weyhill Fair. He took Cobbett to his own house in Southwark, wrote to his father, and tried to persuade William to obey parental orders, which were to return to Farnham. Cobbett refused, so the hop-merchant found employment for him as clerk in an attorney's office in Gray's Inn:[20]

No part of my life has been totally unattended with pleasure, except the eight or nine months I passed in Gray's Inn. The office (for so the dungeon where I wrote was called) was so dark, that, on cloudy days, we were obliged to burn candle. I worked

39

like a galley-slave from five in the morning till eight or nine at night, and sometimes all night long. . . . I never quitted this gloomy recess except on Sundays, when I usually took a walk to St. James's Park, to feast my eyes with the sight of the trees, the grass, and the water.

Too proud to return home he tried to 'improve' himself by learning French, but his ambitions, however vague, and wayward temperament sought a more active life.

So, again, following the impulse of the moment, Cobbett went down to Chatham in February 1784 to go to sea as a marine – but, by mistake, enlisted in a marching regiment serving in Nova Scotia. As the war in America was now over, no great haste was made to send recruits to regiments there, and so he spent a year in Chatham. Here he knew the miserable, hungry existence of a private soldier on sixpence a day: 'I called to mind, almost with tears in my eyes, the hard dumplings and skimmer cakes which I used to eat when I was a boy.'[21] Yet here, too, in his off-duty hours, he began in earnest a rigid process of self-improvement. He subscribed to a circulating library and read avidly, going even hungrier than his fellows in order to buy pen, ink and paper, and in the winter reading and writing by firelight, 'and only my *turn* of that'.[22] Among noisy companions, he copied out Lowth's *Grammar*, got it by heart and repeated it over to himself when he was posted sentinel. The very fact that he had taught himself under such difficulties to write correctly buttressed his not inconsiderable self-confidence, and, once his knowledge of grammar was secure, he was able to look down upon most men better born and more powerful than himself simply because he could always detect some grammatical error in their speech or writings. The study of grammar also, for the present, kept Cobbett out of mischief. This honest, sober, punctual, intelligent, literate soldier was promoted to corporal, and an extra twopence a day, before the spring of 1785 when he sailed to join his regiment in Nova Scotia and, soon afterwards, move with it to New Brunswick.

Soon after his arrival in North America, Cobbett was made clerk to the regiment, and in a short time was responsible for all the returns, reports and other official papers, so that 'neither adjutant, pay-master, or quarter-master, could move an inch without my assistance'.[23] Within a year he was promoted over the heads of thirty sergeants to the rank of sergeant-major (and half-a-crown a day). From his own account he seems to have been a perfect specimen of the higher N.C.O. – hard-working and hard-driving, indispensable to his officers and considerate but firm towards his men. He developed a stubborn passion for good order, discipline, smartness and early rising which was to remain with him through life. In his *Advice to Young Men* (1829–30) he recalled:[24]

> My custom was this: to get up, in summer, at day-light, and in winter at four o'clock; shave [in cold water to save time], dress, even to the putting of my sword-belt over my shoulder, and having my sword lying on the table before me, ready to hang by my side. Then I ate a bit of cheese, or pork, and bread. Then I prepared my report, which was filled up as fast as the companies brought me in the materials. After this I had an hour or two to read, before the time came for any duty out of doors, unless, when the regiment or part of it went out to exercise in the morning. When this was the case, and the matter was left to me, I always had it on the ground in such time as that the bayonets glistened in the *rising sun*, a sight which gave me delight, of which I often think, but which I should in vain endeavour to describe. If the *officers* were to go out, eight or ten o'clock was the hour, sweating the men in the heat of the day, breaking in upon the time for cooking their dinner, putting all things out of order and all men out of humour. When I was commander, the men had a long day of leisure before them: they could ramble into the town or into the woods; go to get raspberries, to catch birds, to catch fish, or to pursue any other recreation, and such of them as chose, and were qualified, to work at their trades.

Characteristically, Cobbett is touched by the beauty of the bayonets in the rising sun, and equally characteristically angered by the incompetence of his superior officers.

Cobbett's years as a sergeant-major formed his character and perhaps did something, too, to shape the brisk, 'parade-ground' peremptoriness of his prose style. They also instilled in him a contempt for artificial distinctions. In his later recollections he tells many stories of his officers' incapacity and the extent to which they depended upon him. For example, when a revised drill-manual was brought into use:[25]

> I had to give lectures of instruction to the officers themselves, the Colonel not excepted; and, for several of them, I had to make out,

upon large cards, which they bought for the purpose, little plans
of the position of the regiment, together with lists of the words
of command, which they had to give in the field. There was I, at
the review, upon the flank of the grenadier company, with my
worsted shoulder-knot, and my great high, coarse, hairy cap;
confounded in the ranks amongst other men, whilst those who
were commanding me to move my hands or my feet, thus or
thus, were, in fact, uttering words, which I had taught them; and
were, in everything except mere authority, my inferiors; and ought
to have been commanded by me. It was impossible for reflections
of this sort not to intrude themselves; and, as I advanced in
experience, I felt less and less respect for those, whom I was
compelled to obey.

But it was the dishonesty of officers, more than what he saw as their
incompetence, indolence, drunkenness or swagger, which he detested;
so, as early as 1787, he began collecting from muster-books and
accounts evidence of certain officers' peculations, with the intention of
bringing them to justice once he was discharged from the Army and
safe in England.

Before long, Cobbett had another reason for wishing to return to
his homeland. He had fallen in love with Ann Reid, daughter of a
sergeant of artillery, after he had seen her out in the snow one February
morning at daybreak scrubbing out a washing-tub – ' "That's the girl
for me", said I' – but the artillery had been posted back to England.
Cobbett had saved one-hundred-and-fifty guineas, a remarkable sum
from four years' soldiering, 'the earnings of my early hours, in writing
for the pay-master, the quarter-master, and others, in addition to the
saving of my own pay', which he gave to Ann to maintain herself and
live without hard work until he could come home to marry her.
When, in November 1791 after four years' separation, the pair were
reunited, Cobbett 'found my little girl *a servant of all work* (and hard
work it was), at five pounds a year ... and, without hardly saying a
word about the matter, she put into my *hands the whole of my hundred
and fifty guineas unbroken!*'[26] In perseverance and dedication to hard
work Cobbett had met his match, and in frugality his undoubted
superior. They were married on 5 February 1792; Ann was nearly
eighteen and Cobbett nearly twenty-nine.

Hoping still to bring his officers to justice he had asked for and
received his discharge from the Army in November 1791, two weeks

after his regiment's return home. In January he sent to the Secretary at War a series of charges against his former commanding officer, adjutant and quarter-master, accusing them of making false musters and returns, and of various forms of misappropriation of public money or soldiers' pay. A court martial was arranged for March 1792 where Cobbett would act as prosecutor, but a few days before it was convened he fled secretly to France. The court sat, the charges were read, but none of the witnesses summoned by Cobbett was prepared to speak, and so, in the absence of the prosecutor, the accused were honourably acquitted. This prosecution had been, from the start, a wild Quixotic venture. Cobbett's charges may have been well-founded, but the social position of himself and his witnesses (who were mostly common soldiers still serving in the regiment) relative to that of the accused officers made it virtually certain that the prosecution would have failed. He feared that the regimental accounts, which had remained in the accused officers' hands between January and March, would have been tampered with, that his witnesses would be intimidated, and, finally, that there was a plot to prosecute him on false charges of sedition. Less remarkable than the panic of his sudden flight is the foolhardy courage that impelled Cobbett to imagine that he could, single-handed, have won this action. The episode foreshadows others in his life as a political fighter: for a while he would display a sublimely innocent self-confidence, then his nerve suddenly failed. Often he was as much a danger to his friends as to his enemies, for we can assume that the witnesses he called to the court martial would subsequently be marked men in the eyes of authority, just as, later, the poor pedlars of Cobbett's *Political Register* were.

It is likely, though, that Cobbett struck another, less ineffective blow against corruption in high places at this time, for he was probably the author of the anonymous pamphlet of grievances, *The Soldier's Friend*, published in June 1792. (He denied authorship in his *Political Register* for 5 October 1805, after it was known that it had circulated among the naval mutineers of 1797, but acknowledged it in the *Registers* of 23 June 1832 and 28 December 1833.) The occasion of the pamphlet was a government request for an extra £23,000 in the Army Estimates in order to raise the private soldier's allowance to three shillings a week. Three shillings was, in fact, the sum already legally assured to the soldier by the annual Mutiny Act, but officers withheld part of this money, so that, as the Secretary at War admitted in the debate of February 1792, 'It had so happened that of late years the soldier had

43

only eighteenpence or two shillings a week'. Cobbett was at this moment attempting to have three officers court martialled, but the government apparently proposed to make the taxpayer bear the expense of officers' peculations.

The author of *The Soldier's Friend* commented, with all the heavy use of iteration and italics that would be characteristic of Cobbett's acknowledged writings:

> It has so *happened*, and for years too! astonishing! It has so *happened* that an Act of Parliament has been most notoriously and shamefully disobeyed for years, to the extreme misery of thousands of deluded wretches (our countrymen), and to the great detriment of the nation at large; it has *so happened* that not one of the offenders has been brought to justice for this disobedience, even now it is fully discovered; and it has *so happened* that the hand of power has made another dive into the national purse, in order – not to add to what the soldier ought to have received; not to satisfy *his* hunger and thirst; but to gratify the whim or the avarice of his capricious and plundering superiors.

He goes on to show in detail how it has so happened, and his explanation of the mechanics of peculation seems to bear closely upon Cobbett's observations in New Brunswick and the specific charges he had made against his own officers. The blunt sarcasm, not to speak of the anti-Semitism, of the mature Cobbett appears when the pamphleteer writes of officers he has known: 'I could mention characters in this *honourable* profession that would shine among the *Seed of Abraham*, or do honour to the society of stock-jobbers.' He writes bitterly upon the hard lot of the common soldier and declares that the government does not prosecute corrupt, plundering officers because 'the ruling Powers look upon your officers as Gentlemen and upon you as Beasts' and because there is a sinister connection between government, 'the ruling Faction', and the commanding officers of that great potential instrument of oppression, a standing army. Like an old-fashioned Commonwealthman, and like the later Cobbett, he asserts the power of Parliament, and of the nation, against the Crown:

> You are a servant of the whole nation, of your countrymen,
> who pay you, and from whom you can have no separate interests.
> I would have you look upon nothing that you receive as *Favour*

or *Bounty* from Kings, Queens, or Princes; you receive the wages
of your servitude; it is your property, confirmed to you by
Acts of the Legislature of your country.

The motto on the title-page 'Laws grind the poor, and rich men rule
the law' is from *The Deserted Village*, 'every word of [which] I could
repeat by heart from the first year that I became a soldier'.[27] Cobbett's
favourite author, Swift, may have provided hints for some of the
rhetoric against stock-jobbers, standing armies and absolutism; but the
pamphlet is full of the influence of Tom Paine's *The Rights of Man*
(1791), which Cobbett had just read.

France, then enjoying its brief heyday of liberty between the fall of the
Bastille and the Reign of Terror, was the readiest haven for a man who,
like Cobbett, feared he was suspected of sedition, but his ultimate
destination was America. As a boy of thirteen he had seen his father at
Weyhill Fair drink success to General Washington against King
George, and as a soldier serving in the most barren, most villainous
piece of wasteland, New Brunswick, he had heard reports of the
beautiful, fertile land to the south. Nevertheless, he was in no hurry.
He and his new wife spent the summer in a small northern village near
St Omer while Cobbett studied the French language. In August they
set off to spend the winter in Paris, but at Abbéville, hearing that Louis
XVI was dethroned and a war between England and France likely, he
made another of his abrupt turns and flights – this time to Le Havre,
and a very uncomfortable voyage across the Atlantic.

They landed in America in October 1792 and, after three months
in Wilmington, moved to Philadelphia, then capital of the United
States, where Cobbett made his living as a translator of French books
and an English tutor to immigrant Frenchmen who had escaped the
Reign of Terror in France or fled from Negro rebellions in the French
West Indies. From these exiles he imbibed a horror of revolutionary
excess, and from these lessons he compiled a highly successful and
profitable textbook, *Le Tuteur Anglais* (1795). But by August 1794 he
had found his lifetime's occupation as a political pamphleteer when he
published, anonymously, his *Observations on the Emigration of Dr.
Joseph Priestley* (enlarged in 1795 by the addition of the allegorical
'Story of a Farmer's Bull'). Priestley was the scientist who had made
notable electrical experiments and investigations into the chemical
properties of gases; he was the Unitarian who was nicknamed 'Gunpowder Priestley' because he had spoken of 'laying gunpowder, grain

by grain, under the old building of error and superstition, which a single spark may hereafter inflame so as to produce an instantaneous explosion'; and he was the 'Friend of the Revolution' whose house in Birmingham had been destroyed on 14 July 1791 by a 'Church and King' mob infuriated by his intention to celebrate the anniversary of the fall of the Bastille. Uneasy in England after the outbreak of war against France, he sailed in 1794 for America where the welcoming public addresses to him from enthusiastic citizens who had 'beheld with the keenest sensibility the unparalleled persecutions which had attended him in England', together with the 'invectives against England' in his replies, irritated Cobbett enough to write these *Observations*, which, while primarily intended to encourage Francophobia in America, were at once reprinted several times in England.

Cobbett's attack on Priestley is vigorous and pungent. He points with scorn to the effrontery of a supporter of the violent and bloody French Revolution who now complains that he had not been given protection by the laws and government of his own country, even when the rioters who burned his house had been punished and he compensated. Looking at the bloodbath in France, Cobbett observes that Priestley had suffered only the mildest form of the mischief that he had himself advocated. It is clear that, having lived in two post-revolutionary societies since reading Tom Paine, Cobbett had now abruptly changed his politics – but if his politics are reactionary so is his satirical technique. His lampoon assimilates Priestley to the butts of Butler and Swift – the fanatical, rebellious Dissenter and the mad projector:[28]

> The Doctor was one of those who entertained hopes of bringing about a revolution in England upon the French plan; and for this purpose he found it would be very convenient for him to be at the head of a religious sect. Unitarianism was now revived, and the society held regular meetings at Birmingham. In the inflammatory discourses, called sermons, delivered at these meetings, the English constitution was first openly attacked. Here it was that the Doctor beat his drum ecclesiastic, to raise recruits in the cause of rebellion. . . .
>
> But the strangest part of the story remains to be told; for when this bustle was all over and settled, and every body thought the perverse fellow was going to take to his church, and get his living in an honest way, what did he do but set to work bottling

up his own f-rts, and selling them for superfine inflammable air, and what's still worse, had the impudence to want a patent for the *discovery*.

Priestley, the wild system-monger, 'the philosophi-theologi-politi-cal empiric' is one of those visionaries who will not take man as they find him and govern him on principles established by experience, but will have him to be 'a faultless monster that the world ne'er saw'. Cobbett says nothing of his own political principles, except to indicate that he is for the monarchy, the common law and the natural growth of institutions; but his bread-and-butter political values perhaps emerge most clearly in the gustative representation of Merry England with which he begins his 'Story of a Farmer's Bull' (the bull is the English people and the troublesome fellow Priestley):[29]

A certain troublesome fellow, who turned his back upon the church, having occasion to pass through a large farm-yard in his way to a meeting-house, met with a fine majestic venerable old Bull lying down at his ease, and basking in the sunshine. This Bull was at times the tamest creature in the world; he would suffer the curs to yelp at him, the flies to tease him, and even some of the mischievous fellows to pull him by the horns. He was at this very moment in one of his gentlest humours ruminating upon past and present scenes of delight; contemplating the neighbouring dairy and the farm-yard, where the milch cows had their bags all distended till they were nearly running over; the calves, and the pigs, and the poultry, were frisking, and grunting, and crowing on every dunghill; the granaries were full, and the barns ready to burst; there was, besides, many a goodly rick of wheat, and barley, and oats, and peas, and beans, and hay, and rye-grass and clover. The dairy was full of curds, and cream, and butter, and cheese of every kind. To be sure there was plenty for the master and his family, and all the servants, and every body belonging to the farm. Nay, those that were poor and needy, and idle, and lazy, and sick, and proud, and saucy, and old, and infirm, and silly, were freely supplied.

Cobbett's first test of good government was that all subjects should have well-filled bellies.

The attack on Priestley provoked many adverse reviews and drew Cobbett into a six-year-long pamphlet battle against the whole pro-

French faction, led by Jefferson and drawing strength from 'Democratic Clubs' and societies of Irish revolutionaries, which wanted the United States to join the French Republic in a crusading war against England and the other monarchies. The Federalist government under Washington's presidency wished to prevent the spread of revolutionary influences in America and preserve abroad a neutrality sympathetic to England, her best trading partner; so that when Cobbett threw himself pugnaciously into controversy with works under such characteristic titles as *A Bone to Gnaw for the Democrats* (January, 1795) and *A Kick for a Bite* (March, 1795 – under the happy pseudonym 'Peter Porcupine'), he did so both as an American federalist and an English patriot. In a typical gesture, on becoming his own publisher and bookseller, he opened his bookshop in July 1796 with a display of prints of kings, queens, princes, nobles, English cabinet ministers, bishops, judges and admirals, all calculated to vex the Philadelphian 'Jacobins'.

Cobbett's target, beyond the American democratic clubs and their press, was France, which was still, as it had been in Cobbett's youth, England's 'natural enemy'. His pamphlets are full of accounts of the atrocities said to have been committed by these 'free and enlightened French republicans' during the Revolution and during Bonaparte's campaigns in Italy and Germany. The 'infamous' Tom Paine is now damned (though for this Cobbett would later make strange expiation) and, along with him, the other members of Jefferson's circle of philosopher-politicians, including Priestley, David Rittenhouse the astronomer, and, particularly, Benjamin Rush, chemist, medical practitioner and land-speculator. Such men are foolish *virtuosi*, but dangerous when they meddle in politics, because the effect of their revolutionary theories is to dehumanize not only themselves but the mobs who are their creatures. Enlightened, democratic, theoretic liberty becomes in practice anarchy or tyranny. Republican liberty, whether French or American, is 'flummery and mush', while English liberty under the throne is 'roast beef and plumb pudding'.[30] Cobbett is not stretching a metaphor; he believes that English constitutional liberty under a monarch whom all obey and who protects the many against the tyranny and rapacity of the aspiring, rich and avaricious few, does in fact secure roast beef and plum-pudding for the people.

Though *A Tale of a Tub* may be their distant model, the little fables and allegories with which Cobbett peppers and salts his pamphlets are always transparently simple. He rarely attempts to imitate the complexity of Swift's satire. Perhaps occasionally there is a hint of Swift's damning 'fairness' by which an enemy is cleared of one charge so that he may be convicted on another; thus, demonstrating that Whigs and Republicans are the worse species of fanatics, he remarks that the Methodist 'now and then, indeed, makes use of the cloak of religion for the purposes of fraud or seduction; but, nine times out of ten, he has no other object in view than that of obtaining an easy comfortable living, without manual labour'.[31] With the body metaphor in *A Bone to Gnaw for the Democrats* (where the 'crumena' is the seditious hack-pamphleteer's empty purse) he attempts a more obviously Swiftian manner:[32]

> We are told, that there is, or ought to be, about every human body, a certain part called the *crumena*, upon which depends the whole oeconomy of the intestines. When the *crumena* is full, the intestines are in a correspondent state; and then the body is inclined to repose, and the mind to peace and good neighbour-hood: but when the *crumena* becomes empty, the sympathetic intestines are immediately contracted, and the whole internal state of the patient is thrown into insurrection and uproar, which, communicating itself to the brain, produces what a learned state physician calls the *mania reformationis*; and if this malady is not stopped at once, by the help of an hempen necklace, or some other remedy equally efficacious, it never fails to break out into Atheism, Robbery, Unitarianism, Swindling, Jacobinism, Massacres, Civic Feasts and Insurrections.

Here Cobbett goes a little way towards assuming a Swiftian mask, the *persona* of those philosophers who are his targets; but such indirection is rare. Cobbett usually enters battle without disguise, armed only with his flair for sarcasm and ready, energetic vituperation, and with a rock-like self-esteem that is simple and strong enough to constitute a kind of integrity. Determined to be recognized for what he is, he sometimes breaks off his personal attacks upon his political adversaries in order to reflect upon the wholeness and wholesomeness of his own life, and to muse with unconcealed pride upon his rise from obscurity to distinction. Thus in his monthly periodical, *The Political Censor*, for September 1796, he introduces his review of a group of hostile pamphlets as follows:[33]

> Dear, Father, when you used to set me off to work in the morning, dressed in my blue smock-frock and woollen spatterdashes, with

my bag of bread and cheese and bottle of small beer swung over
my shoulder on the little crook that my old god-father Boxall
gave me, little did you imagine that I should one day become so
great a man as to have my picture stuck in the windows, and have
four whole books published about me in the course of one week.
... When I had the honour to serve King George, I was elated
enough at the putting on of my worsted shoulder-knot, and,
afterwards, my silver-laced coat; what must my feelings be then,
upon seeing half a dozen authors, all *Doctors* or the devil knows
what, writing about me at one time.

Such self-esteem and the specific need to refute charges that he was
an agent in the pay of the British government and that he had behaved
with base ingratitude towards his first American publisher, Thomas
Bradford, were the occasion for Cobbett to write *The Life and Adventures of Peter Porcupine* (1796) which is the freshest of the American
pamphlets because the most free from polemical dust and heat. In
passages such as those already quoted (pp. 35-6, 38-9) where in memory
he recreates the honest pride and happy days of youth in Farnham or
an experience of patriotic rapture on Portsdown Hill, Cobbett blends
his sense of the unique value of his own life into an attractive, idealized
vision of Old England. Like his Romantic contemporaries in that age
of autobiographies, he has found that his own life has a representative
significance.

Peter Procupine continued to shoot his quills against French Jacobins
and their friends the American Democrats until he brought upon
himself a libel action which ended in December 1799. Judgment was
made against Cobbett to the extent of $5,000 in damages, nearly as
much again in costs, and a further fine for his breach of good behaviour
in connection with an earlier libel case. The action arose because he had
called Dr Benjamin Rush a quack, but plaintiff and judge alike were
Cobbett's political enemies, and he, justifiably, concluded that the
heavy sentence was politically motivated. Damages, costs and fine
were eventually paid by a public subscription among the loyalists of
Nova Scotia and New Brunswick, but for a while Cobbett was short
of money. His position was further weakened by the passage of the
Aliens Act which gave the Federal government power to deport
British subjects who fell foul of the law. So, although he had set up a
new bookseller's business in New York in October 1799, his eyes now
turned towards England where nearly all his American pamphlets had

been reprinted and well received by the government – and where, he was assured by the British Embassy in Philadelphia, he could have powerful friends if he wished. In July 1800 the Cobbetts returned to their native country.

3

A One-man Country Party: 1800–10

Seven years of war against revolutionary France had taken their toll of such prosperity and liberty as the English lower orders had once enjoyed. Fearful of Jacobinism at home, the Government under Pitt had taken measures to curb the freedom of the Press, to suppress 'seditious societies' and to prevent workmen's combinations to increase wages. Habeas Corpus had been suspended. While there were men among the lower orders who wished to reform or even overthrow by force existing political institutions, most of the popular disaffection which the government stigmatized as 'Jacobinism' was the complaint of empty bellies in a period when prices were rising much faster than wages. To meet the enormous expense of the war, as much as one-sixth of the national income was taken in taxation, mostly in the form of customs and excise duties which drove up prices already high on account of wartime interruptions of trade and the draining of resources for use in the Army and Navy. With her rising industrial population, England had lost her agricultural self-sufficiency and so become more susceptible to economic influences from outside. Gold reserves were depleted and, after a run on the banks in the invasion scare of 1797, the Bank of England suspended the redemption of its notes in gold; the number or notes in circulation was thereupon greatly increased (not so much by the Bank as by many gimcrack but plausible country banks) and inflation aggravated. The overall increase in population contributed to food scarcity, and hence to high prices, though this was a fact that contemporaries were slow to recognize and that Cobbett himself never would admit. Despite an increase of arable land with widespread enclosure of wastes and some improvement of yield with improved farming methods, England during the war often stood, or thought she stood, on the verge of famine, and such apprehension itself was sufficient to drive prices still higher, so that after the two poor harvests of 1799 and 1800 the average price of wheat soared to well over twice its prewar level. High agricultural prices greatly benefited landlords, tithe-owners and farmers, but not agricultural labourers, and least of all in enclosed parishes and districts where domestic industry had been destroyed by competition from the factories. Without the waste the day-labourer's family was entirely dependent upon purchased food, and without domestic industries they had only his agricultural wage to live on, so that in the agricultural counties of the South and East an unprecedented number of labourers came on to parish relief (under the 'Speenhamland System' of a sliding scale based upon the price of bread and the size of the family), not because they were unable to work but because the wages they received were well below subsistence level. Wages were higher in the towns but the settlement laws encouraged rural labourers to stay in their own parishes and receive the paupers' dole.

Cobbett would learn all about this soon enough, but in the summer of 1800, back in England, fresh from his verbal battles against French and American Democrats, he was aware only of the overriding need to win a just war against the traditional enemy who had been made more hateful by the atrocities of the Revolution and more terrible by the military genius of Napoleon. The government had welcomed Cobbett's anti-Jacobin pamphleteering in America and was eager to enlist his help at home, so, within days of arriving in London, he was dining with Pitt at the house of William Windham, the Secretary at War, and had been offered the editorship of a government daily newspaper – which offer he declined. When he set up again as publisher and issued in May 1801 a twelve-volume collection of his American writings, under the title of *Porcupine's Works*, the list of 750 subscribers was headed by the Prince of Wales and all the royal dukes, and included many leading members of the government.

Windham, the political heir of Burke, encouraged Cobbett, who may at the time have seemed the obvious successor to Burke as anti-Jacobin journalist, to start his own daily paper, the *Porcupine* (October 1800–December 1801). When it failed, Windham advanced £600 to set up the weekly which, under various titles but best known as the *Political Register*, continued from January 1802 until after Cobbett's death. The *Porcupine* took up where the American pamphlets of 'Peter Porcupine' had left off, and was as virulently anti-Jacobin as the government could have wished. Cobbett, for instance, reprints a handbill which had called on working men to gather on Kennington

Common 'to petition the King and Parliament to reduce the price of provisions, and raise their wages, or to furnish them with the means to emigrate to some country where they may be able, by the exercise of their industry, to keep their families from perishing by famine', and remarks that its author 'would nowhere find it so easy a matter to maintain a family by the fruits of his industry (if indeed he be industrious, which we very much doubt) as in England'. The real purpose of the writer of this 'inflammatory paper' was to collect a mob by any means whatever:[1]

> Be that as it may, the vigilance of the Police Magistrates rendered the attempt abortive ... the moment a mob began to form it was dispersed by their officers. ... We are happy to know, that in consequence of the excellent distribution of the loyal military associations, who were yesterday prepared to act, at a minute's notice, and of the extreme vigilance of the government, every effort of the Jacobins to aid the cause of their republican friends in France ... will be defeated as soon as made.

There is hardly a dreary word of this that Cobbett would not in a few years regret.

The main political issue argued in the *Porcupine* was peace with France, and here Cobbett's line was Windham's but not the Government's. Pitt, with Grenville, Windham and other ministers had resigned in February 1801 over the King's refusal to grant emancipation to Roman Catholics, and had been replaced by Addington and a band of nonentities. Britain was war-weary, and, though Napoleon was master of western and southern Europe he required a truce during which he could prepare to renew war. The French negotiators of the Peace of Amiens easily out-manoeuvred the panicky British Foreign Secretary Lord Hawkesbury, so that Britain restored most of her colonial conquests while France retained in Europe the hegemony that Louis XIV had only dreamed of. Britain had failed in her war-aim to achieve security. However, the general reaction to the Peace among a people driven to distraction by high taxes and high prices was relief – even hysteria – so that when the windows of London's shops and houses were illuminated to celebrate the preliminaries of the Peace, in October 1801, and its ratification the following March, and Cobbett left his stubbornly unlit, the mob duly smashed them. As in Philadelphia, he pugnaciously set himself alongside an unpopular minority, in this case the 'New Opposition' led by Grenville and Windham, who had at once seen the Peace for the danger that it was. Cobbett repeatedly proclaimed that peace under these terms was for Britain a feeble, foolish and unnecessary capitulation to an enemy who 'has erected her colossal empire on the ruins of moral order',[2] and who remained a perilous threat.

Cobbett and his fellow scaremongers proved right. It soon appeared to the English that Napoleon had made peace only to secure a better position for waging war. On the outbreak of war in May 1803 Cobbett wrote his *Important Considerations for the People of this Kingdom,* which was published under royal authority by the Association for Preserving Liberty and Property, and was sent out as a handbill for display and distribution in every parish in England and Wales. This little work, with its catalogue of the Corsican Ogre's atrocities, is mostly grating chauvinism, but it concludes with a nobler appeal to that simple, inbred, instinctive patriotism by which a man identifies himself with the land itself:[3]

> The sun, in his whole course round the globe, shines not on a spot so blessed as this great, and now united Kingdom; gay and productive fields and gardens, lofty and extensive woods, innumerable flocks and herds, rich and inexhaustible mines, a mild and wholesome climate, giving health, activity, and vigour to fourteen millions of people; and shall we, who are thus favoured and endowed; shall we, who are abundantly supplied with iron and steel, powder and lead; shall we, who have a fleet superior to the maritime force of all the world, and who are able to bring two millions of fighting men into the field; shall we yield up this dear and happy land, together with all the liberties and honours, to preserve which our fathers so often dyed the land and the sea with their blood?

No less sincere, direct, passionate and simple is Cobbett's filial devotion to the monarchy, as he rhapsodizes in 1802:[4]

> The crown is the guardian of the people, but more especially is its guardianship necessary to those who are destitute of rank and of wealth. The King gives the weakest and poorest of us some degree of consequence ... in his justice, his magnanimity, his piety, in the widsom of his councils, in the splendour of his throne, in the glory of his arms, in all his virtues, and in all his honours, we share, not according to rank or to riches, but in

proportion to the attachment that we bear to the land which gave
us birth, and to the sovereign, whom God has commanded us
to honour and obey.

The notion that the Crown could be an effective guardian of the
people had been out of date when Bolingbroke published his *Idea of a
Patriot King* in 1749; it was preposterous in 1802. Though always a
monarchist of sorts, Cobbett would, before long, change his opinion
of this royal family, but he would never lose his tendency to be
dazzled by the ideal forms of his own romantic imagination, just as he
would never lose his feeling for tradition, his reverence for an idealized
past and a faith in the national character of England.

Romantic reverence for the King did not extend to the King's
ministers. Within three weeks of the rhapsody just quoted, Cobbett
was levelling at them the good old accusation that 'Court' was in
league with 'City' against those old landed men who were the true and
reliable trustees of the nation's wealth and honour:[5]

> The ancient nobility and gentry of the kingdom have, with a very
> few exceptions, been thrust out of all public employments. . . . A
> race of merchants and manufacturers, and bankers and loan-jobbers
> and contractors, have usurped their place, and the government is
> fast becoming what it must be expected to become in such hands.

Shortly before Pitt again became Prime Minister, in 1804, Cobbett
addressed a patriotic appeal to him, and added a caution: 'We must be
great again, or we must be nothing; and, greatness is not to be re-
acquired by implicitly yielding to the councils of merchants, manufacturers, and bankers.[6] Before six months had passed, however, he
declared that he was henceforth to be Pitt's 'assailant', no longer his
'eulogist'. Jacobinism was no longer the real danger abroad or at home.
As the war against France had changed its character to bring England
into conflict not with republicanism but with Napoleonic despotism,
so at home Englishmen needed to resist the despotism of a Prime
Minister. The general drift of Cobbett's feeling is more clear than his
logic though when he compares Napoleon – newly made Emperor –
with Pitt. Napoleon's assumption of the imperial title, writes Cobbett,[7]

> not only removes the danger before to be apprehended from the
> prevalence of notions in favour of liberty, but tends to excite
> apprehensions of a different kind, to make us fear that, by means
> of the immense and yet growing influence now deposited in the

hands of the minister by the funding and bank-note system, we may, in fact, though not in name, become little better than slaves, and slaves, too, not of the king, but of the minister of the day.

Cobbett's shouts of defiance against Napoleon gradually faded away, and had ceased altogether well before the end of the war. The real enemy was not France at all but the moneyed interest, and what Cobbett in 1805 identified as the 'Pitt System':[8]

The system of upstarts; of low-bred, low-minded sycophants usurping the stations designed by nature, by reason, by the Constitution, and by the interests of the people, to men of high birth, eminent talents, or great national services; the system by which the ancient Aristocracy and the Church have been undermined; by which the ancient gentry of the kingdom have been almost extinguished, their means of support having been transferred, by the hand of the tax-gatherer, to contractors, jobbers and Jews; the system by which but too many of the higher orders have been rendered the servile dependents of the minister of the day, and by which the lower, their generous spirit first broken down, have been moulded into a mass of parish fed paupers.

Henceforth, the state of the lower orders would be Cobbett's chief concern and all his political shifts and turns designed to better their state. For the present, still concerned with the war, he asks why should the lower orders, so oppressed and reduced to pauperism, be expected to risk their lives in defence of their country? 'Love of country', Cobbett declared in his new, more thoughtful definition of patriotism,[9]

is founded in the value which men set upon its renown, its laws, its liberties, and its prosperity; or, more properly speaking, perhaps, upon the reputation, the security, the freedom from oppression, and the happiness, which they derive from belonging to such country. . . . Amongst men who set a high value upon reputation, whether for talents or for courage, the renown of their country will be an object full as interesting as its liberties or its prosperity; but, amongst the mass of the people, freedom from oppression, and that happiness which arises from a comfortable subsistence, will always be the chief objects of attachment, and the principal motives of all the exertions which they will make in defence of their country.

This was written after Cobbett had finally broken with Windham, who had joined the new government on Pitt's death in 1806, but had made no attempt to destroy the hated 'Pitt System' of paper-money, stock-jobbing, taxation, placemen and sinecurists. Cobbett had discovered (or rediscovered, cf. p. 6 above) that there were no true political parties at Westminster, but only coalitions of selfish men bent on plunder and power. Whig and Tory, in office or out, were alike 'Court' parties – and, what was worse, in league with the City. Years later, relating this discovery, he wrote:[10]

> The Crown had one party in *possession* and another party in *expectancy, while the people had no party at all.* . . . Formerly there were a *Court Party* and a *Country Party*, the latter of which was always ready to defend the rights of the people; to oppose every attempt at encroachment on the part of ministers of the Crown.

Cobbett was the nearest thing to a one-man 'country party' on the nineteenth-century political scene; he adapted to the revolutionary world of 1800 many of the notions of a Tory squire of 1700 and in the process became, without any consciousness of inconsistency, a leader of industrial, working-class Radicalism.

Ultimately he would come to hate the so-called 'landed interest' as cordially as he hated the moneyed interest, but his cherished values were always those of the 'land', so it was natural that, after the *Political Register* was firmly and profitably established, he should buy his own stake in those 'gay and productive fields' which he had eulogized in his *Important Considerations*. Towards the end of 1804 Cobbett acquired a house in Botley, Hampshire, where he was chiefly to make his home until his bankruptcy in 1820. It is evident from a letter to Windham, in August 1805, that he saw Botley's rich soil and wholly agricultural society as the heartland of Old England:[11]

> Botley is the most delightful village in the world. It has everything in a village, that I love; and none of the things I hate. It is in a valley. The soil is rich, thick set with woods; the farms are small, the cottages neat; it has neither workhouse, nor barber, nor attorney, nor justice of the peace. . . . Two doctors, one parson. No trade, except that carried on by two or three persons, who bring coals from the Southampton Water, and who send down timber. All the rest are farmers, farmers' men, millers, millers' men, millwrights, publicans who sell beer to the farmers' men and

the farmers; copse-cutters, tree-strippers, bark-shavers, farmers'
wheelwrights, farmers' blacksmiths, shopkeepers, a schoolmistress,
and in short, nothing but persons belonging to agriculture, to
which indeed, the two doctors and the parson belong as much as
the rest.

More to Cobbett's purpose, there were no great families in this corner
of Hampshire, so that he was able quite rapidly to enlarge his landholding in a way that would have been impossible for him in, say, the
northern part of the county where whole parishes were in the hands
of a few wealthy men.

The desire for country air and country recreations probably dictated
Cobbett's purchase of Botley House with its four acres in 1804; and a
wish to settle his brother, Thomas, made him buy a farm in neighbouring Droxford in 1805. Even so, the speed and extent of his subsequent purchases suggest that William was alive to the investment value
of land in a period when wartime inflation seemed likely to continue. In
the space of five years he paid out nearly £30,000 (some from *Register*
profits, but most borrowed on mortgage) to buy farms and small
estates in Botley and two adjoining parishes, and it is possible that in
the same period he spent as much again in improvements, planting,
cottage-building and stocking those farms he took into his own hands.
In May 1810 he wrote to his brother-in-law as having just:[12]

> closed the bargain for an estate as large as all I now possess; one
> half of the parish of Durley. Three fine farms, two small ones,
> and some detached parcels of property, some in house and some
> in land, including a fine chalk-pit, and having as much timber
> upon it as I already have. The leases of the farms will be out in
> four years time. Some of the lands are let at will.

The price agreed was £15,000, but Cobbett's affairs were so disrupted
by his trial and imprisonment (cf. pp. 75–6 below) that he could not
complete the transaction; had it gone through he would have owned
well over 1,000 acres altogether. Like other city booksellers, and even
authors, before him, he was buying his way into the ranks of the lesser
landed gentry; but the fact that Cobbett was a former ploughboy and
sergeant-major made this case of social advancement, to say the least,
unusual.

By 1810 Cobbett had turned farmer, but there is no evidence to
suggest that his residence at Botley was first conceived as anything but

recreational. He spent heavily on walling and planting the four acres of grounds and building new stables at Botley House, and from the beginning, pursued eagerly the usual field-sports of hunting, coursing (which he liked best of all), shooting and fishing. As the owner of land worth a hundred pounds a year, Cobbett had shooting rights under the Game Laws and went to great trouble and expense to preserve his pheasants and other game. Part of a contract made in 1809, under which one of his farm servants undertook to destroy vermin reads:[13]

> 6d. for each magpie or crow: 1s. stoat, weazle, polecat or cat: 2s. hawk, kite, and 1s. for each young one: 5s. dog and fox cub: 10s. for each old fox: 20s. for each fox with cubs in her: 40s. for each poacher, or shooter, that shall be prosecuted to conviction, if I pardon him: and the whole of the penalty, if I take the penalty.

The inclusion of foxes, which at this date were being eagerly preserved and even imported by some hunts, may imply that Cobbett preferred the socially exclusive sport of shooting to fox-hunting where there was less class-distinction. If this is so, Cobbett's tastes would change as the Game Laws became harsher.

Like the old-fashioned landowner he was, Cobbett encouraged the traditional 'manly sports'. In October 1805 he organized at Botley the first of a series of great singlestick matches when young men were drawn from a wide area in healthy contention to break one anothers' heads 'so that the blood may run an inch', for 'fifteen guineas and a gold-laced hat' and other prizes. Such events 'which string the nerves and strengthen the frame, which excite an emulation in deeds of hardihood and valour, and which imperceptibly instill honour, generosity, and a love of glory, into the mind of the clown'[14] were part of that ideal old rural England, with all its virtues of community, and of the decent subordination implied in the word 'clown'. In 1804 he vociferously supported Windham's opposition to a parliamentary bill outlawing boxing, bull-baiting and certain other sports – a bill, Cobbett said, 'which goes to the rearing of puritanism into a system'.[15] Like the politicians of the previous age, and the age before, Cobbett believed there were six stages of national degradation: 'Commerce, Opulence, Luxury, Effeminacy, Cowardice and Slavery.' A sure symptom of effeminacy was to be seen in these attempts to extirpate boxing, wrestling, quarter-staff, singlestick, bull-baiting and 'every exercise of the common people ... that tends to prepare them for deeds of bravery of a higher order ... to preserve the independence and the liberties of their country'. The 'system of effeminacy ... includes the suppression of mirth as well as of hardy exercises, and indeed of everything that tends to produce relaxations from labour and a communication of ideas of independence among the common people'.[16] Here he has found a real enemy. Methodist and Evangelical preachers and such bodies as the Society for the Suppression of Vice, led by Pitt's 'moral lieutenant', William Wilberforce, were already beginning to dim, if not extinguish, the poor's traditional amusements, with the scarcely disguised motive of making the poor clean, sober and punctual wage-slaves. Singlestick at Botley could play its small part in preserving the old national character, and retarding the slide into cowardice and slavery. Cobbett from the first identified Wilberforce with a morose and debilitating Puritanism. Later he would accuse the great philanthropist of hypocrisy, because a sanctimonious concern for the liberty of Negroes seemed to Cobbett to consort oddly with Wilberforce's support for repressive measures by Pitt and Lord Liverpool at home.

When he bought Botley House, Cobbett had intended to spend at least three months of every year in London, but after June 1806 Botley became his regular home, and the day-to-day management of the *Political Register* was left to his London assistant, John Wright. Cobbett enlarged his landholding with the purchase in 1807 of the 260-acre farm of Fairthorn (the place with which his name is most associated, though it does not seem that he ever lived there) and in 1808 of the 270 acres of Raglington. When the leases ran out he took the land into hand, and began farming in earnest, though he reserved a considerable area for plantations. Cobbett's great variety of exotic seedlings from North America (including the 'locust' or false acacia that he was to make so famous) aroused the respectful interest of the Board of Agriculture's surveyor,[17] but his wife and neighbours thought him crazy to use rich land in this way when prices for wartime farm-produce were so high. On a modest scale Cobbett was following the example of Earl Bathurst, Henry Hoare and all those other eighteenth-century landowners who had taken to heart the injunctions of John Evelyn's *Sylva* and had planted trees to beautify the countryside, increase the material wealth and naval strength of the nation, and make provision for their posterity. Surtees wrote, 'We remember when the wise ones used to counsel a man to stick trees in his fences at every yard, and used to calculate to a fraction what they would be worth at the end of the world',[18] and Cobbett calculated in 1808 that his planta-

tions would in twenty years have appreciated in value between fifty-
and one-hundred-and-twenty-fold and would ensure a fortune for
his children; but, as it happened, the children did not come into this
patrimony.

For all his plantations, Cobbett farmed on a large scale, too. By 1810,
just before imprisonment disrupted all his schemes, he had taken in
hand over 500 acres of the land he owned, had rented at least one other
sizeable farm, had lavishly stocked his various farms and had bought
many implements (including one of those threshing-machines so much
disliked by out-of-work labourers). Using a seed-drill of the type
advocated by Jethro Tull he won a wheat-growing wager against a
neighbouring gentleman-farmer (a barrister) whose fields were sown
broadcast. To provide better access to markets he helped to plan, carry
through and finance a new turnpike road from Winchester to Portsmouth by way of Botley and his own farm gates. With his energy and
vision, his heavy capital outlay, use of machinery, and understanding
of scientific crop-rotation and stock-breeding, Cobbett was one
of the new race of enlightened, liberal 'high farmers' (with the distinction that he was a landowner, not a tenant). Had he been able to farm
uninterrupted for a long period he may well have made farming pay,
but, as it was, he lost money at Botley; and his pen, like Arthur
Young's, had to make good the losses of the plough.

Cobbett's own farms were enclosed, but he enjoyed rights of common over some neighbouring wastes and was sufficiently alive to the
interests of small farmers and cottagers to agitate fairly consistently
against the enclosure of wastes. He took the old view that waste-land
was the nursery of population:[19]

It helps to rear, in health and vigour, numerous families of the
children of labourers, which children, were it not for those
wastes, must be crammed into the stinking suburbs, amidst filth
of all sorts, and congregating together in the practice of every
species of idleness and vice. A family reared by the side of a
common or a forest is as clearly distinguishable from a family
bred in the pestiferous stench of the dark alleys of a town, as one
of the plants of Mr. Braddick's wheat [drilled according to Tull's
principle] is distinguishable from the feeble-stemmed, single-
eared, stunted stuff that makes shift to rear its head above the
cockles, and poppies, and couch-grass, in nine-tenths of the
broadcast fields in the kingdom.

This is the kind of paradoxical but persuasive figure that frequently occurred to Cobbett in the heat of controversy; it implies that morally and socially the town is the weedy wilderness, the true 'waste-land', and that the rural 'waste' is the home of true cultivation. When he went to Botley, he found on the skirts of near-by Horton Heath about thirty cottages and gardens, 'the latter chiefly encroachments on the common, which was waste (as it was called) in a manor of which the Bishop [of Winchester] was the lord'. These cottagers raised on the common cows, sheep, pigs, poultry and bees; they had vegetables, apple trees and 'black-cherry trees, called by them "merries", which was a great article in that part of Hampshire'. Altogether, on 150 acres of waste they produced as much for themselves and for the market as any neighbouring 200-acre farm, but according to Cobbett's old-fashioned view their chief merit was that they produced children: 'Was it a "waste" when a hundred, perhaps, of healthy boys and girls were playing there of a Sunday, instead of creeping about covered with filth in the alleys of a town?'[20] Cobbett vigorously, but unsuccessfully, opposed the enclosure of Horton Heath. In another neighbouring parish, Bishop's Waltham, where he owned property, Cobbett proposed to the vestry meeting that they should petition the Bishop of Winchester – the lord of this manor, too – to grant an acre of waste-land to any married labourer who would enclose and cultivate and live on it. However, Cobbett's proposal was voted down by the other landholders who took a conventional masters' view that to give the labourers a bit of land would make them 'saucy' or encourage them to breed more children who would eventually come to parish relief.[21]

Cobbett's own high farming and 'engrossing', for he was surely an engrosser of farms, albeit on a modest scale, did not cause unemployment; neither did they force him to modify his laments, couched in traditional terms (cf. p. 19 above), over the decline of small farms, which he saw now as part of the 'Pitt System':[22]

The taxing and funding, or, in other words, the *paper* system, has, and from its very nature, it must have, drawn the real property of the nation into fewer hands; it has made land and agriculture objects of speculation; it has, in every part of the kingdom, moulded many farms into one; it has almost entirely extinguished the race of small farms; from one end of England to the other, the houses which formerly contained little farms and their happy families, are now seen sinking into ruins, all the windows except one or two stopped up, leaving just light enough for some labourer, whose father was, perhaps, the small farmer, to look back upon his half-naked and half-famished children, while, from his door, he surveys all around him the land teeming with the means of luxury to his opulent and over-grown master . . . we are daily advancing to that state in which there are but two classes of men, *masters* and *abject dependents*.

Cobbett's own experience at Botley should, perhaps, have taught him to modify this well-worn generalization. Some of his own labourers lived in the farm houses which he had bought, while others lived in cottages he built for them, each with a garden. Cobbett was undoubtedly master on his own estate, but his dependants were anything but abject; there is independent evidence to confirm his constant assertion that he was a good employer.

Cobbett would employ no one who received parish relief, but the men who did work for him were guaranteed employment all the year round, in health and sickness, and were paid at rates between twelve and sixteen shillings a week (six to eight shillings for boys), with more at harvest-time. These were good cash wages for the period (1808-10) and area, particularly as in some cases they were accompanied by such perquisites as a rent-free cottage 'having an oven to bake in' and plenty of fuel carried to the door, two rods of garden, and 'twenty bushels of potatoes a year'. (After reading Cobbett's anathemas upon the potato as an article of human diet, one may be surprised to read such an entry in his farm accounts and to learn that one or two fields or potatoes were included in his crop-rotation, but perhaps the 'lazy root' was to be consumed by the fowl and pigs of Botley.) Presumably his labourers worked hard, but Cobbett was opposed in principle to a rigidly imposed 'puritanical' work-discipline, as distinct from the *self*-discipline of labour:[23]

as to imposing the necessity of never-relaxing toil and care upon the lower classes of the people, in order, as the expression is, to keep them out of mischief, it is a maxim that never could have been engendered in any mind not by nature formed for the exercise of the worst of tyranny.

Cobbett kept the old holidays and the usual traditional festivals of the rural year, and, as we have seen, encouraged 'manly sports'. His purchase of 128 rats at twopence each from the 'rat-merchant' in May 1808 was, no doubt, to provide sport for the farm dogs, but it is not known for what purposes of divination or diversion he employed a 'conjuror' in April 1810 and, according to the farm accounts, paid him five shillings for two days' work. Those unmarried farm servants who, according to the good old custom, lived in Cobbett's house were ruled paternally. On one occasion his efforts to instil the virtues of punctuality and early-rising into one of these servants caused an *imbroglio*, as a result of which Cobbett's political opponents tried to picture him as an oppressor, but there is no reason to doubt that some truth lay behind his boast:[24]

> Those who have been long employed by me, not only like my employment, but they like me personally better than they like any other man in the world; and this, not from any cant about humanity; but on account of the frankness and sincerity which they always experienced from me, that freedom in conversation, that unrestrained familiarity, and that absence of anything like superciliousness or austerity, which have always marked my character, and, in all which, to the surprise of most observers, I indulged with my children as well as with all others under me, without at all lessening my authority.

Some of his men stayed with him for many years. John Dean, for instance, was farm-carpenter at Botley, then effectively bailiff while Cobbett was in prison, then kept Cobbett's shop in London and worked as a 'newsman'; later he worked in Cobbett's seed businesses in Kensington and Barn-Elm and accompanied his master on several 'rural rides', eventually becoming his farm manager at Ash.

Cobbett claimed that he was as familiar with his children as with his servants, and the children's reminiscences of Botley confirm the picture that he was to paint in his *Advice to Young Men* of his kind authority as a father (see below, pp. 161–2). He often writes proudly of a warm and satisfying family life; for all his busy involvement in public affairs, family affections lay at the heart of his world as the root of those enduring social affections that constituted his idea of patriotism. Thus when he writes to Windham in November 1804, shortly after settling in Botley, and expresses his heartfelt desire to see the end of the 'Pitt System' and the restoration of Old England's traditional virtue and glory, Cobbett moves by the most natural transition to his hopes for, and joys in, his own children:[25]

then should I hope once more to see my country great and glorious; then should I be cheered with the prospect of being able to say to my sons, 'I leave England to you as I found it, do you the same by your children.' This, speaking of sublunary things, I can, as I often have to you, most sincerely declare to be the first wish of my heart, and the very thought of it now almost brings tears of joy from my eyes as the boys are playing round the table.

Botley House and its attendant farms could be havens of health and delight out of the storm of national politics, but they also embodied the values that Cobbett brought into politics. As Pope did at Twickenham, so Cobbett at Botley shaped a setting that expressed much of his personality as a man and writer, and gave a large measure of material reality to an imaginative other-world, opposed at every point to Court and City. As in Pope's case, the rural estate or the garden earned by profits of the pen becomes a meeting-place for opposition politicians and the moral base for a political stance. The *Political Register* papers dated from Botley implicitly and explicitly contrast that scrap of Old England on his farms with all the misery and degradation that flows into the nation at large out of the febrile corruptions of the City and the Pitt System. The *Advice to Young Men* shows the domestic regimen and family pieties of the Botley household as ideals to which others should strive. Cobbett's various writings on husbandry refer to his activities at Botley in the light of the old rural philosophy as it is refracted by his own distinctive prejudices:[26]

it is more honourable, and attended with more happiness, to be provided with competent and secure fortunes by the sowing and the planting of trees, than by endeavouring to succeed in attaining that object after the manner of the base Jews and Jobbers, who win their half-millions by 'watching the turn of the market'.

He compares the state of labourers elsewhere, pauperized by the Speenhamland System, with the state of labourers on his own farms, and declares that if other farmers cannot follow his own example and pay a living wage it is because they too are suffering under the Pitt System which enables a vast army of fundholders and 'tax-eaters' to live in idleness upon the fruit of the labour of others. Mere reform of the Poor Law would be useless or worse. In reply to Whitbread's well-intentioned parliamentary bill of 1807 proposing the hiring out of pauper labour by the parishes in order to reduce charges on the poor rate, Cobbett opposed his own Swiftian 'Modest Proposal' – 'I should not be at all surprised if someone were to propose selling of the poor, or the mortgaging of them to the fundholders' – and concluded roundly, 'I wish to see the poor men of England what the poor men of England were when I was born.'[27]

As the whole parish of Botley 'belonged to agriculture' and every one of its 600 inhabitants lived without dependence on foreign trade (apart from a few men who in the coppice-cutting season made hoops for West Indian rum barrels), so, Cobbett claimed in some of his most extravagantly physiocratic writing, could England. Overseas trade impaired the virtue, honour, national spirit and security of England, and, by creating great inequalities of wealth, increased the sufferings of the poor. France was powerful because she had an almost wholly agricultural economy, with a tiny National Debt, 'and, which is the same thing, she has no paper money; none of that sort of property which gives to its owners an interest at variance with the rest of the country'.[28] So, by an exercise of doggedly perverse logic, Cobbett came to welcome the 'Continental System' of blockade and embargo by which, after 1806, Napoleon sought to cripple England's export trade. Under mottoes from *The Deserted Village* and the coat-trailing title 'Perish Commerce' – a phrase which had caused outrage when Windham uttered it in a parliamentary speech – Cobbett wrote a series of *Political Register* articles[29] in the winter of 1807–8 showing that England could be self-sufficient and would be economically and morally healthier without overseas trade in anything but a few essential naval stores such as turpentine, pitch and some timber. Her mineral resources and her land were enough; she could grow all her own food; industry should provide for home needs and nothing more; places such as Manchester could not possibly be for the national good; and persons now engaged in export manufactures should return to the land which '*always* calls for labour, and never fails to yield a grateful return'. Cobbett's naïve, nostalgic, utterly unrealistic, agrarianism invokes a Virgilian feeling for the land itself, the *volentia rura*, a patriotic pride, a farmer's practical commensense, physiocratic economics, and, above all, an instinctive hatred of Court, City and all foreigners that would have delighted the noisiest 'October Club' Tory squire of Queen Anne's day.

Cobbett argues that for the most part all we obtain by foreign trade is a heap of debilitating luxuries, such as tea, tobacco, wines and spirits, which we should be better off without, while in exchange we part with such valuable necessaries as hardware and cloth. All true wealth comes from our own land; commerce is merely a diversionary channel through which such wealth can flow for the enrichment of the few and the ultimate impoverishment of the nation:

> the great tendency of the commercial system is to draw the real
> wealth of the whole country towards the metropolis, there, upon
> the labour of the working classes, to maintain, in idleness and
> luxury, innumerable swarms of place-men, pensioners, tax-
> gatherers, jews, jobbers, singers, parasites, and buffoons.

In this last phrase there is a touch of satirical 'yoking' which Cobbett may have learned from Swift, just as his characterization of the typical merchant as 'Sir Baalam' a little later is perhaps from Pope. Again, early-eighteenth-century fears about the growth of London, the distaste with which Gay, Pope and others regarded *nouveau-riche* patronage of Italian opera, and that dread of national 'effeminacy' proclaimed in Brown's *Estimate* of 1757, all blend into Cobbett's simple chauvinism when he attacks the 'effeminating luxuries' of the metropolis, such as those 'squeaking wretches' the Italian singers and their retinue who have consumed '[this year] two or three thousand quarters of corn':

> the singers and their crew are not only useless in themselves, but
> spread about at large their contagious effeminacy. This
> mis-application of the surplus produce of the country proceeds from
> commerce; from that intimate connection and almost intermixture
> with foreign nations, which our extended commerce has produced.

The trading interest, the moneyed interest and the Court work hand in glove: 'every thing connected with commerce is *necessarily* on the side of the minister of the day. The commercial and the funding systems are inseparable. One cannot go to any mischievous length without the other.' It was the constant theme of Bolingbroke and Swift that wealthy men are sordid, mean, selfish and unpatriotic, but the *Political Register* states this with a bluntness that makes even the *Examiner* and the *Craftsman* appear models of courteous moderation. Cobbett singles out for special attack the East India Company – by no means a new target. The possession of India is 'a terrible evil', and 'there is no glory attending such conquests and their accompanying butcheries', while:

> *'fortunes brought from India'*, which some of the Nabobs represented to be an addition to the wealth and prosperity of the nation, were the result of an operation, half parliamentary and half commercial, which conveyed the amount of those fortunes from the land and labour of England into the pockets of East India adventurers, who came home, and with the very money which they had drawn from our land and our labour, obtained the estates of those who had paid away the value of them in taxes, and became the lords of the labourers, who had, substantially, been rendered slaves by the same operation.

And again, one of Cobbett's mottoes from Goldsmith's *The Deserted Village* is

> The wealth of climes where savage nations roam
> Pillag'd from slaves to purchase slaves at home.

Cobbett denies that taxes levied on East Indian trade and traders are a real addition to national wealth, and his argument, typically, is couched in the form of a little fable about Nokes, who gains ten thousand a year by selling tea to a thousand landed Timkins. If tea imports were stopped, then what the government previously took in tax from Nokes it could now take from all the Timkins who would be wealthier (and healthier) when deprived of tea. Nokes would lose his fine house and park and hot-houses and carriages which never would have existed but for commerce; the race of Timkins would use Nokes's erstwhile profits to support useful agriculture – a course that could be regretted only by those who preferred French valets to English labourers. Significantly, another of Cobbett's 'Perish Commerce' mottoes from *The Deserted Village* is the 'man of wealth and pride' passage.

Cobbett's protest against the moneyed interest in his 'Perish Commerce' papers takes him beyond such personal heroes as Bolingbroke and Chatham, who always distinguished between the muck-worm, parasite stock-jobber and the great, liberal merchant (see p. 12 above), but elsewhere his main target remains the moneyed man as Swift and Bolingbroke had defined him. If supporters of the landed interest in the 1720s had been frightened by a National Debt of £50 million, Cobbett had cause for alarm when in the thirty years preceding the

Peace of Amiens the Debt had risen fourfold, from £150 to £600 million. As a result of Pitt's ingenious but often short-sighted and piecemeal financial projects to meet wartime expenses, the government found itself in the opening decade of the nineteenth century borrowing at a high rate of interest in order to repay loans made at a low rate. Perpetual and ever-growing interest charges upon the National Debt could be met, it seemed, only by ever-growing taxation. As early as 1806 Cobbett was proposing that interest payments on the Debt should be lessened and then discontinued. In his opinion, the Debt and the paper-money system obscenely engendered each another. As every government loan occasioned a fresh batch of paper-money to pay the interest upon it, so that batch of paper-money caused a depreciation of the currency which necessitated yet more paper-money, and so on. While all the placemen, pensioners, stock-jobbers, bankers, fundholders and every other species of 'tax-eater' grew fat, the labouring classes suffered under taxation, rising prices and currency depreciation.

Paper-credit was a mystery to Swift, but not to Cobbett who understood all as soon as he finished reading Tom Paine's *The Decline and Fall of the English System of Finance* (1796). That Cobbett read this work as early as 1803 shows that his anti-Jacobin phase did not long survive his return to England, but it was not until 1810 that he used Paine's ideas systematically in his own treatise, *Paper against Gold*, first published as a series of thirty-two letters in the *Political Register*, under a motto from Swift's letter on moneyed men (quoted p. 10 above). The immediate occasion for *Paper against Gold* was the government Bullion Committee's report that currency had depreciated since the Bank stopped gold payments in 1797, and their recommendation that gold payments should be resumed as soon as possible. Cobbett believed that it was not just to repay in gold a debt contracted in depreciated paper, and that when gold payments were resumed, interest payments on the National Debt should cease; otherwise, when prices fell, and taxes to pay this interest did not, the real burden of the Debt would greatly increase, and, like all burdens, would have to be carried by the labouring classes, while the moneyed men would be more prosperous than ever before.

Paper against Gold was conceived as a plain man's guide to a hellish mystery. Couched in the form of letters to 'the tradesmen and farmers in and near Salisbury' – where a country bank had recently failed – it opens:[30]

Gentlemen,
During the last session of parliament, a Committee, that is to say, ten or twelve members, of the House of Commons were appointed to inquire into the cause of the high price of Gold *Bullion*, that is, Gold *not coined*; and to take into consideration the state of the circulating medium, or money, of this country. This Committee have made a *Report*, as they call it; but, it is a great book that they have written, and have had printed; a book much larger than the whole of the New Testament.

Cobbett bluntly turns technical terms into common speech, while the jibe on the Report's length reminds his readers that, in money matters, the teachings of the economists are different from Christ's. Throughout his treatise Cobbett's language remains blunt, direct and energetic; by studiously refusing to use economists' jargon he claims, in effect, that, as the operation of national economic policies has a direct bearing upon the daily life of common men, common men have the right to discuss these policies. He is crude and passionate in reaction against the cold abstractions of all respectable practitioners of the dismal science; so he allows alliteration and rhythm to reveal his agitation – 'This vile paper money and funding system, this system of Dutch descent, begotten by Bishop Burnet and born in hell' – or engages in insolent dialogue with some imagined opponent:[31]

the corn and the grass and the trees will grow without paper-money; the Banks may all break in a day, and the sun will rise the next day, and the lambs will gambol and the birds will sing and the carters and country girls will grin at each other and all will go on just as if nothing had happened. 'Yes', says some besotted Pittite, 'we do not suppose, that the destruction of the paper-system would put out the light of the sun, prevent vegetation, or disable men and women to propagate their species: we are not fools enough to suppose that.' Pray, then, *what* are you fools enough to suppose?

Again, the language of the imagined economist is nicely differentiated from Cobbett's own.

In *Paper against Gold*, Cobbett tried to probe to the bottom of the Pitt System of paper-money, National Debt, taxation and tyranny, where the financial power of the City propped up a Court party – whether Whig or Tory – enabling it to divide fat sinecures and pensions among its supporters, while this same Court party remained permanently in office through its control of rotten boroughs and passed laws to give moneyed men their privileged position; and all the time the labouring people were reduced further to pauperism and slavery. The Constitution had been undermined, and Cobbett, quoting Blackstone on the separation of powers (cf. pp. 4–5 above) and using the Act of Settlement clause against 'placemen' as his motto, joined the movement for Parliamentary reform, 'from the want of which it is my firm opinion, and, I believe, the opinion of a great majority of the nation, that great part of our calamities have arisen'.[32]

Talk of Parliamentary reform had continued since the days of Wilkes, but agitation had become more difficult since the repressive 'anti-Jacobin' legislation of the 1790s, while the continuing war had made it certain that neither the Tory government nor a large part of the official Whig opposition would countenance reform for the present. Despite the existence of underground 'Corresponding Societies' and other democratic clubs for working people, the Reform movement was virtually monopolized by men of wealth and consequence. At the time Cobbett joined, its leader was Sir Francis Burdett, disciple of Bentham, country gentleman of ancient family, and, by his alliance with the banking family of Coutts, immensely wealthy. In 1802 Cobbett, still beneath the hangover of his American anti-Jacobinism, had viewed with dismay Burdett's election for Middlesex – 'It will embolden and increase the disorderly and dishonest part of this monstrously overgrown and profligate metropolis' – but in 1804 when the 'disorderly' mobs were out again in their 'Wilkes and liberty' mood to support Burdett and Reform at another Middlesex election, Cobbett was on their side and Burdett's. Cobbett supported him at the Westminster election in 1806 and again in 1807 when, sensationally, Burdett and another reformer, Lord Cochrane, defeated the two official candidates, one Whig and one Tory. Westminster was a rare example of an 'open constituency' with a household franchise which admitted some artisans and journeymen to the vote, so, in this election, men who were not regarded by Burke as part of the political 'people' or 'public' (cf. p. 3 above) had spoken for reform, and made their voices heard.

The case was different in other constituencies, as Cobbett knew to his cost. In June 1806 he had intervened in the by-election at Honiton, Devon, first as a candidate and then as a supporter of Cochrane. Cobbett's and Cochrane's single issue was the heavy tax burden due to improper expenditure on placemen and pensioners, and they promised never to receive bribes or to give them. The electors of Honiton took a different view and openly sold their votes to Cochrane's opponents. Such corruption was doubly offensive to Cobbett in so beautiful a country; the old rural England was defiled:[33]

> In quitting this scene, looking back from one of the many hills that surrounded the fertile and beautiful valley in which Honiton lay, with its houses spreading down the side of an inferior eminence crowned by its ancient and venerable church; in surveying the fields, the crops, the cattle, all the blessings that nature could bestow, all the sources of plenty and all the means of comfort and happiness, it was impossible to divest myself of a feeling of horror at reflecting upon the deeds which the sun witnessed upon this one of his most favoured spots.

So it was to the Westminster artisans and journeymen and their like that Cobbett increasingly turned, and for the next seven or eight years he acted as a kind of sergeant-major for Burdett, keeping the reform troops on their toes. His views on reform now coincided with Burdett's: a reformed Parliament should be elected on a wider and more equitable franchise, but still something short of the full, adult manhood suffrage called for by that doughty old reformer, Major Cartwright. The intention was to 'restore the Constitution', and to:[34]

> restore to the people of the whole kingdom their constitutional share in the government; that will, in other words give to every man, *paying direct taxes*, that is to say, to every *man of real property*, in fee or by lease, a voice in the choosing of the persons, who are to impose those taxes, to cause them to be levied, and to dispose of them when levied.

Such tax-paying, propertied householders would 'naturally choose *gentlemen of fortune* and *good character*' as their Members of Parliament. Cobbett does not yet have any democratical notion of enfranchising the mob. He merely wishes to restore the Constitution and place political power once again in the hands of the 'natural magistracy' – in Hume's phrase, frequently repeated by Cobbett – of public-spirited, disinterested and uncorrupt country gentlemen.

Reform would not sweep away the traditional governing class, then, it would rather free it from corruption. More democratical notions were, however, beginning to creep into Cobbett's mind, and they seem to have arisen out of his reflections upon another aspect of the

73

Constitution – the freedom of the Press. In 1809 he wrote: 'Of the *constitution* of England the *liberty of the press* constitutes an essential part.'[35] Few people would refuse lip-service to this belief, but many of Burke's 'public' were outraged by Cobbett's interpretation of liberty. Francis Jeffrey, the most distinguished of an army of journalists who tried to 'write down' Cobbett deplored, in 1807, the facts that the *Political Register* had more influence than any journal had ever exercised before upon 'that most important and most independent class of society, which stands just above the lowest', and that Cobbett was working up a 'very general spirit of discontent, distrust, and contempt for public characters, among the more intelligent and resolute portion of the inferior ranks of society'.[36] Jeffrey feared the consequences of Cobbett's successful effort to widen the area of political consciousness among the 'people', defined in a far wider sense than Burke's.

Freedom of the Press meant 'the acknowledged *legal right*, of freely expressing our opinions, be they what they may, *respecting the character and conduct of men in power*; and of stating anything, no matter what, if we can prove the *truth* of the statement'.[37] But this was a difficult right to assert when the law of seditious libel made it an offence to bring into hatred or contempt, or to create disaffection towards, the King, his heirs, his ministers, and the administration of justice. 'Vice and folly, of whatever description, hate the light,' Cobbett wrote; 'publicity is their natural enemy.'[38] All that needed to be said in justification of the freedom of the Press had been said in Pope's *Epilogue to the Satires*, and Cobbett, in drawing his pen for truth and freedom, is the self-proclaimed heir of Swift and Pope. Cobbett's never-ending praise for those two satirists was in keeping with respectable conservative literary taste up to the 1830s (while his counterbalancing denunciation of Milton, 'pensioner' Johnson, and the punning, smutty Shakespeare were consciously eccentric),[39] but his insistence that Pope, as well as being 'the brightest genius that England ever produced', was one of 'the most independent and virtuous'[40] of men indicates an understanding of Pope's moral position as satirist that was, perhaps, less common in Cobbett's day.

The enormous bulk of Cobbett's own writings and the compilations which he edited or published gave substance to his often-proclaimed ideal to let the whole truth be available for general political debate. In 1804 Cobbett began serial publication of *Parliamentary Debates*, which grew into today's *Hansard*. Other comparable projects initiated by

Cobbett were a *Parliamentary History* in thirty-six volumes (1806–20), which gathered together records of political proceedings between 1066 and 1803, and a *Complete Collection of State Trials* in thirty-three volumes (1809–26), all three series passing out of his control in 1812. In 1806 Cobbett boasted that the *Political Register* was the only paper to print all the documents relating to foreign affairs, while in 1809 he began, though he did not long continue, the somewhat more tendentious practice of printing, instead of the motto at the head of each *Register*, a list of government pensioners and the sums each one received.

Cobbett believed that the liberty of the Press gave him the right to comment on the doings of men in power, whoever they might be, and throughout the first decade of the century he became increasingly outspoken about the extravagant pensions given to younger members of the royal family and about the military incompetence of the royal dukes. Joining in a general hue and cry by opposition newspapers, Cobbett wrote many thousands of words in 1809 on the sale of army commissions and church preferments by the Duke of York's mistress; but it was not until he violently condemned the flogging of five English militia-men at Ely under the guard of German mercenary troops after the militia-men had complained about a stoppage in their pay, that the government charged him with seditious libel. Behind Cobbett's protest lay not only a widespread hatred of the German troops quartered in England, but his personal recollections of the cheating and ill-treatment that English soldiers regularly suffered. The charge of seditious libel was kept hanging over Cobbett's head for some months. On eventually being called to trial in June 1810, he conducted his own defence ineptly and was found guilty. In the days between verdict and sentence, Cobbett's nerve failed him and he sought to make peace with the government by offering to give up the *Political Register* and all political activity in exchange for freedom, but nothing came of these negotiations and on 9 July he was duly sentenced to two years' imprisonment with a fine of a thousand pounds, together with bail and sureties for his keeping the peace for a further seven years.

4

The Botley Demagogue:
1810-17

Cobbett was wealthy enough to mitigate the discomforts of two years in Newgate. He rented private quarters at twelve guineas a week, received many visitors, had one or other of his older children with him most of the time as amanuensis, and was frequently visited by his wife. He contrived to manage his estate by sending instructions down to Botley at least once a week, but his schemes there suffered by his absence. He suffered financial loss, too, when he belatedly attempted to sort out the tangle of his very informal partnership with the book-seller John Wright. Cobbett felt the prison sentence as an attack upon his fortunes, his farming and upon that close-knit family life which supplied the moral centre of his life. He felt this with particular strength when his wife came to child-bed in lodgings near Newgate and the baby was still-born. Physically comfortable as his imprisonment was, it greatly embittered him. However, the only difference that it made to his writing was that the *Political Register* appeared for a while twice a week because he had more time to write, and that editorial articles were dated from 'State Prison, Newgate' with as much emphatic pride as they had been previously from Botley. On 8 July 1812 Cobbett ended his last article from gaol with the flourish: 'State Prison, New-gate, where I have just paid a thousand pounds fine to the King; and much good may it do his Majesty.' On his release, Cobbett was fêted and returned in triumph to Botley where he resumed his gentleman-farmer's life in a smaller house upon diminished acreage.

In October 1812 Cobbett issued a series of *Addresses to the Hampshire Electors*,[1] tentatively inviting nomination of himself as a Reform candidate for one of the county seats, but in the event he did not contest the election. In the *Political Register* he continued to denounce the bad old abuses in vigorous terms and to call for a return to the good old constitution. By the following year, with Napoleon's retreat from

Moscow and his defeat at the Battle of Leipzig, Cobbett had come to oppose any continuation of the war in order to achieve the Allies' aim, which (as he saw it) was to restore all the old despotisms in Europe. The territorial ambitions of France had been checked, and if the French people preferred Napoleon to Louis XVIII they were entitled to keep him. The chief issue now was that prolongation of war meant a rising National Debt (the figure was already nine-hundred millions) and consequently greater suffering for the poor, and it meant a further postponement of the vital matter of parliamentary reform. Cobbett also opposed the desultory and futile war of 1812-14 against the United States, retracted the insulting language he had used in his 'Peter Porcupine' days and earned many American friends on this account.

Cobbett had long claimed that the struggle for Reform at home was more important than war abroad, and it might appear that Lord Liverpool's Tory government was inclined to agree when in the summer of 1812 it stationed 12,000 troops in the counties disturbed by Luddite riots. Riots and machine-breaking were the work of industrial workers unemployed or suffering wage cuts and faced with starvation, but the reaction of the panic-stricken government, ever alive to sedition and treason, was forcible repression. Cobbett scoffed bitterly at the government's claim that all these troubles were proof of a treasonable conspiracy:[2]

> I do not wish to justify the woman who, according to the
> newspapers, committed *highway robbery* in taking *some potatoes out
> of a cart at Manchester*, and, who, according to the newspapers,
> was hanged for it, [but] I cannot and I will not allow, that her
> forcibly taking some potatoes out of a cart at Manchester, was
> any proof of a *treasonable design* and of hatred against the whole
> form of our government.

There was no plot said Cobbett; rather than suppressing the riots by force, the government ought to attempt to end the misery that caused the riots. Characteristically and naïvely, his specific advice was that the authorities should enforce a reduction in the price of bread and find work on the land for unemployed industrial workers.

The end of the war in 1815 brought even more unemployment and wage cutting on top of the continuing ills of high taxes, and there was renewed rioting in many parts of the country, agricultural as well as industrial. Cobbett commented on the 'Bread or Blood' riots in East

Anglia in 1816, when starving agricultural labourers calling for a minimum wage were put down with maximum force:[3]

> It may be proper to call the offending persons '*insurgents, savages, villains, monsters, &c.*' as the Courier news-paper does. But, then, there are a great number of Englishmen, who are insurgents, savages, villains and monsters. There is no getting out of this dilemma. The fact is, they are people in *want*. They are people who have *nothing to lose, except their lives*; and of these they think little, seeing that they have so little enjoyment of them. . . . The present riots have clearly arisen out of want; out of the want of food, which will make even dumb animals break down, or leap over, fences.

Bread was dear largely on account of the new Corn Laws, which in the changed circumstances after the war operated far more inequitably than the old. The Corn Laws, which had continued with various modifications since the reign of Charles II, provided that in plentiful seasons when the price of corn was low in England there should be a bounty on the export of grain and a high duty on imports, but that in times of dearth when the price was high export was forbidden, and if the supply continued inadequate imports were allowed at a low rate of duty or duty-free. During the greater part of the eighteenth century, these laws had ensured that in an average season England had grown more than enough grain for her slowly growing population and that this was sold at tolerably steady and fair, if never extremely low, prices. The Corn Laws had no direct effect on prices during the Revolutionary and Napoleonic Wars, because other factors such as population growth, poor harvests and interruption of trade ensured that dearth or the constant fear of dearth kept prices very high. During wartime, landlords had enclosed wastes which could be cultivated profitably only if these high prices continued; substantial tenant-farmers had sunk capital in land-reclamation, and other improvements, too, and renewed their leases at high rents which they would not be able to pay if prices came down. So, in a dismal panic, a landlord-dominated Parliament passed in 1815 a new, wholly protectionist, Corn Law which placed almost prohibitively high duties on imported grain. This was done at a time when home population was outstripping home supply even in years of good harvest, and when cheaper foreign sources of grain were becoming available.

Petitions against the Corn Bill of 1815 poured in from all the industrial areas, where the workers hated high food prices and their employers feared that dear food might compel them to pay higher wages; Cobbett sent his petition, too, on behalf of all the lower orders, including agricultural labourers, and of farmers and other payers of poor-rates. Low prices, he claimed, would mean an end to widespread pauperism and bring economic, but above all moral, benefit to rural society at large:[4]

> pauperism, kept in check for a long series of years by the native
> spirit of the people, was let loose like a torrent over the land by
> the enormous prices during the late wars, which, in depriving
> men of their food, deprived them, and even their children of that
> shame, which had before kept them from the Poor-List; and
> therefore, your Petitioner cannot but view with profound sorrow,
> that a legislative act should be in contemplation, having, as he
> firmly believes, a tendency to prevent for ever the restoration of
> the labouring classes to their former state of comfort, of
> independence of mind, and of frankness and boldness of manners.

This Bill was against nature: 'There is something so monstrous in the idea of compelling people to purchase their food dear, when they can purchase it cheap, that human nature revolts at it.' But behind it lay the yet more monstrous 'System': 'It is the Government, and not the Farmer, who stands in need of high priced corn.' Cobbett saw that the evil lay in the Debt, the pensions, the army and all other unnecessary government expenses which called for high taxes, which could only be paid if prices were high. At one end of a chain of corruption labourers paid dearly for their scanty food; at the other end the fund-holders and pensioners grew fat.[5]

It was the 'System' which had unduly raised the large farmer's standard of living, so that now he had:[6]

> A fox-hunting horse; polished boots; a spanking trot to market;
> a 'Get out of the way or by G–d I'll ride over you' to every poor
> devil upon the road; wine at his dinner; a servant (and sometimes
> in *livery*) to wait at his table; a painted lady for a wife; sons
> aping the young 'squires and lords; a house crammed up with
> sofas, pianos, and all sorts of fooleries.

Cobbett's point that farmers so circumstanced are not likely to make common cause with their own labourers to reduce agricultural prices is valid, but his old-fashioned attack upon rich farmers reads too much

like a tetchy diatribe against newfangledness, all the more uncon-
vincing because Farmer Cobbett himself – thanks to journalism
rather than profitable farming – enjoyed a standard of living comparable with the one he describes with so much disgust.

As the rich farmers were involved in the 'System', so to an even
greater degree were the old landed families who had once formed the
'natural magistracy'. At the height of his patriotic fervour just after the
war was resumed in 1803, Cobbett had approvingly printed a letter
prophesying that:[7]

> The strength and value of the landed interest will be once more
> duly appreciated; and the false splendour of mercantile wealth
> no longer monopolize the attention of the legislature and the
> government. . . . The days of the Veres, and Percies, and
> Cliffords, and Nevilles must return; and the glory of leading
> *vassals* into the *field.*

But, as had been remarked on another occasion, the Age of Chivalry
was dead, and Cobbett soon came to recognize the fact. By 1812
Cobbett recognized that the country gentlemen of England had
abdicated their responsibilities both to their vassals and their nation:[8]

> The gentlemen of England seem to have given up the country
> to the minister of the day. Each seems to care for nobody but
> himself; and to think himself pretty well off, if he has weight
> enough left to secure him the permission to have a sufficiency
> to live upon. . . . The natural magistracy, as Hume calls it, is
> extinguished. All authority now proceeds immediately from the
> government. There is not a village in England where the
> Surveyor of Taxes is not a more powerful man than the Lord
> of the Manor.

Cobbett would grow to hate and despise the landed gentry more and
more during the next twenty years. In his view, not only were the
landed men giving way before the moneyed, but they were the agents
of their own ruin, for it was they who supported the whole hideous
web of parliamentary corruption. Whatever the iniquities of stock-
jobbers and fundholders, the small body of 'boroughmongers' who
could buy and sell parliamentary seats were worse: 'The Boroughmongers, 23 of whom have from 140 to 200 votes, are our real rulers.'
It suits the boroughmongers to have the throne occupied by a member
of a despicable foreign family because such a creature can be no rival

for their power; he 'is neither more nor less than a passive tool in the hands of those who own the seats in Parliament, and who, in fact, appoint all the Ministers, Ambassadors, Judges and Commanders.' As the Crown is in the boroughmongers' pocket, so is the Church. After describing the impious, solemn farce of the *congé d'élire* Cobbett observes:

> it is not the *king*, but some Borough-monger, in virtue of some bargain for votes, who has really nominated the Bishop; ... the *king*, the Minister, the Dean and Chapter, and the Holy Ghost proceeding, are neither more nor less than so many tools in the hands of the said Borough-monger.

After referring to Blackstone on the Constitution, with its wise system of divided powers, its checks and balances, Cobbett asks what is the real constitution at present:[9]

> It is neither a monarchy, an aristocracy, nor a democracy; it is a band of great nobles, who by sham elections, and by the means of all sorts of bribery and corruption, have obtained an absolute sway in the country, having under them, for the purposes of *show* and execution, a thing they call a *king*, sharp and unprincipled fellows whom they call *Ministers*, a mummery which they call a *Church*, experienced and well-tried and steel-hearted men whom they call *Judges*, a company of false money-makers whom they call a *Bank*, numerous bands of brave and needy persons whom they call *soldiers and sailors*; and a talking, corrupt, and impudent set, whom they call a *House of Commons*.

By 1816, then, Cobbett had declared himself at war with the 'usurpation' of the boroughmongers. The worst consequences of this usurpation had appeared in his lifetime, but the circumstances that had made it possible had been created in the 'most villainous rebellion' of 1688, when the aristocracy, with the aid of a Dutch army and the passive acquiescence of the people, overthrew the mild rule of the Stuarts and created a new despotism whose tools included the Bank of England, the Debt, paper-money and the corruption of Parliament by the boroughmongers. Nevertheless, according to Cobbett's myth of history, the natural wealth of the land and the natural strength of the people ensured that for the greater part of the eighteenth century:[10]

> We were a nation famed throughout the world not less for the goodness of our dress, the plenty and solid quantity of our food,

the decency, neatness and comfort of our household stuff and our
dwellings, than for our freedom and our valour. English
hospitality; the roast beef of old England; the Englishman's beer
and beef and the Frenchman's soup-meagre and frogs . . . were
common, proverbial sayings.

Frequently in these immediately post-war years Cobbett elaborates
his picture of a golden age in rural England fifty years before:

Well do I remember, when old men, common labourers, used
to wear to church good broad-cloth coats which they had worn
at their weddings. They were frugal and careful, but they had
encouragement to practise those virtues. The household goods of
a labouring man, his clock, his trenchers and his pewter plates,
his utensils of brass and copper, his chairs, his joint-stools, his
substantial oaken tables, his bedding and all that belonged to
him, form a contrast with his present miserable and worthless
stuff that makes one's heart ache but to think of. His beer and
his bread and meat are now exchanged for the cat-lap of the
tea-kettle, taxed to more than three-fourths of its prime cost, and
for the cold and heartless diet of the potato plant.

The comfortable condition of common people in Cobbett's childhood,
as he remembered it, was the norm. This, indeed, so Cobbett claims,
was their condition in the fifteenth century, for Burdett had shown him
a description of England by Henry VI's Lord Chief Justice, Sir John
Fortescue, which said that the English common people had abundance
of all sorts of flesh and fish, were clothed in good woollens had woollen
bedding and plenty of household goods, and in all ways were more
prosperous and more free than the French.[11] Now all was changed;
the common people were starving and groaning beneath oppressive
laws, and everyone was subject to crushing taxation in order to support
wealthy sinecurists. A conspiracy of politicians, fundholders and
boroughmongers, moneyed men and landed men, had subverted the
good old Constitution, so that it could now be restored only by a
thoroughgoing reform of Parliament.

Cobbett still referred repeatedly to the checks and balances of some
ideal old English form of government, just as Swift and Bolingbroke
had done, but he no longer trusted the landed gentry as guardians of
the Constitution. The guardians must be the 'people', which included
the common people. If the principle were accepted that no man ought

to be taxed without his own consent, then it should be remembered that '*every* journeyman and labourer paid *ten pounds a year in taxes* out of every *eighteen* pounds that he earned and expended.'[12] Property should be represented directly, rather than 'virtually', and every man had indubitable property in the labour of his head and hands. Cobbett had come under the influence of the patriarch of English Radical reformers, Major John Cartwright, who had been a prominent figure in every lawful agitation for reform since 1776, when his pamphlet *Take your Choice* had called for a return to the true 'Gothic' constitution by way of annual parliaments, manhood suffrage and voting by ballot; so by the beginning of 1817 Cobbett was advocating the full Cartwright programme (and justifying universal male suffrage by a very sophistical interpretation of Sir John Fortescue's and Blackstone's legal writings).[13]

Cobbett repudiated what he now saw as the mild, Whiggish reformism 'from above' of Burdett, and in a series of *Political Register* articles towards the end of 1817 denounced his former friend and leader for alleged inconsistencies. Even so, between 1803 and 1817, Cobbett had changed his own opinions far more than Burdett had. What appeared to be Burdett's snobbish unwillingness to accept support from the common people aroused Cobbett's scorn: 'Is not a ploughman or a journeyman artisan as *respectable* as a farmer or shopkeeper of the same morals and manners? Is not a coal-heaver as respectable as a Lord, if their minds and morals are upon a level?'[14] Cobbett's own life and character were an unequivocal answer, if answer were needed to this rhetorical question. He had always been a foe to empty distinctions, but it was only after his active alliance with Major Cartwright, and with 'Orator' Henry Hunt about the same time, that he began seeking to enlist the common people themselves in the cause of that parliamentary reform from which they would benefit. Even so, he disliked any notion of a working-class or even a Radical party, and, naturally, he would have nothing to do with the tavern-clubs where small groups of latter-day Jacobins among the lower orders plotted active rebellion. He deplored on the one hand Henry Hunt's wild talk, and on the other Burdett's squeamishness. He wanted to involve the common people in the cause of reform using, as Cartwright advised, the old eighteenth-century constitutional tools (which Johnson so despised) of public meetings and petitions to Parliament for redress of grievances, but at the same time doubted their efficacy. It was impossible to believe that the boroughmongers,[15] men so vested with power, and having a great standing army at their nod, would ever give up this mass of power and this mass of possessions, merely at the *solicitation* of an unarmed people. It was like petitioning an able man to give up his talents to you, or a handsome woman to give you up her beauty.

This defeatist conclusion was penned after Cobbett had fled to America in 1817, but in the previous October he had been convinced that a direct push by way of agitation and petition for reform would succeed, and that his own *Political Register* must play a vital part in this. For some years Cobbett's journal had been gaining circulation in the politically conscious industrial towns of the North, where it was read not only by men in the middle classes but was taken in by many working men's clubs and reading-rooms. This was in spite of its high price, 1s. 0½d., on account of the stamp tax of fourpence a copy and the fact that it received no government advertizing. However, taking advantage of a loophole in the stamp regulations, Cobbett began on 2 November 1816 the separate publication of leading articles from past or current *Political Registers* in the form of open sheets, or, after a few weeks, as octavo pamphlets under the title *Cobbett's Weekly Political Pamphlet*. As these pamphlets contained no news they incurred no duty, apart from a small tax on the entire impression, so the price could be twopence a copy, with low-quantity rates for those who desired to distribute. Cobbett knew that though three or four working men could not afford a shilling between them every week to read the *Political Register*, they could spare a halfpenny each, and the expense would be less than going to a public-house to hear it read. Always the family man, Cobbett saw other advantages:[16]

> The *children* will also have an opportunity of reading. The wife can sometimes read, if the husband cannot. The women will understand the causes of their starvation and raggedness as well as the men, and will lend their aid in endeavouring to effect the proper remedy. Many a father will thus, I hope, be induced to spend his evenings at home in instructing his children in the history of their misery, and in warming them into acts of patriotism.

Domesticity is the fount of patriotism and the hearth the foundation of public virtue.

As the unstamped weekly *Pamphlet*, soon christened 'Twopenny

Trash' by Castlereagh, could not be sent by post, Cobbett made elaborate and remarkably successful arrangements for its distribution. He invited shopkeepers and others all over the country to become newsvendors; they should send a regular weekly order, giving 'very plain' directions concerning the coach by which the parcel should be sent. As the wholesale price was 12s. 6d. a hundred (or £5 10s. a thousand), the profit on a substantial sale could support a family, and Cobbett pointed to certain successful acts of salesmanship, such as the case of the cottager who made seventy-five shillings within two or three weeks on the sale of 1,800 copies of the twopenny *Pamphlet*, hawking them around the neighbouring towns and villages. A correspondent of Lord Sidmouth (formerly Addington, now Home Secretary) wrote on 16 March 1817 about Cobbett's newsvendor in Hull: 'He runs about with them and sells about 1500 per week at three guineas per week profit. He employs *underagents* in Hull, Sculcoats and Holderness. Every cobler shop is supplied, and women who could never talk on politics are now warm for Cobbett.'[17] A government spy wrote, 'Cobatt hath done more with his Twopenny papers than any Thousand beside him, as any one can get them, the price being so low and contains so much matter as the children purchase and read them.'[18]

The first of the twopenny *Pamphlets* was a reprint of an article appearing in the full *Political Register* of the same date (2 November 1816). It was an 'Address to the Journeymen and Labourers', and opened:

Friends and fellow countrymen,
Whatever the Pride of rank, of riches or of scholarship may have induced some men to believe, or to affect to believe, the real strength and all the resources of a country, ever have sprung and ever must spring, from the *labour* of its people; and hence it is, that this nation, which is so small in numbers and so poor in climate and soil compared with many others, has, for many ages, been the most powerful nation in the world: it is the most industrious, the most laborious, and therefore, the most powerful. Elegant dresses, superb furniture, stately buildings, fine roads and canals, fleet horses and carriages, numerous and stout ships, warehouses teeming with goods; all these . . . spring from *labour.* . . .
As it is the labour of those who toil which makes a country

abound in resources, so it is the same class of men, who must, by their arms, secure its safety and uphold its fame. . . .

With this correct idea of your own worth in your minds, with what indignation must you hear yourselves called the Populace, the Rabble, the Mob, the Swinish multitude; and with what greater indignation, if possible, must you hear the projects of those cool and cruel and insolent men.

Cobbett goes on to discuss in the plainest language the causes of present misery – taxation, sinecures, the Debt, paper-money and the rest – and proclaims that the only remedy is to be found in a reformed Parliament, for which the journeymen and labourers should petition in a peaceable and lawful manner. Cobbett adds a warning against agitators who 'would persuade you, that, because things have been perverted from their true ends, there is *nothing good* in our *constitution and laws*. For what, then, did Hampden die in the field, and Sidney on the scaffold? . . . We want *great alteration*, but we want *nothing new*. . . .' Cobbett has a respect for the past, and even for property, which is almost Burkeian, but the perspective in which these are regarded is certainly not Burke's. He flings back those unlucky words 'swinish multitude', and, further to emphasize the inhumanity of the cool and cruel and insolent men now in power, he links Burke's phrase with a kind of 'Modest Proposal': 'As some have called you the *swinish multitude*, would it be much wonder if they were to propose to serve you as families of young pigs are served?' (This is in the course of a sharp rejoinder to that detestable 'Parson Malthus' who believed that the sufferings of the poor were a consequence of their excessive fertility.) The steady, measured rhythms and grave language in which Cobbett writes of the working man's labour as the source of all wealth and national greatness, themselves express the dignity of labour, so that it becomes no absurdity to see the labourer of 1816 as Hampden's heir. The wistful fancy of Gray's *Elegy*, and all the other eighteenth-century platitudes concerning noble peasants and the liberty of the common man, here becomes strongly felt convictions and a spur for political action.

The style of the 'Address' is as sturdy and direct as the traditional, even conservative, attitudes which underly its Radicalism. By contrast, the 'Letter to Luddites' (in *Pamphlet* and *Register*, 30 November 1816) is evasive and contorted. Cobbett has the worthy aim of directing popular discontent away from the sporadic and unproductive violence of bread-riots and machine-breaking into a controlled, continuous, peaceful agitation for Reform. He argues that paper-money, taxation and sinecures, not machines, have caused the labourers' misery, and that when government newspapers attempt to inculcate notions hostile to machinery they are winding a Machiavellian plot to provoke acts of violence which will make an excuse for cruel repression by the government. Pointing to examples in the home and on the farm, the places best known to him, Cobbett tries to prove that, as machines made work easier and 'cheaper', they operated to the benefit of everyone, including all workpeople. Cobbett's style lacks conviction, however. It shifts from the cheap verbal trickery of the *reductio ad absurdum* – 'hand mills are *machines*. Come, then, let us resort to Robinson Crusoe's *pestle and mortar*. No: those are machines. Why, then, let us, like cattle, grind the corn with our *teeth*!' – to the cold abstraction of any modern political arithmetician – 'it is the *quantity of the demand* for goods that must always regulate the *price*, and the price of the goods must regulate the *wages* for making the goods'. Cobbett frequently betrays an unhappy tendency to faggot his political notions as they fall in line with the argument of the moment, and consistency was never his dominant characteristic, but here his eagerness to prevent any rioting which might harm the Reform cause leads him into some unexpected attitudes. Thus, like any cotton-lord, he declares that national prosperity depends upon the cheap export of manufactured goods – 'while the destruction of machinery would produce *no good* to you with regard to the *home* trade, it would produce a great deal of *harm* to you with regard to the foreign trade; because it would make your goods so *high in price*, that other nations, who would very soon have the machinery, would be able to make the same goods at a much *lower price*' – and, in order to defend bakers against the age-old charge of profiteering, he demonstrates that home-baking is uneconomical, not only on account of the cost of ovens and fuel, but because it keeps the wife at home when she could be out working. All this comes oddly from the author of 'Perish Commerce' and the future author of *Cottage Economy*; in the heat of his argument, Cobbett has forgotten the virtues, public and domestic, of his old England.

Cobbett had staked all on Reform, and was confident that it must come quickly. These were exciting times. For a few months the circulation of the twopenny *Pamphlet* rose to forty or fifty thousand copies a week – a figure many times larger than that of any other newspaper, and one that must be multiplied by, perhaps, ten, to estimate roughly the number of readers. There had been nothing comparable in popular Radical writing since Tom Paine's *The Rights of Man* (1791). Cobbett recalled:[19]

> I had put myself before the wind, which I well knew would prove too strong to suffer me to stop, or to slacken my pace. It was impossible now, in this new scene, to remain at Botley. I went off to London in a few days [from November 2nd], and remained there until my final departure for Liverpool [22 March 1817]; and, of the eventful days of my wonderful life, these were certainly the most eventful.

Samuel Bamford, weaver, poet and Radical, wrote:[20]

> At this time the writings of William Cobbett suddenly became of great authority; they were read on nearly every cottage hearth in the manufacturing districts of South Lancashire, in those of Leicester, Derby, and Nottingham; also in many of the Scottish manufacturing towns. Their influence was speedily visible; he directed his readers to the true cause of their sufferings – misgovernment; and to its proper corrective – parliamentary reform. Riots soon became scarce. . . . The Labourers . . . soon became deliberate and systematic in their proceedings.

In the twopenny *Pamphlet*, Cobbett did possibly more than any other man of his age to arouse working-class consciousness of political issues, and, indeed, to create the 'working class' as a political force. When the higher ranks enunciated the grand principle of subordination and told the labourer to be obedient and grateful to those set in authority over him, Cobbett declared that the labourer, if properly informed, was capable of thinking for himself, that he was a man, and by bearing himself manfully he would gain his rights.

There was still no nationally organized Radical movement, or any regular and continuous leadership of Reform agitation. Leadership fell to the most prominent demagogue of the day, and in the winter of 1816–17 this was Cobbett, who was for a while what Hazlitt called him, 'a kind of *fourth estate* in the politics of the country'.[21] Cobbett exercised his leadership solely through his writings and not by means of any political organization. Corresponding societies and other such bodies to further Radical ends had been outlawed, but Cobbett would have as little as possible to do with legitimate societies, for he shared the traditional 'Country' dislike of all political cabals: 'I advise my countrymen to have nothing to do with any *Political Clubs*, any secret

Cabals, any *Correspondencies*; but to trust to *individual exertions* and *open meetings*.'[22] In this he differed from Cartwright who was busy touring the provinces setting up 'Hampden Clubs', which were livelier, working-men's counterparts to the upper-class and always feeble Hampden Club for Reform in London.

In the event Cobbett's mistrust of clubs was justified, for they were all too easily penetrated by spies and agents whose reports could justify the government's repressive measures. The reverential attitude of the provincial Hampden Clubs:[23]

> towards a mythically powerful headquarters in London was to prove one of the greatest dangers which arose out of the attempt of the London Radicals to proselytize and organize the provinces. Any gentleman of ostensible respectability with a plausible story, coming among the provincial workmen in the name of 'The Hampden Club in London', was assured of credence. He came in 1817, and he was Oliver the Spy.

Oliver, and the miserable Derbyshire Rising which he in large part engineered and then betrayed, checked the Reform movement in 1817, but the reformers' own divisions damaged their cause, too.

On 15 November a great open-air meeting in Spa Fields, London, elected Burdett and 'Orator' Hunt to carry a reform petition to the Prince Regent. The petition called for universal male suffrage, annual parliaments and the ballot, and Burdett would not handle it. Hunt was refused admission to the Prince, and a second meeting was held at Spa Fields in protest against such contemptuous treatment of the people's petitioner. On this occasion a group of extremist 'Spencean Philanthropists' who were present called for revolution, marched away to seize the Tower of London and were taken up by a magistrate and five constables. This finally alienated Burdett from Hunt and Cobbett, and strengthened the government's suspicions of a widespread revolutionary plot. These suspicions were given further colour when delegates from the provincial Hampden Clubs met at the Crown and Anchor Tavern in the Strand on 22 January 1817. The very orderliness of their assembling from all parts of the country into a kind of extra-Parliamentary convention unsettled a civil authority which had been tutored to see the common people as the mobility or swinish multitude. Burdett, though he was chairman of the London Hampden Club and had convened the meeting, stayed away from the Crown and Anchor, but Cobbett, with some initial misgivings, attended and announced his conversion to the cause of universal suffrage. Major Cartwright was chairman, and Lord Cochrane carried from the meeting to the House of Commons reform petitions with half-a-million signatures. But that morning a projectile had treasonably broken the glass of the Prince Regent's coach as he went to open Parliament. The following month the Parliamentary Committees of Secrecy opened their 'Green Bags' of secret information, and reported that they had evidence to show that the Hampden Clubs were involved alongside the Spencean and other Radical organizations:[24]

> to infect the minds of all classes of the community, and particularly of those whose situation most exposes them to such impressions, with a spirit of discontent and disaffection, of insubordination, and contempt of all law, religion, and morality, and to hold out to them the plunder and division of all property, as the main object of their efforts, and the restoration of their natural rights; and no endeavours are omitted to prepare them to take up arms on the first signal for accomplishing these designs.

On the strength of these reports Parliament, in March, passed Bills to suspend habeas corpus, and considerably to strengthen existing legislation against seditious meetings, against tampering with the loyalty of the armed forces of the Crown, and against reading-rooms keeping literature which any magistrate might consider to be 'of an irreligious, immoral, or seditious tendency'. In the debates, Whigs and Tories in both Houses harped upon the mischief of a seditious Press and of twopenny pamphlets in particular. These 'Gagging Acts' were supplemented by the Home Secretary Lord Sidmouth's circular letter to all Lords-Lieutenant declaring (erroneously as the law stood) that a magistrate could arrest and imprison anyone hawking seditious literature. Publishing Sidmouth's letter, the ministerial newspaper *The Courier* said that the government 'had adopted a measure that would at once put an end to publications such as *Cobbett's Political Register* which had too long been permitted to poison the minds of weak and thoughtless people'.[25] Cobbett was blamed for the Derbyshire Rising of 1817 by the defence counsel, who castigated the 'Address to the Journeymen and Labourers' as 'one of the most malignant and diabolical publications that ever issued from the English Press'.[26]

But by then Cobbett had fled. Arguing that the Gagging Acts and suspension of habeas corpus were directed primarily against his own liberty, and not relishing another spell in prison, Cobbett had left secretly at the end of March for the United States, but not before he had made a half-hearted attempt to seek protection from the Whigs – admitting in interview with Lord Holland 'his distrust of his own nerves, and dread of behaving meanly and basely if arrested'.[27] As he travelled north to take ship at Liverpool and passed through settled, rural England in the early spring, Cobbett fumed at the spectacle of human misery among plenty, but saw in the wonderfully fertile beauty of the landscape itself a warrant that this misery must come to an end:[28]

> The road very wide and smooth; rows of fine trees on the sides of it; beautiful white-thorn hedges, and rows of ash and elm dividing the fields; the fields so neatly kept; the soil so rich; the herds and flocks of fine fat cattle and sheep on every side; the beautiful homesteads and numerous stacks of wheat! Here is wealth! Here are all the means of national power, and of individual plenty and happiness! And yet, at the end of these ten beautiful miles, covered with all the means of affording luxury in diet and in dress, we entered that city of Coventry, which, out of *twenty thousand inhabitants*, contained at that very moment upwards of *eight thousand miserable paupers*. . . .
>
> The beautiful country through which I have so lately travelled, bearing upon every inch of it, such striking marks of the industry and skill of the people, never can be destined to be inhabited by slaves. To suppose such a thing possible would be at once to libel the nation and to blaspheme against Providence.

Cobbett's flight brought dismay and demoralization to many supporters of the Reform movement, but the main effect was upon himself, for he never fully regained his authority as a Reform or working-class leader. The place of the *Political Register* was taken by such other unstamped journals as T. J. Wooler's *Black Dwarf*, William Hone's *Reformists' Register* and W. T. Sherwin's *Political Register*. The *Black Dwarf*, against all the repressive measures of the government even achieved a circulation of twelve thousand and for some years quite eclipsed Cobbett. Though Cobbett's flight was heavily criticized by Wooler and other Radicals, Cobbett himself compared it to those made in similar circumstances by Algernon Sidney, Voltaire and Tom Paine, and argued that he could do more good to the cause of English Reform in America than in an English prison.[29] In the event not as many Radical journalists went to prison as the government had hoped. In 1817 there were twenty-six prosecutions of Radicals for seditious and blasphemous libels and sixteen *ex officio* informations filed by the Crown's law officers, but when cases were brought on, the juries usually refused to convict. In that hectic year of prosecution and counter-ridicule, Wooler escaped sentence by proving that he did not *write* libels but that, such was his fluency, he composed them directly into type; Hone convulsed the court with laughter by his reading of other men's parodies no less 'seditious' than his own; and Sherwin gleefully obtained in the courts freedom to republish Southey's *Wat Tyler*, a piquant reminder of the Tory Poet Laureate's republican, Jacobin youth, and a work he now desperately wished to suppress. Had Cobbett stayed he might have joined in all this dangerous fun, but one trial for seditious libel and one taste of prison was enough for him – as it might be for any man.

Cobbett may have been in danger, he certainly was in debt, and his enemies seized upon this as the principal motive for his flight. According to the Tory *Quarterly Review*, he fled from his creditors: 'That he should do this is perfectly natural; the thing to be admired is, that such a man should have creditors to flee from. Had he staid at Liverpool another tide, he would have been brought back, and consigned to Newgate or the King's Bench for the remainder of his life.'[30] According to the extreme Radical Richard Carlile (writing after a quarrel with Cobbett):[31]

> His farming at Botley consisted in a series of new schemes and projects that were begun today and abandoned tomorrow. His career was described as ruinous by all who were acquainted with it, until in the year 1817, he had worked himself into a crisis with debts, and was obliged to abandon them by a flight to America. ... No man has made more show in the country upon credit and paper money than William Cobbett; and no banker, no 'rag rook', has cheated his creditors in a more scandalous manner than William Cobbett has done.

This was not the first or last time that Cobbett was in financial difficulties, but his state was one of pecuniary vexation rather than embarrassment – if we may judge by the peremptory tone of his request to creditors for time in which to pay his debts:[32]

> I hereby publicly give notice to every person with whom I may have any pecuniary engagements, that, if they proceed to any acts of legal malice; that if they give any obstruction to the

performance of anything that may be to my advantage, and that may tend to alleviate in some small degree, the blow which the Borough-mongers have given me in a pecuniary way; I hereby solemnly give notice to all such persons, be they who they may, that I will not only never pay them one single farthing, if I should have heaps of money, but that, on the contrary, I shall consider them as *aiders and abetters of the Borough-mongers*, and that whenever the day of justice shall arrive, I will act towards them accordingly.

He was, of course, in America when he wrote this.

5

American Farmer and English Grammarian: 1817-19

Cobbett's attitude towards the United States and its people had changed as completely between 1800 and 1817 as had most of his political opinions. In the *Political Register*, he had strongly supported the Americans throughout the quarrel which erupted into the war of 1812–14; much of his voluminous writing on this quarrel was reprinted in New York, Philadelphia and Boston, while for six months in 1816 he had issued *Cobbett's American Political Register* and had there published articles he thought unsafe to be printed in England.

Unlike his earlier stay in the United States, this visit, which was to last two-and-a-half-years, was marked by no intervention into American domestic politics. Immediately upon his arrival he announced his intention of living as a farmer, gaining his food and drink 'from the *untaxed* earth; which is never niggardly towards those, who will apply to her with earnestness and with care',[1] and very soon he had leased a farm called Hyde Park on Long Island. He found his new surroundings delightful, and wrote in a letter to his old Hampshire neighbour, farmer Richard Hinxman:[2]

> If this untaxed, beautiful, fertile, and salubrious island were inhabited by Englishmen, it would very far surpass the garden of Eden; for here the trees produce golden fruit, and we are forbidden to eat none of them. I have such good servants in my man Churcher and his wife, and I hear their Hampshire tongues so often, that I almost conceit myself at home; only the fine sun, the fine roads, the fine fruits and the happy labourers tell me I am not there.

He felt the absence of Englishmen because there were no cottage gardens here, 'which form so striking a feature of beauty in England,

and especially in Kent, Sussex, Surrey, and Hampshire, and which constitute a sort of fairy-land, when compared with those of the labourers in France'.[3] In these near-paradisal surroundings he never forgot the serpents in the Eden across the Atlantic. Farming was a healthful and virtuous diversion, but Cobbett's main energies still went into writing against Old Corruption at home. Within three days of his arrival on Long Island he sent off copy for a *Political Register* article; this was printed in London on 12 July 1817, and thereafter an issue of the *Register*, either written by Cobbett in America or improvised by his London printer from earlier writings, appeared during almost every week of Cobbett's stay on Long Island.

The slow double-journey of news across the Atlantic meant that Cobbett could comment on events in England only four or five months after they had occurred. His first articles were in a large part devoted to 'A History of the Last Hundred Days of English Freedom', that is, an account of the repressions which culminated in the Suspension of Habeas Corpus Act and his own retreat to America. In these articles he hurled abuse at critics, Tory, Whig or Radical, who might condemn his flight, and denounced a government which had now assumed powers no less arbitrary than those possessed by 'the Dey of Algiers, or by any Bourbon that ever existed'.[4] After he had learned of the miserable, abortive Derbyshire Rising of 9 June[5] and the trial of the 'rebels' at Derby in October 1817 (where Cobbett was named by defence counsel as an instigator of rebellion by his incendiary writings), he never allowed his readers to forget the names of the detested Oliver, spy, government agent and true fomenter of the Rising, or of Jeremiah Brandreth, its unfortunate leader, who had been hanged. Whether or not the 'Address to the Journeymen and Labourers' was as subversive as counsel had claimed at the Derby trial, some of Cobbett's writings from America do advocate the right of rebellion:[6]

> the Derby men knew very well what they were about; they were betrayed; they were deceived; but they knew what they were about very well, and all the grounds upon which they proceeded. They knew well, that according to law as well as reason, *Resistance of Oppression* is a Right, and not a Crime. . . .
> What did Brandreth do more than was done by the Whigs at the Revolution?

As E. P. Thompson has observed, Cobbett (and Wooler and 'Orator' Hunt) 'were adept at pitching their rhetoric just on the right side of treason; but they laid themselves open . . . to the charge of encouraging other men to take illegal or treasonable actions, from the consequences of which they themselves escaped'.[7]

Burdett could not be open to such a charge. He was asked by Henry Hunt to use the Derby trial as an opportunity to attack the whole government spy-system, but he washed his hands of the Derbyshire rebels completely. This inflamed yet further the smouldering quarrel between him and Cobbett. Already, in 'A History of the Last Hundred Days of English Freedom', Cobbett had scathingly condemned Burdett's inactivity during the massive peaceful reform agitation of winter 1816–17, and had thrown the entire blame for failure upon him; but he was not altogether fair in further berating and blackguarding Burdett for being in Melton Mowbray or Brighton or Ireland, instead of in the battle-smoke at Westminster, when Cobbett himself was thousands of miles away on Long Island. When, in 1817, Cochrane announced his decision to resign his Westminster seat in order to join the freedom-fighters in South America, Burdett refused to support the candidature of either Major Cartwright or Henry Hunt, the extreme Radical choices. The fact that his first nominee had been Brougham was a clear enough indication that Burdett had thrown in his lot with the middle-class, moderate Whig reformers, and Cobbett duly called him 'an understrapper of the Whig oligarchy'. As a result of such divisions the Radicals lost one of the Westminster seats in the 1818 election, nor were they able to regain it in 1819. Not everyone was prepared to blame Burdett. Shelley wrote to Peacock in April 1819 about the Westminster election: 'There is little hope. That mischievous Cobbett has divided and weakened the interest of the popular party so that the factions who prey upon our country have been able to coalesce to its exclusion.'[8]

Upon political differences was superimposed the sad tangle of Cobbett's financial affairs, for he owed Burdett about £3,000. On 20 November 1817 he wrote to Burdett from America, enclosing a copy of a letter to Tipper, a stationer and paper-maker to whom he owed another £3,000, stating his inability to pay at present and even claiming, in tones oddly foreshadowing the proudly self-righteous Mr Cypress in the following year,[9] that, as 'society' had failed to protect him by its laws, he had no further obligations towards members of that society:

I hold it to be perfectly just, that I should never, in any way whatever give up one single farthing of my future earnings to the payment of my debts in England. When the society is too weak or unwilling, to defend the property, whether mental or of a more ordinary and vulgar species, and where there is not the will or the power in the society to yield him protection, he becomes clearly absolved of all his engagements of every sort to that society; because in every bargain of every kind, it is understood, that both the parties are to continue to enjoy the protection of the laws of property.

Burdett replied indignantly to this impudent bluster, and the correspondence found its way into print in Leigh Hunt and John Hunt's *Examiner* in January 1819. In the event Burdett was never repaid; Cobbett on some occasions admitted a debt, and on others claimed that the money was a gift for political expenses. The breach between the two men never healed. By his new writings in America, notably the *English Grammar*, and by a continuing sale in cheap pamphlet-form of such popular *Political Register* pieces as *Paper against Gold* and the 'Address to the Journeymen and Labourers', Cobbett was contriving to reduce his debts, but, in every sense of the word, his credit was low in England for a long time after his flight.

Cobbett, though, would lose no sleep over Burdett. His American farming journal for 1817–18 reveals an almost constant state of well-being:[10]

It is impossible for any human being to lead a pleasanter life than this. How I pity those who are *compelled* to endure the stench of cities; but, for those who remain there without being compelled, I have no pity. . . . Drink about twenty good tumblers of milk and water every day. No ailments. Head always clear. Go to bed by day-light very often. Just after the hens go to roost, and rise again with them. . . . I fight the Borough-villains, stripped to my shirt, and with nothing on besides but shoes and trowsers. Never ill; no head-aches; no muddled brains.

Out of this farming journal grew a discursive blend of agricultural treatise, travel book, Radical pamphlet and autobiography which he published in London and New York (1818–19) under the title, *A Year's Residence in the United States of America* 'Treating of the Face of the Country, the Climate, the Soil, the Products, the Mode of Cultivating the Land, the Prices of Land, of Labour, of Food, of Raiment, of the Expenses of House-keeping, and of the usual manner of Living; of the Manners and Customs of the People; and of the Institutions of the Country, Civil, Political and Religious.' In the Preface to this work Cobbett offers his credentials with a characteristic mixture of political polemic and warm nostalgia:[11]

> The account, which I shall give, shall be that of actual *experience*. I will say what I *know* and what I have *seen* and what I have *done* . . . every thing which appears to me useful to persons intending to come to this country shall be communicated; but, more especially that which may be useful to *farmers*; because, as to such matters, I have ample experience. Indeed, this is the *main thing*; for this is really and truly a *country of farmers*. Here, Governors, Legislators, Presidents, all are farmers. A farmer here is not the poor dependent wretch that a Yeomanry-Cavalry man is, or that a Treason-Jury man is. A farmer here depends upon nobody but *himself* and on his own proper means; and, if he be not at his ease, and even rich, it must be his own fault. . . .
>
> I shall give an account of what I have done; and, while this will convince every good farmer, or any man of tolerable means, that *he* may, if he will, do the same; it will give him an idea of the climate, soil, crops, &c., a thousand times more neat and correct, than could be conveyed to his mind by any general description, unaccompanied with actual experimental accounts.
>
> As the expressing of this intention, may, perhaps suggest the reader to ask, how it is that much can be known on the subject of *Farming* by a man, who, for *thirty-six* out of *fifty-two* years of his life has been a *Soldier* or a *Political Writer*, and who, of course, has spent so large a part of his time in garrisons and in great cities, I will beg leave to satisfy this natural curiosity beforehand.
>
> Early habits and affections seldom quit us while we have vigour of mind left. I was brought up under a father, whose talk was chiefly about his garden and his fields, with regard to which he was famed for his skill and his exemplary neatness. From my very infancy, from the age of six years, when I climbed up the side of a steep sand-rock, and there scooped me out a plot four feet square to make me a garden, and the soil for which I carried up in the bosom of my little blue smock-frock (or hunting-shirt), I have never lost one particle of my passion for these healthy and rational and heart-cheering pursuits, in which

every day presents something new, in which the spirits are never suffered to flag, and in which industry, skill, and care are sure to meet their due reward. . . .

I was bred at the plough-tail, and in the Hop-Gardens of Farnham in Surrey, my native place, and which spot, as it so happened, is the neatest in England, and I believe, in the whole world. All there is a garden. The neat culture of the hop extends its influence to the fields round about. Hedges cut with shears and every other mark of skill and care strike the eye at Farnham, and become fainter and fainter as you go from it in every direction. I have had, besides, great experience in farming for several years of late; for, one man will gain more knowledge in a year than another will in a life. It is the *taste* for the thing that really gives the knowledge.

To this taste, produced in me by a desire to imitate a father whom I ardently loved, and to whose every word I listened with admiration, I owe no small part of my happiness, for a greater proportion of which very few men ever had to be grateful to God. These pursuits, innocent in themselves, instructive in their very nature, and always tending to preserve health, have been a constant, a never-failing source of recreation to me; and, which I count amongst the greatest of their benefits and blessings, they have always, in my house, supplied the place of the card-table, the dice-box, the chess-board and the lounging bottle. Time never hangs on the hands of him, who delights in these pursuits, and who has book on the subject to read. Even when shut up within the walls of a prison, for having complained that Englishmen had been flogged in the heart of England under a guard of German Bayonets and Sabres; even then, I found in these pursuits a source of pleasure inexhaustible. To that of the whole of our English books on these matters, I then added the reading of all the valuable French books; and I then, for the first time, read that Book of all Books on husbandry, the work of Jethro Tull, to the principles of whom I owe more than to all my other reading and all my experience. . . .

I wish it to be observed, that, in any thing which I may say, during the course of this work, though *truth* will compel me to state facts, which will, doubtless, tend to induce farmers to leave England for America, I *advise* no one so to do. . . . I myself am bound to England for life.

Cobbett's patriotism is both national and local for it is allied to family piety, so he has to pay tribute to Farnham and allude to the affectionate bonds of family life in his father's house and in his own, and the healthful pursuits in which those affections were exercised. He will write only directly from his own experience and will make himself the measure of all things. He flashes upon the reader some awareness of the shining wholeness of his own life, as it is contrasted with the shadows – the yeomanry-cavalry, the packed jury, the mercenary army – which threaten or have threatened him and the homeland of which he feels himself to be an embodiment.

A Year's Residence in the U.S.A. is mostly observation and advice on farming matters; and a very considerable portion of it is devoted to describing the culture and virtues of a single vegetable – the swede. Although the widespread introduction of the field turnip into crop-rotations had helped to revolutionize agriculture in the eighteenth century, this useful vegetable was vulnerable to a succession of frosts and thaws. In the Farnham area itself in Cobbett's youth Gilbert White had noted: 'vast rime on the trees all day. The naked turnips suffer, especially where the fields incline to the sun; they are frozen, and then thawed, and so rot.'[12] The answer to this problem was the Swedish turnip, introduced into Scotland in the 1780s and cultivated in many parts of Britain during the Napoleonic Wars, which was harder and drier than the ordinary turnip and far less likely to rot in frost and thaw. Cobbett taught his Long Island neighbours the swede's virtues and learned from them the great advantage of oxen over most breeds of horses for ploughing and other purposes (a practical confirmation of Jethro Tull's wisdom), the cultivation of Indian corn or maize, and more about the fast-growing 'locust tree' or false acacia which he had already experimented with at Botley. Both the locust and maize were already being grown in various parts of Britain, but, after he returned home, Cobbett made great efforts as propagandist[13] and nurseryman to spread their cultivation.

As he advised and observed, Cobbett never forgot the borough-mongers, or the contrasts in laws, government and taxation, and therefore in the spread of human happiness, as between England and the United States. Thus a journal entry describing farmhouses seen on a journey through Pennsylvania easily and inevitably expands into agitated reflections upon England's deserted villages. As remembrance wakes with all her busy train the effect is not unlike the turning on of a tap:[14]

It is a curious thing to observe the *farm-houses* in this country.
They consist, almost without exception, of a considerably large
and a very neat house, with sash windows, and of a *small house*,
which seems to have been *tacked on* to the large one; and, the
proportion they bear to each other, in point of dimensions, is,
as nearly as possible, the proportion of size between a *cow* and
her calf, the latter a month old. But, as to the *cause*, the process has
been the opposite of this instance of the works of nature, for it is
the larger house which has grown out of the small one. The father, or
grandfather, while he was toiling for his children, lived in the
small house, constructed chiefly by himself, and consisting of rude
materials. The means, accumulated in the small house, enabled a
son to rear the large one. . . . What a contrast with the farm-
houses in England! There the *little* farm-houses are falling into
ruins, or, are actually become cattle-sheds, or, at best, *cottages*, as
they are called, to contain a miserable labourer, who ought to
have been a farmer, as his grandfather was. Five or six farms are
there *now* levelled into one. . . . The *farmer*, has, indeed, *a fine
house*; but, what a life do his labourers lead! The cause of this sad
change is to be found in the crushing taxes; and the cause of
them, in the Borough usurpation, which has robbed the people
of their best right, and, indeed, without which right they can
enjoy no other. They talk of the *augmented population* of England;
and, when it suits the purpose of the tyrants, they boast of this
fact, as they are pleased to call it, as a proof of the fostering
nature of their government; though, just now, they are
preaching up the vile and foolish doctrine of Parson Malthus,
who thinks, that there are *too many* people, that they ought
(those who *labour*, at least) to be *restrained from breeding so fast*.
But, as to the fact, I do not believe it. . . . It is a curious and a
melancholy sight, where an ancient church, with its lofty spire or
tower; the church sufficient to contain a thousand or two or three
thousand of people conveniently, now stands surrounded by a
score, or half a score of miserable mud-houses, with floors of
earth, and covered with thatch; and this sight strikes your eye in
all parts of the five Western counties of England. . . . Let any man
look at the *sides of the hills* in these counties, and also in
Hampshire, where *downs*, or open lands, prevail. He will there see,
not only that those hills were formerly cultivated; but that *banks*
from distance to distance, were made by the *spade*, in order to

E

form little flats for the plough to go, without tumbling the earth down the hill; so that the side of a hill looks, in some sort, like *the steps of a stairs.* Was this done, *without hands,* and without *mouths* to consume the grain raised on the sides of these hills? The Funding and Manufacturing and Commercial and Taxing System has, by drawing wealth into great masses, drawn men also into great masses. London, the manufacturing places, Bath, and other places of dissipation, have, indeed, wonderfully increased in population. Country seats, Parks, Pleasure-gardens, have, in like degree, increased in number and extent. And, in just the same proportion has been the increase of Poor-houses, Madhouses, and Jails. But *the people of England,* such as Fortescue described them, have been *swept away* by the ruthless hand of the Aristocracy, who, making their approaches by slow degrees, have, at last got into their grasp the substance of the whole country.

A second reference to Fortescue underlines Cobbett's account of the way his neighbours still practise 'old English hospitality';[15] but the paradisal spectacle of Long Island as the home of freedom, independence, prosperity and all the old English rural virtues did not turn him into an American; rather it served further to increase his indignation against the condition of labourers in England, and his determination that it should be bettered.

One path to betterment lay through education. In open letters to William Benbow, one of the printers recently imprisoned under the 'Gagging Acts', Cobbett wrote, late in 1817, of his plan:[16]

for assisting in the acquirement of book-learning all those against whom the Boroughmongers have, in a great degree, closed the door to such learning, and whom they have the insolence to denominate the 'Lower Orders'. To effect this object it is my intention to publish, at a very cheap rate (though the word *cheap* may shake the nerves of Sidmouth and Canning to jelly) – at a very cheap rate it is my intention to publish – First, 'An English Grammar for the use of apprentices, plough-boys, soldiers, and sailors.' Second, 'A History of the Laws and Constitution of England', for the use of the same description of persons. Third, 'A History of the Church and of Religion in England, in which will be seen the origin of the present *claims* of the clergy, and in which their *duties* will also be shown,' for the use of the same description of persons. Fourth, 'A view of the present state of the Income,

Debt, and Expenses of the Kingdom; its Population and Paupers; its causes of Embarrassment and Misery, and the means of its Restoration to ease and happiness,' for the use of the same description of persons.

Not all of this programme was fulfilled. The second and fourth projects were never completed in these forms, though material for them had appeared and would continue to appear in the *Political Register* and would find a place in the 'Legacies' (cf. p. 184 below); the third eventually appeared in 1824 as *A History of the Protestant 'Reformation'* (cf. p. 136 below); the first was the famous *Grammar of the English Language* (1818).

Cobbett's *Grammar* was written in a series of letters to his third son, who, at the age of fourteen, copied and learned them by heart according to his father's directions and became 'a grammarian at once'. Such a form of direct and sometimes intimate address gives a freshness and effect of spontaneity unusual in writings on this subject, but the grammatical categories and 'rules' are those common to other *Grammars* of the day – that is, for all Cobbett's contempt for the 'learned languages', they are based upon Greek and Latin. Cobbett's *Grammar* is descriptive and prescriptive, and no more. His aim is to enable the reader, 'not only to express our meaning fully and clearly, but so to express it as to enable us to defy the ingenuity of man to give to our words any other meaning than that which we ourselves intend them to express'.[17] Cobbett has no time or use for the historical study of language:[18]

> deep inquiries regarding the origin of these words are more curious than useful. . . . It is for monks, and for Fellows of English Colleges, who live by the sweat of other people's brows, to spend their time in this manner, and to call the result of their studies *learning*; for you, who will have to earn what you eat and what you drink and what you wear, it is to avoid every thing that tends not to real utility.

Although Cobbett's own work is not without error – for instance, he confuses prosody with pronunciation, and etymology with accidence – Cobbett devotes much space in his *Grammar* to the mistakes of other grammarians, not excluding Bishop Lowth whose *Grammar* had first instructed young Private Cobbett on long nights of sentry-duty, but concentrating upon Lindley Murray, the Pennsylvanian Quaker settled in England, whose *English Grammar* (1795) was used in schools to the exclusion of almost all other grammar-books. Murray had conceded exceptions to grammatical 'rules' in the usage of great, established writers, but Cobbett will not, and he gleefully pounces upon examples of false grammar and unclear syntax in the works of Johnson, Addison, Hugh Blair and other eighteenth-century patterns of good writing. Two entire letters are devoted to the exposure of errors in Johnson's *Rambler*, Isaac Watt's *Logic* and a recent King's speech. Cobbett is at his favourite game of cutting the great and famous down to size. Of Hugh Blair's celebrated *Lectures on Rhetoric*, he writes:[19]

> Here is a *profound scholar*, a teacher of rhetoric, discussing the comparative merits of Greek and Latin writers, and disputing with a French critic: here he is, writing English in a manner more incorrectly than you will, I hope, be liable to write it at the end of your reading of this little book. . . . With what propriety, then, are the Greek and Latin languages called the '*learned* languages'?

Cobbett's many references to the 'learned languages' display nothing but philistine contempt. In 1807 he had challenged 'the *learned* gentlemen of the two universities' to debate in the pages of the *Political Register* his assertion 'that what they call the *learned languages* are improperly so called; and that, as a part of general education, they are worse than useless'.[20] The universities did not respond to this challenge, but many contributors to the correspondence columns did, and Cobbett was able to enjoy a good knock-down verbal fight, which, as usual, he shifted on to political grounds. He believed that incompetence and corruption in government were, in part, traceable to the type of 'liberal education' bestowed upon the 'leisured classes': 'Having had their education under *word-mongers*, they are extremely fortunate if they ever get completely rid of the love of dealing in the same ware themselves.' Their want of public spirit, manliness and independence is partly due to the fact that they were taught, when young, to admire the work of those 'base, servile, self-degraded wretches, Virgil and Horace'; Virgil, especially, was a 'crawling and disgusting parasite, a base scoundrel, and pandar to unnatural passion'.[21]

In the *Grammar*, too, Cobbett loses no opportunity to score a political point. Thus, in the course of a few paragraphs warning the soldier, sailor, apprentice or plough-boy reader to look at his nominative before putting verb to paper, he offers as examples of correct usage:[22]

> 'a soldier *or* a sailor, who *has* served his country faithfully, *is* fairly entitled to a pension; but who will say, that a prostituted peer, a pimp, *or* a buffoon, *merits* a similar provision from the public?' . . .
>
> 'The borough-tyranny, with the paper-money makers, *have* produced misery and starvation.' And not *has*, for we mean that the two have *co-operated*. . . .

and of faulty:

> 'Neither the halter *nor* the bayonets *are* sufficient to prevent us from obtaining our rights.' . . .
>
> 'The gang of borough-tyrants *is* cruel, and *are* also notoriously as ignorant as brutes;' (using nouns of multitude, such as '*mob, parliament*, gang'). . . .

Such sentences apart, the whole *Grammar* is a political act, since by writing it Cobbett hoped to be able to create 'numerous formidable assailants of our insolent, high-blooded oppressors'.[23] In his own life he had shown dramatically that mastery of language brought political consciousness and power. With Radical logic he now attempted to make some of that power available to soldiers, sailors, apprentices, ploughboys and other members of the lower orders.

By the end of 1822 Cobbett claimed that 50,000 copies of his *Grammar* had been sold, and 100,000 by 1834. In 1823 he augmented it by 'Six lessons, intended to prevent Statesmen from using false grammar, and from writing in an awkward manner', and in 1831 he published a companion work for young children, *A Spelling Book . . . with a Stepping-Stone to English Grammar*. For fairly obvious reasons Cobbett's *English Grammar* was never widely accepted as a schoolbook, and, though often reprinted, never rivalled the success of Lindley Murray's, but Cobbett found the readers he wanted outside the schools. The popular sales of his *Grammar* fairly indicate that in the years after Waterloo a new culture was growing within what was virtually a new class of politically conscious, self-taught working men.[24]

A Year's Residence in the U.S.A. and the *English Grammar* were the best works to come out of the American visit, but Cobbett also wrote there a handbook, *The American Gardener* (1821), to teach Americans to cultivate gardens as well as Englishmen could. He revised his old textbook, *Le Tuteur Anglais* (1795), for teaching French people English, began a *Grammar of the French Language* (1824), for teaching English people French, and started collecting materials for a new, eulogistic *Life* of Tom Paine which might make amends for the scurrilous *Life* he had edited and published in 1796. But his chief energies went as always into the *Political Register*. Week by week he battered away at borough-mongers and spies, at paper-money, taxes and tithes, at sinecures and standing armies, at Sidmouth, Castlereagh, Canning, Eldon, Wilberforce and Malthus.

The attack on the last-named, in an open letter 'To Parson Malthus, on the Rights of the Poor, and on the cruelty recommended by him to be exercised towards the Poor' (*Political Register*, 8 May 1819) is intemperate even by Cobbett's standards:

> Parson,
> I have during my life, detested many men; but never any one so much as you. . . . Priests have, in all ages, been remarkable for cool and deliberate and unrelenting cruelty; but it seems to be reserved for the Church of England to produce one who has a just claim to the atrocious pre-eminence. No assemblage of words can give an appropriate designation of you; and, therefore, as being the single word which best suits the character of such a man, I call you *Parson*, which, amongst other meanings, includes that of Boroughmonger Tool.

In his *Essay on the Principle of Population* (1798, and five more editions in Cobbett's lifetime), Malthus had enunciated a principle, a 'law of nature', that there was a constant tendency for population to outstrip the means of subsistence, but that this tendency was, in practice, countered by certain positive or preventive checks upon population. Positive checks were all causes of mortality outside the individual person's control or what Malthus called vice and misery: 'Under this head may be enumerated all unwholesome occupations, severe labour and exposure to the seasons, extreme poverty, bad nursing of children, large towns, excesses of all kinds, the whole train of common diseases and epidemics, wars, plagues, and famine.' Preventive checks included the reprehensible devices of sexual perversity and artificial contraception, and – the only permissible one – 'moral restraint', that is the postponement of marriage until a man could well afford to support a family, together with strict continence before marriage. According to the bleak Malthusian parable,

A man who is born into a world already possessed, if he cannot get subsistence from his parents, on whom he has a just demand, and if the society do not want his labour, has no claim of *right* to the smallest portion of food, and, in fact, has no business to be where he is. At Nature's mighty feast there is no vacant cover for him.

Parish relief countered the operation of this natural law, because it encouraged the poor to marry early and create a further surplus of population which would lead ultimately only to greater misery for all the poor. Malthus therefore advocated a gradual abolition of the Poor Law:[25]

> To this end I should propose a regulation to be made, declaring, that *no child* born from any marriage taking place after the expiration of a year from the date of the law: and no illegitimate *child* born two years from the same date, should ever be entitled to parish assistance. After the public notice, which I have proposed, had been given, to the punishment of nature he should be left; the punishment of severe want; all parish assistance should be rigidly denied him. He should be taught that the laws of nature had doomed him and his family to starve; that he had no claim on society for the smallest portion of food.

Until 1806 Cobbett had supported and promulgated Malthus's principle of population,[26] but he changed his attitude sharply in 1807 when Samuel Whitbread, the Whig Reformer, attempted to have the Poor Law amended along Malthusian lines. In March and May of that year, Cobbett printed in the *Political Register* the first three of the letters that went into the making of Hazlitt's *Reply to the Essay on Population*,[27] and added his own first attack on Malthus.

In the first place, Cobbett refused to believe that population was increasing as Malthus claimed; but if any classes of people could be described as 'surplus population' these were the pensioners, sinecurists and other 'tax-eaters' and drones who consumed the wealth created by the labouring poor. A corrupt government counteracted natural law by taking subsistence from those who worked and giving it to those who did not. If Malthus wanted to argue the laws of nature, Cobbett would do so, too:

> The laws of nature, written in our passions, desires and propensities; written even in the organization of our bodies;

these laws compel the two sexes to hold that sort of intercourse, which produces children. Yes, say you: but nature has *other laws*, and amongst these are, that man shall live by *food*, and that, if he cannot obtain food, he shall *starve*. Agreed, and, if there be a man in England who cannot find, *in the whole country*, food enough to keep him alive, I allow that *nature has doomed him to starve*. If, in no shop, house, mill, barn, or other place, he can find food sufficient to keep him alive; *then*, I allow, that the laws of nature condemn him to die.

'Oh!' you will, with Parsonlike bawl, exclaim, 'but he must not commit *robbery* or *larceny*!' Robbery or larceny! what do you mean by that? Does the law of *nature* say any thing about robbery or larceny?. . . . So, you will quit the law of nature *now*, will you? You will only take it as far as serves your purpose of cruelty. . . .

Your muddled Parson's head has led you into confusion here. The *law of nature* bids a man *not starve* in a land of plenty, and forbids his being punished for taking food, whereever he can find it. Your law of nature is sitting at Westminster, to make the labourer pay taxes, to make him fight for the safety of the land, to bind him in allegiance, and when he is poor and hungry, to cast him off to starve, or, to hang him if he takes food to save his life! That is your law of nature; that is a Parson's law of nature.

Malthus is the tool of the rich boroughmongers and the contriver of a philosophy that would bolster the 'System', He proposes to relieve the rich of the burden of the poor-rates and offers them plausible reasons for hardening their hearts as they sit at the feast of nature, but, says Cobbett, if the rich cast off their responsibility to the poor, why should not the poor cast off their responsibility towards the rich? In a retaliatory fable against Malthus he touches upon that old and rankling rural grievance, the emparking enclosure:

If in process of time, the land get into the hands of a comparatively small part of the people, and if the proprietors were to prevent, by making parks, or in any other way, a great part of the land from being cultivated, would they have a right to say to the rest of the people, you shall *breed no more*; if you do, *nature* has doomed you to starvation? Would they have a right to say 'We leave you to the *punishment of nature*'? If they were fools enough to do this, the rest of the people would, doubtless, snap

them at their word, and say, 'Very well, then; *nature* bids us live
and love and have children, and get good food for them from the
land; here is a pretty park, I'll have a bit here; you take a bit
there, Jack; and so on.'

Cobbett is indulging his habit of suggesting illegal action while not
supporting it. Concluding his letter to Parson Malthus he declares that
he does not advocate such a redistribution of property according to the
'laws of nature', but stands, as always, by the old 'Laws of England'
which say 'that no person shall be without a sufficiency of food and
raiment'.[28]

Cobbett has strong and clear political reasons for opposing Malthus,
but the violence of his many attacks on the detested Parson arises from
Cobbett's sense that family affections lie at the heart of life, and, in no
small part, from simple prudishness:[29]

> for, as to preaching the Malthusian doctrine of restraint to the
> country girls, only let the nasty *feelosophers* go and state the
> doctrine to them *in plain terms*; let them state the unnatural, the
> beastly, the nasty ideas in *plain, unvarnished language*; let them do
> this, and see how soon their heads will be tied up in their aprons,
> and their filthy brains knocked out against the posts of the cow-
> cribs.

As usual the *Political Register* contained frequent pronouncements
upon England's financial affairs. In August 1818 Cobbett suggested
that the Bank of England and the whole paper-money system could be
annihilated by the wholesale forgery and distribution of banknotes:[30]

> If the nation should, one of these fine mornings, find itself
> amidst abundance of bank-notes, *picked up in the street*, or taken
> out of *post-letters*, who, from that day forth, would ever *take a
> bank-note*? Who is to detect the *utterer*? The object enchants by
> its grandeur! However, I shall neither do the thing myself nor
> advise others to do it; but content myself with saying, *that I think
> it likely it will be done.*

It is difficult to determine from this, or from his later references to this
financial 'Modest Proposal', whether Cobbett here is jocular or desperate,
but the scheme was by no means impossible in those days when the
method of printing banknotes made forgery so easy. In December
1818, Peacock wrote to Shelley:

> There have been four capital trials for forgery of Bank Notes, and the Jury has found the prisoners 'Not Guilty', expressly declaring that they could not believe the evidence of hired informers who betrayed men into crime; that they could not themselves distinguish the forged notes from the true; and that unless they were furnished with some certain criterion, they would not take the *ipse dixit* of the Bank Inspectors that the notes were forged.

Shelley, a regular reader of the *Political Register*, replied: 'Your news about the Banknote trials is excellent good. Do I not recognize in it the influence of Cobbett?'[31]

Holding the views he did, Cobbett might have been expected to support the 'sound money men' who, after the war, advocated a return to the gold standard which had been abandoned in 1797 (see above, p. 52), but, on the contrary, he was a highly vociferous opponent of Peel's Act of 1819 which provided for a return to cash payments in several stages over three years. Cobbett called it a 'wild and visionary project', and paid a characteristic tribute to the political economist whose ideas lay behind it:[32]

> I see that they have adopted the scheme of one Ricardo (I wonder what countryman he is) who is, I believe, a converted Jew. At any rate, he has been a change-alley man for the last fifteen or twenty years. If the old Lord Chatham were now alive, he would speak with respect of the muckworm, as he called the change-alley people. Faith! they are now become *everything*. Baring assists at the Congress of Sovereigns, and Ricardo regulates things at home. .... The Muckworm is no longer a creeping thing: it rears its head aloft, and makes the haughty Borough Lords sneak about in holes and corners.

Cobbett had repeatedly declared that any attempt to make gold repayments against paper without first enforcing a reduction in the interest paid on the National Debt, and in government salaries, sinecures and pensions, would have the effect of drawing all the nation's wealth into the hands of the moneyed men. It was downright madness for a Parliament largely composed of landowners to countenance such action:[33]

> Ask them whether they do not recollect, that I told them, in 1803, that, if the *Muck Worm* were not speedily *crushed*, it would

devour both *Church* and *Aristocracy*. – Oh! infatuation! A Nobility and a Hierarchy crying aloud against imaginary Republicans, and Deists, and, at the same time, cherishing a race of men, who are actually *taking away their estates*! What! One house filled wholly with Landowners, and the other four sixths filled with their their relations; and both agree in adopting and enforcing measures, which *must* make all the lands change owners! The Hindoo (I believe it is) Wife, is not a more self-devoted victim.

Written in 1821, this passage (from a 'Letter to Peel', who was a new kind of Tory) shows that Cobbett, for all his Radicalism, is stuck in the 'Country Party' attitudes of over a hundred years earlier. Cobbett still sees political society in terms of interests rather than classes, despite the fact that his own popular writings had already done much to shape class-consciousness.

A Debt which had been contracted during the war in inflated paper-money should not, and indeed, according to Cobbett, could not, be repaid in solid-gold coin during this period of post-war deflation. It would, in effect, mean giving now the equivalent of four-and-a-quarter bushels of wheat for every one-and-three-quarters that the fundholder had lent during the war;[34] Cobbett always found analogies from farming easiest to handle. If this feat were actually performed, Cobbett declared, 'I will give Castlereagh leave to put me upon a gridiron, while Sidmouth stirs the fire, and Canning stands by making a jest of my writhing and my groans.'[35] Cobbett believed that the only possible course was an 'equitable adjustment' or reduction of interest, by which the Debt could be scaled down to the 'real' value which it had at the time it was contracted: but, his prophecy notwithstanding, there was full return to the gold standard in the 1820s with no reduction of interest on the Debt. Enlarged money incomes of many people (though not the people for whom Cobbett was most concerned, the agricultural labourers) and the mercantile activity stemming from rapidly increasing industrialization served to carry the great weight of taxation and the Debt. Furthermore, the banks developed the cheque system to increase the supply of money without formal abandonment of the gold standard. So the complete disaster which Cobbett forecast did not ensue. Nevertheless there was much hardship: taxes remained high although labourers' wages and landlords' rents and farmers' profits were generally lower, and indirect taxation of commodities still pressed unduly hard upon the poor. Whenever there was any hint of a national financial crisis Cobbett claimed that his prophecy of disaster had come true. From time to time, even as late as 1835, Cobbett placed the engraving of a gridiron at the masthead of the *Political Register*, and in 1826, following the Bank of England's re-issue of the small notes which it had withdrawn a few years earlier, he organized public 'Feasts of the Gridiron' in various parts of England.

If we are to believe Cobbett, his return to England was occasioned not by the loss of his Long Island farmhouse by fire in May 1819, nor by the imminence of the King's death which would entail a general election at which Cobbett would fight Coventry (where he had already been adopted as Radical candidate), but by the passage of Peel's Act for gold repayments. Cobbett described in detail the circumstances of his decision to return, and the setting – a temporary shack built near the site of his burnt-out farmhouse:[36]

> [in August 1819] this copy of the Bill and of the Report were delivered to me in a tent, the walls of which were made of *Morning Chronicles* and *Couriers* pasted on upon laths that were a foot asunder, and the roof of which consisted of thatch, the eaves being brought out six feet beyond the walls, in order to protect those walls from violent rain and winds. In this tent, with a large mahogany slab, supported by stakes driven into the ground, for a table, and with four young oaks driven into the ground, and connected by four rails, with boards laid across upon them, having upon the boards a truss of rye-straw in a species of sack, with a pillow of the same, and with one sheet below and another above, for bedding: with this furniture for use and for decoration, and sitting in this tent, with a shirt and pair of trowsers for dress, I received the copies of this celebrated Bill and Report. . . . I hastily ran my eye over them; and in five minutes time I had resolved to return to England the next fall.

Cobbett never doubted that his readers were profoundly interested in his every thought, word and deed. There is a Robinson Crusoe-like concern for every practical detail (just how the building was constructed) and a grandly unaffected self-dramatization. He assumes here the role of a tough, campaign-hardened general in the field, alert to every move of the enemy, and rapidly deciding upon his countermovements. The only difference is that that walls of his tent were not hung with, but were actually composed of, the trophies of his former campaigns against other journalists.

Cobbett's last act in America was a strange expiation for his savage libels on Tom Paine twenty years earlier. He exhumed Paine's bones which, as befitted the remains of a notorious atheist (or, at best, Deist), had been deposited in unhallowed ground on a farm. These Cobbett brought to England, intending to raise over them a mausoleum which would be the object of pilgrimage for reformers. For some months after his return to England he filled the *Political Register* with offers to exhibit the bones or to sell gold rings, each with a lock of Paine's scanty hair, and with requests for money to build the mausoleum, but Cobbett's strange, theatrical, superstitious–pious (and possibly mercenary) act provoked nothing but ridicule. Byron's was one of many squibs:[37]

> In digging up your bones, Tom Paine,
>   Will. Cobbett has done well;
> You visit him on earth again,
>   He'll visit you in hell.

The bones remained in Liverpool from the time of Cobbett's landing there on 20 November 1819 until after his death, but were later mislaid. No mausoleum was built.

Even without the farce of Tom Paine's bones, Cobbett's return would have attracted considerable public attention. The magistrates at Manchester, their memories of Peterloo only three months old, forbad his planned great public meeting in that town, but elsewhere Cobbett drew large crowds of working-class reformers as he made a leisurely progress by way of Coventry and London (where he was arrested for debt and had to be bailed out by Henry Hunt and Dolby, the publisher of the *Political Register*), eventually reaching Botley in December, where 'The farm was in very neat order, the turnpike perfectly good, the trees monstrously grown; the American trees of finer growth than any that I ever saw in America of the same age.'[38]

6

Candidate, Courtier, Preacher, Teacher and Historian: 1819–29

During Cobbett's absence from England there had been great distress and unrest, particularly in the North. A wave of strikes in 1818 showed the determination of industrial workers to act together to better their conditions, and by the beginning of 1819 the old leaders of Reform, Cartwright and Henry Hunt among them, were back in the industrial areas, directing this working-class unrest once more into agitation for universal suffrage, annual parliaments and the rest. A series of great, peaceful, open-air meetings culminated in Manchester with the 'Peterloo Massacre' in August 1819, when, as a result of panic among the magistrates and incompetence among the yeomanry-cavalry, a peaceable crowd of men, women and children was ridden down and eleven people were killed. Peterloo on the one hand gave resolution and vigour to the Reform movement, which had been languishing since the fiasco of early 1817, and on the other provoked the government to its last and fiercest flurry of repressive measures.

A week after Cobbett landed in Liverpool the first of a series of coercion bills was moved in Parliament, and very early in 1830 all of the so-called 'Six Acts' were on the statute-book. Two of these provided against armed revolution by prohibiting any assembly for drilling or other military exercise, and by empowering magistrates to search for and seize arms. Another made more summary the procedure for dealing with alleged political offenders. Two more stiffened the existing statutes against blasphemous and seditious libels and against seditious meetings. The last of the Six Acts, the Newspaper Stamp Duties Act, compelled payment of the fourpenny newspaper stamp duty on all pamphlets containing any public news or remarks thereon, or upon any matters in Church or State, printed for sale and published periodically, or in parts or numbers at intervals not exceeding twenty-six days and costing less than sixpence or containing less than two whole sheets. Certain official papers and publications used in schools or containing only matters of piety, devotion or charity, were exempted from stamp duty. This was an act directed specifically against Cobbett's twopenny *Pamphlet* and all the other Radical twopennies. In the debate in the Lords, Ellenborough explained the Government's attitude:[1]

> It was not against the respectable Press that this Bill was directed, but against a pauper Press, which, administering to the prejudices and the passions of a mob, was converted to the basest purposes, which was an utter stranger to truth, and only sent forth a continual stream of falsehood and malignity, its virulence and its mischief heightening as it proceeded . . . such that it threatened the most material injury to the best interests of the country, unless some means were devised of stemming its torrent.

The Act compelled Cobbett to raise the price of the *Pamphlet* from twopence to sixpence, and thus put it beyond the pockets of most of the people he wanted to reach. The abortive Cato Street Conspiracy in February 1820 seemed to the Government to be a justification for the passage of the Six Acts, and by the summer many of the leading Radicals were in prison or awaiting trial. The fight for the freedom of the Press went on and Cobbett played his share, but he was no longer beside Carlile and Wooler in the front line. Much of his abundant bellicosity went into the unedifying, rancorous quarrel with Burdett and what he called the 'Westminster Rump' of Burdett's supporters.

Though Cobbett still had considerable debts on both sides of the Atlantic, he had enough ready cash from the sale of his American property, agricultural and literary, to re-establish his family and business in England, but not enough, he thought, to fight 'Old Corruption'. On 6 January he announced 'Cobbett's Fund for Reform', and called for five thousand pounds, or twopence each from 600,000 men and women, to be[2]

> lodged in my hands; to be used solely by me *of course*, and without the *check or control* of any body; and without any one ever having a right to ask me what I am going to do with it. It is my firm conviction, that, with this sum of money at my command, I could do more, in the space of *six months*, for the benefit of the whole nation, than I shall be able to do without it, in the whole course of my life.

At the end of January he launched a daily newspaper, *Cobbett's Evening Post*, but it died after two months. In February he appealed for money to fight the forthcoming election at Coventry, firstly to the common people:

> My good, honest, and kind country-people – the Industrious Classes – you have long been deceived by artful and interested men. The means of restoration are easy. *If I were in Parliament*, I I would point out the means. . . . There, however, I cannot be, without *your assistance*! What will be the sum required, I cannot exactly say – Two Thousand Pounds, perhaps; or a little more.

And then to seventy chosen gentlemen:

> if you, together with the rest of the seventy, send us, each of you, *ten pounds*, I shall, *to a certainty*, be returned a member for Coventry. I wish to see my country again free and prosperous; and I am convinced that, *in one month*, I should be able to suggest the means of effecting, in a comparatively short time, her complete restoration.

Such ineffective antics could only delight his enemies and dismay his friends.

The Coventry election was fought in March 1820 and the Radicals had high hopes of Cobbett. Thus Leigh Hunt wrote in the *Examiner* (alluding to the Cato Street Conspiracy and other, rumoured, plots to murder Cabinet ministers):[3]

> There has been a great talk of grenades, and of the confusion which their explosion would have made among the Members of Government. But of all implements to be pitched among a set of Ministers, and to confuse and scatter their faculties, commend us to the Cobbett.

But Cobbett was ineffective on the hustings at Coventry, and lost his voice. The contest was rough and brutal even by the standards of that age of manly sports. One of Cobbett's daughters recalled a savage mob bursting into the family lodging, 'calling out for the "miscreant" to kill him. We were in the bedroom and heard the noise, and we pushed the bedstead against the door and hid the fire-irons.'[4] At the end of it all Cobbett came bottom of the poll.

Immediately afterwards Cobbett was once against arrested for an old

Botley debt incurred before he went to America. This, on top of the debts incurred in the Coventry election and in his unsuccessful launching of *Cobbett's Evening Post*, brought his affairs to crisis and forced him in April to declare himself bankrupt. Most of his creditors treated him generously, and the wealthy and long-suffering Burdett, towards whom Cobbett still displayed no gratitude, waived all rights, but five-thousand-pounds worth of debts were proved before the commissioners, and the last piece of Botley property went to the mortgagee, never to return to him. As if this were not enough, Cobbett had involved himself in a series of libel actions. In 1808, before his alliance with 'Orator' Hunt, he had written to his printer John Wright, warning him to have nothing to do with Hunt, whom he described as riding 'about the country with a whore, the wife of another man, having deserted his own'. During disputes among the Radicals at the Westminster election of June 1818, Wright gave this letter to a member of Burdett's committee, the celebrated Francis Place, who gave it at once to Thomas Cleary to read on the hustings in order to discredit Hunt and destroy the value to him of Cobbett's support. Cobbett, from America, disavowed the letter, denounced it as a forgery, and violently caluminated both Wright and Cleary.[5] Hunt bore no malice on account of the original letter (which, though offensive, was true), but as soon as Cobbett landed in England Wright and Cleary brought libel actions for his attacks on them in the *Political Register*. In December 1820 these actions came on, with Brougham prosecuting for Cleary, and James Scarlett, the most successful advocate of the period, for Wright; and Cobbett, as usual, conducting his own defence. Henry Crabb Robinson went along to the King's Bench to hear the case, *Wright v. Cobbett*, and gives, in his Journal, a portrait of the defendant:[6]

> Cobbett was cool and impudent, with affected ease. His examination of witnesses was not at all able or judicious and his speech to the jury chiefly remarkable for assurance. He abandoned the justification of his libel, which charged Wright with forgery, cheating, etc., but in his speech by no means abandoned the charge. He was acute and bitter, and able too, on extraneous matters; attacked Scarlett and Brougham, etc. He was forced to call his sons to prove that it was not himself but one of them who was the author of the libel. I understand that on cross-examination they proved plaintiff's case, and £1,000 were given against Cobbett, to my great pleasure, for he is a superlative

scoundrel. But though my opinion of him is so bad,
while he was speaking his good-humoured manner nearly
disarmed me. His manner is almost puerile occasionally, and at
times he has a simple air, the effect of which is heightened by a
cast of the eye. His voice and manner vary much, indications of
insincerity and falsehood, which certainly do not fail here. He lied
egregiously during his speech, and even of his speech.

The damages and costs were paid by George Rogers of Southampton,
who on several previous occasions had helped Cobbett generously, but
Cobbett's reputation was greatly harmed by his unsavoury attempt
to shift on to his son's shoulders the blame for the libel, and by the
production in court of a letter and an article written by Cobbett in
1810 – but retracted after a few days – in which he offered to discontinue the *Political Register* if the government would not proceed with
the charges they had made on account of the article on the Ely floggings.
Cobbett's fortunes, his credit and his reputation had now reached their
lowest point since he had first become a public figure.

In the sixteen months following the return from America the Cobbetts had, at different times, lived at Botley and occupied lodgings in
semi-rural Chelsea and Brompton, but in April 1820, after the bankruptcy, they took a house on Kensington High Street with a garden of
four acres where they established a tiny farm, with five cows, a hundred
pigeons, some pigs and poultry, fruit and vegetables for the family,
and exotic nursery plants such as maize, cranberry and false acacia (from
seed imported from America) for sale. As usual with Cobbett's farming, all was carried on in the most costly manner. Come what may,
Cobbett *would* be a farmer. A year after moving to Kensington he
wrote to his friend Samuel Clarke, a Norfolk farmer:[7]

> Nature made me for a farmer certainly; and that I will be again,
> in spite of the Devil. . . . I like the company of farmers. They
> talk about something *rational*, except when they get out of their
> sphere. A carter or hedger is a more edifying companion than a
> '*politician*'. But, I would, indeed, prefer a farmer of some science.
> And, therefore, I want to have a talk with you.

Nature may have made Cobbett for a farmer, but at the time he wrote
this letter he found himself in the unusual role of courtier – dancing
attendance on Queen Caroline.

The colourful private lives of Queen Caroline and King George IV had long excited the nation. George, then Prince of Wales, had separated from his consort in 1796, and in 1806 had instigated a parliamentary inquiry – the so-called 'delicate investigation' – into her alleged adultery, but this inquiry had exonerated her from all charges except that of 'levity of conduct'. In 1813 she came to public attention again when she protested to Parliament against the restrictions placed by the Privy Council upon her access to her daughter, Princess Charlotte. During 1806 and 1813, there was some popular agitation on Caroline's behalf, and a crop of seditious writings and prints drawing attention to the Prince's notoriously dissolute habits. On coming to the throne in January 1820, George determined that his wife should not be recognized as Queen, and insisted that his ministers should, on fresh evidence of her adulteries, bring in a 'Bill of Pains and Penalties' to deprive her of her title and to dissolve the marriage. The Bill passed the House of Lords in November by so narrow a majority that the government dared not move it in the Commons. In July Caroline tried to force her way into the Coronation at Westminster Abbey but was repulsed. In August, to the immense relief of the King and his ministers, she died.

For the eighteen months or so after George IV's accession the 'Queen's case' monopolized public attention; Caroline was a national heroine, the idol of the London mob, and a very convenient stick with which the Radicals could belabour the government. Hazlitt summed it up:[8]

> The Queen's trial . . . was the only question I ever knew that excited a thorough popular feeling. It struck roots into the heart of the nation; it took possession of every house or cottage in the kingdom; man, woman, and child took part in it, as if it had been their own concern. Business was laid aside for it: people forgot their pleasures, even their meals were neglected, nothing was thought of but the fate of the Queen's trial. . . . There was the cant of loyalty, the cant of gallantry, and the cant of freedom mixed altogether in delightful and inextricable confusion. She was a Queen – all the loyal and well-bred bowed to the name; she was a wife – all the women took the alarm; she was at variance with the lawful sovereign – all the free and independent Electors of Westminster and London were up in arms. . . . City patriots stood a chance of becoming liege men, and true to a Queen – of their own choosing. The spirit of faction was half merged in the spirit of servility.

Cobbett had supported Caroline in 1813, and now, displaying all the varieties of cant in Hazlitt's list, he came forward as one of her leading champions. He devoted the *Political Register* wholly to her cause, writing many of the 'loyal addresses' to her from county and town meetings, and also penning her replies. Cobbett wrote the famous letter of remonstrance which she sent to the King in August 1820. It was returned unopened, but within two weeks had been printed in almost every journal in the country. The nation had cast Caroline in the role of a tragedy queen and Cobbett wrote for her the appropriate lines:[9]

> You have cast upon me every slur to which the female character
> is liable. Instead of loving, honouring, and cherishing me,
> agreeably to your solemn vow, you have pursued me with hatred
> and scorn, and with all the means of destruction. You wrested
> from me my child, and with her my only comfort and consolation.
> You sent me sorrowing through the world, and even in my
> sorrows pursued me with unrelenting persecution. Having left me
> nothing but my innocence, you would now by a mockery of
> justice, deprive me even of the reputation of possessing that. The
> poisoned bowl and the poniard are means more manly than
> perjured witnesses and partial tribunals; and they are less cruel,
> inasmuch as life is less valuable than honour. If my life would have
> satisfied your Majesty, you should have had it on the sole
> condition of giving me a place in the same tomb with my child;
> but since you send me dishonoured to the grave, I will resist the
> attempt with all the means which it shall please God to give me.

The reader of all this might be tempted to ask: 'What's Hecuba to him?' The simple answer is that Caroline was a pretext for agitation against the government which might bring Reform a little closer and might at the same time regain for Cobbett that leadership of the Reform movement which he had forfeited by his flight to the United States. But Cobbett seems genuinely to have been touched by the pathos of the Queen's situation and sincerely to have believed her innocent. His own vanity, too, may have drawn him into the strange role of a courtier. Cobbett's daughter recalled that he would dress himself out in unaccustomed finery to wait upon and 'kiss the pretty little hand' of a woman who, on any objective reckoning, had scarcely any of the qualities he admired or respected in a woman.

Though Cobbett insisted that the Queen's affair was only an '*inci-*

dent in the Great Drama, of which the workings of the Funds, or Debt, is the *plot*', it monopolized the *Political Register* for eighteen months, almost to exclude entirely the well-loved topics of paper-money and parliamentary reform. His position as a kind of public-relations officer for the Queen, organizing and presenting petitions in her support from all manner of local associations, won back for him some authority in working-class Radical circles. As the circulation of the *Political Register* was severely cut by the Six Acts, Cobbett more and more went out to public meetings in order to address the men he would formerly have reached by the printed word, and, after the Queen's death had allowed him to return to his principal concerns, he began to travel the country-side systematically to see agricultural distress for himself, and to address farmers on the subject of Reform. So, in the winter of 1821–2, Cobbett journeyed into Herefordshire, Kent, Norfolk, Suffolk, Sussex and Huntingdon, keeping a journal of his travels and publishing it serially in the *Political Register*. Away from the theatre of Westminster-mob politics, his 'tragedy queen' forgotten, he places his eye firmly upon the objects that really matter – the land and its workers.

The first printed extract from the journal opens *in media res* with Cobbett approaching Newbury amid 'Fog that you might cut with a knife'; at once he is reminded of other fogs and clouds, which he describes with the care of a Gilbert White; the Six Acts tug at his attention and so do recollections of America; he recalls a precept of his grandmother, and at once his mind darts forward to those 'old grannies' his political opponents. This is Cobbett's characteristic gunpowder train of association, by which the nostalgic vision of himself as a smocked child explodes into political diatribe:[10]

There are no two things in *this world*; and, were it not for fear of *Six-Acts* (the 'wholesome restraint' of which I continually feel) I might be tempted to carry my comparison further; but, certainly, there are no two things in *this world* so dissimilar as an English and a Long Island autumn. – These fogs are certainly the *white clouds* that we sometimes see aloft. I was once upon the Hampshire Hills, going from Soberton Down to Petersfield, where the hills are high and steep, not very wide at their base, very irregular in their form and direction, and have, of course, deep and narrow valleys winding about between them. In one place that I had to pass, two of these valleys were cut asunder by a piece of hill that went across them and formed a sort of bridge from one long hill to another. A little before I came to this sort of bridge I saw a smoke flying across it; and, not knowing the way by experience, I said to the person who was with me, 'there is the turnpike road (which we were expecting to come to;) for, don't you see the dust?' The day was very fine, the sun clear, and the weather dry. When we came to the pass, however, we found ourselves, not in dust, but in a fog. After getting over the pass, we looked down into the valleys, and there we saw the fog going along the valleys to the North, in detached parcels, that is to say, in clouds, and, as they came to the pass, they rose, went over it, then descended again, keeping constantly along just above the ground. And, to-day, the fog came by *spells*. It was sometimes thinner than at other times; and these changes were very sudden too. So that I am convinced that these fogs are *dry clouds*, such as those that I saw on the Hampshire-Downs. Those did not *wet* me at all; nor do these fogs wet any thing; and I do not think that they are by any means injurious to health. – It is the fogs that rise out of swamps, and other places, full of putrid vegetable matter, that kill people. These are the fogs that sweep off the new settlers in the American Woods. I remember a valley in Pennsylvania, in a part called *Wysihicken*. In looking from a hill, over this valley, early in the morning, in November, it presented one of the most beautiful sights that my eyes ever beheld. It was a sea bordered with beautifully formed trees of endless variety of colours. As the hills formed the outsides of the sea, some of the trees showed only their tops; and, every now-and-then, a lofty tree growing in the sea itself, raised its head above the apparent waters. Except the setting-sun sending his horizontal beams through all the variety of reds and yellows of the branches of the trees in Long Island, and giving, at the same time; a sort of silver cast to the verdure beneath them, I have never seen anything so beautiful as the foggy valley of the Wysihicken. But, I was told, that it was very fatal to the people; and that whole families were frequently swept off by the '*fall-fever*'. Thus the *smell* has a great deal to do with health. There can be no doubt that Butchers and their wives fatten upon the smell of meat. And this accounts for the precept of my grandmother, who used to tell me to *bite my bread and to smell my cheese*; talk, much more wise than that of certain *old grannies*, who go about England crying up '*the blessings*' of paper-money, taxes, and national debts.

Cobbett's eye is for the land; when he writes he is literally 'upon his own ground'. It is 'nice country' around Hurstbourne Tarrant in Hampshire, where on the hills the soil 'has great tenacity; does not *wash away* like sand, or light loam. . . . Bears sainfoin well, and all sorts of grass, which make the fields on the hills as green as meadows, even [in November]; and the grass does not burn up in summer.' On the borders of Surrey and Sussex: 'the genuine *oak-soil*; a bottom of yellow clay to any depth, I dare say, that man can go. No moss on the oaks. No dead tops. Straight as larches. The bark of the young trees with spots in it; sure sign of full growth and great depth of clay beneath.' In contrast, the stony soil around Cirencester makes 'miserable country. Any thing so ugly I have never seen before'; and, on Ashurst Forest near Uckfield in Sussex, 'the most villainously ugly spot I ever saw in England . . . barren soil, nasty, spewy gravel, heath', and even 'black, ragged, hideous rocks' as ugly as those in Nova Scotia. Cobbett comments upon ancient monuments such as the Wansdike, and upon modern follies such as Brighton Pavilion, and a Mr Montague's pretentious tiny landscape garden with its gimcrack 'Gothick' arch in Scotch firwood. He makes a pilgrimage at Shalbourne in Berkshire, where Jethro Tull used the first seed-drill. He inveighs against paper-money, absentee clergy, taxes and the Debt, and against the great parks and over-large farms which have squeezed out the small farmer. He describes the way in which he and his Radical friends cultivate the swede, and makes the appropriate analogy:[11]

> Our system of husbandry is happily illustrative of our system of politics. Our lines of movement are fair and straightforward. We destroy all weeds, which, like tax-eaters, do nothing but devour the sustenance that ought to feed the valuable plants. Our plants are all *well fed*; and our nations of swedes and of cabbages present a happy uniformity of enjoyments and of bulk, and not, as in the broad-cast system of Corruption, here and there one of enormous size, surrounded by thousands of poor little starveling things, scarcely distinguishable by the keenest eye, or, if seen, seen only to inspire a contempt of the husbandman. The Norfolk boys are, therefore, right in calling their swedes *Radical Swedes*.

Cobbett's main concern is with the condition of rural workers. Near that abominable pocket borough, Great Bedwin, in Wiltshire, not far from the 'extensive and uncommonly ugly park and domain of Lord Aylesbury, who seems to have tacked park on to park, like so many outworks of a fortified city' swallowing up '50 or 100 farms of former days', he saw a group of reapers and their women-helpers:[12]

> There were some very pretty girls, but ragged as colts and as pale as ashes. The day was cold too, and frost hardly off the ground; and their blue arms and lips would have made any heart ache but that of a seat-seller or a loan-jobber. . . . [They] presented such an assemblage of rags as I never before saw even among the hoppers at Farnham, many of whom are common beggars.

Whatever men of taste might think of landscape gardens, Cobbett always found such relatively unproductive land as 'ugly' as barren heath or mountain or the 'spewy gravel' favoured by suburban house-builders. He writes elsewhere of a 'rural war' between rich and poor, and here Lord Ailesbury's garden at Tottenham Park, for all the pastoral dreams that may have inspired it, appears as the alien, fortified city where some invader sits behind his walls, lodges and gamekeepers, while, outside, the pitiful, pale ragged girls exist like refugees or a conquered people. This is the effect of the 'System', or the 'Thing', whose agents are suitably dehumanized in Cobbett's rhetoric.

But the 'Thing', Cobbett ever-confidently exclaimed, is doomed. Such symptoms of it as the shabby-genteel houses on a recently enclosed common at Dartford, the garrison town in Kent, are perversions which must be temporary:[13]

> This is a little excrescence that has grown out of the immense sums, which have been drawn from other parts of the kingdom to be expended on Barracks, Magazines, Martello-Towers, Catamarans, and all the excuses for lavish expenditure, which the war for the Bourbons gave rise to. All things will return; these rubbishy flimsy things, on this common, will first be deserted, then crumble down, then be swept away, and the cattle, sheep, pigs and geese will once more graze upon the common, which will again furnish heath, furze and turf for the labourers on the neighbouring lands.

The effect of this passage is not unlike Pope's lines in the *Epistle to Burlington* prophesying that Timon's vain and costly garden will, one day, by natural process decline into usefulness – except, of course, that Pope was right about Cannons, whereas Cobbett's prophecy about Dartford has not come true, yet. Perhaps it is the effect of fresh air and country sights, but Cobbett's diatribes in the journal descriptions of his travels, written in inns or at friends' houses each evening, are less sour or savage than the ones he wrote at his Fleet Street desk. He knows that, whatever sufferings the borough-mongers may have inflicted upon the rural labourers, the land itself is sound.

The journeys of 1821–2 were made mostly by coach, but in the following winter Cobbett went over most of the same counties on horseback, making the first of what he called his 'Rural Rides'. Such travels helped him to recover his equilibrium after the demoralization of the Coventry election and his bankruptcy.

The last of the Six Acts, the one which had priced the twopenny *Register* reprints out of the pockets of most working men, contained a clause exempting from stamp duty publications containing only matters of 'piety, devotion or charity'. Cobbett was not slow to slip through this loophole, and in March 1821 he began the publication of a series of *Cobbett's Monthly Religious Tracts*, changing the title in June to *Cobbett's Monthly Sermons*. He would, 'for his part, gladly see the affairs of religion left to the management of the Clergy; but, since Societies of lay persons have taken upon them to school the nation in matters of religion, he sees, as yet, nothing to prevent him from taking a small share in the concern.'[14] This promise to take a 'small share' is uncharacteristic mock-modesty; by the time the twelfth and last sermon of the series had appeared in March 1822, he was proudly claiming translations into French and Italian and an English sale of 100,000 copies: 'I have done more in the cause of *morality* and real religion, than I believe to have been done by all the parsons in the kingdom within the last hundred years.'[15]

The first of Cobbett's *Sermons*, 'Naboth's Vineyard; or God's Vengeance against Hypocrisy and Cruelty', was aimed directly against those rival tract-writers whom he saw as false religious teachers who hypocritically preached contentment and other-worldliness to the poor in order the better to plunder them. It was Wilberforce, that object of Cobbett's undying hatred, who, in 1797, had expounded 'the grand law of subordination', and had advised religious instructors on how they should teach the poor[16]

that their more lowly path has been alotted to them by the hand of God; that it is their part faithfully to discharge its duties and contentedly to bear its inconveniences; that the present state of things is very short; that the objects, about which worldly men conflict so eagerly, are not worth the contest.

Cobbett's second Sermon, on 'The Sin of Drunkenness in Kings, Priests, and People' was largely an oblique, but unmistakable, attack upon George IV:[17]

> That the lowest and most degraded of mankind should yield themselves up to such a vice ought to appear surprising; because it is a vice committed against nature herself. What, then, must be our decision as to *Kings*, who should thus debase themselves, degrade the character not only of the King but of the man, and set the commands of the Almighty at defiance, when they ought to be an example and an ever-living light to guide the steps of their people. . . . And, when was the drunkard mindful of the law? When was he mindful to discharge his duties? When did he do justice to any? When did he ever discover a merciful disposition? When did he consider the case of the afflicted? When did he evince that he had one particle of humanity in his bosom? The sensual man is always unfeeling towards others; and this imputation more particularly applies to the drunkard and the glutton. Subjects, neighbours, wife, children; all that ought to occupy a great portion of his affections; all are cast aside to make way for his inordinate and beastly appetites.

Drunkenness among the established clergy was no less disgraceful; nor was it to be tolerated among working people, because it was important for the cause of Reform that working men should be respectable and responsible and be seen to deserve the political rights which Cobbett was claiming for them.

Succeeding Sermons took for their subjects 'The Fall of Judas or God's Vengeance against Bribery', 'The Rights of the Poor and the Punishment of Oppressors', 'God's Judgement on unjust Judges', 'The Sluggard' (who practised what was, in Cobbett's eyes, one of the worst of vices), 'God's Vengeance against Murderers', 'The Gamester', 'God's Vengeance against Public Robbers', 'The Unnatural Mother' (on the virtue of breast-feeding), and 'The Sin of Forbidding Marriage' (directed against Malthus, of course). Throughout, Cobbett's aim is to show the common people their rights, and to fortify their self-respect. In *Sermon* IV, on the rights of the poor, he notably, and against all the economic orthodoxy of the day (cf. pp. 26-7 above), asserts human values in the market-place:

> labour is not merchandize, except, indeed, it be the labour of a slave. It is altogether personal. It is inseparable from the body o ʃ the labourer; and cannot be considered as an article to be cheapened, without any regard being had to the well-being of the person who has to perform it.

The last of the *Sermons* was on 'Parsons and Tithes'. Cobbett detested the Established Church for its wealth and privilege and unfailing support of the Tory government, but his denunciation of pluralism and non-residence is couched in traditional terms. Cobbett carries on his argument with perfect propriety in the context of Biblical teaching; while, despite their modern political-polemical intent, his sermons link themselves naturally to a tradition of religious teaching older and more honourable than Wilberforce's or Hannah More's – the tradition of Langland and Latimer:[18]

> The Prophet Zechariah, in the words of a part of my text, has, manifestly, such a result in his eye when he cries, 'Woe on the shepherd that *leaveth* his flock.' And the Prophet Ezekiel, in the other parts of my text, clearly means to impress the same thing on the minds of the priests. What, indeed, can be more just, than that *woe* should fall upon those, who '*eat the fat* and clothe themselves with the *wool*', but who feed not the flock . . . when we see a man taking the income of two or three livings, and seldom, or never go near either of them, are we still to look upon him as a follower of the Apostles, and intitled to the respect and reverence that is due to their memories and names?

Cobbett's *Sermons* were an insolent retaliation against censorship in the Six Acts, but their purpose was serious and positive; Cobbett was a religious teacher of sorts. The government, invoking the names of Paine, Owen, Carlile and Hone, tried to make out that Radicals were, as a matter of course, atheists and blasphemers, but Cobbett was never open to this charge, and, indeed, his influence was all the wider than Carlile's or Owen's simply because it was always evident that he shared the common religious beliefs of most of the lower orders. Religion is not a matter of revelation or of grace, but of moral law. So he writes in *Sermon* II:

To practise justice, mercy, charity and other virtues, is natural to uncorrupted and unperverted human beings. That which strengthens this natural propensity, or arrests the effects of corruption and perversion, and does this through the means of reverence for God and an expectation of future rewards and punishments, is called Religion. So that, religion means *virtue* arising from considerations connected with a Supreme Being and with hopes and fears as to another world.

There is, of course, nothing specifically Anglican – or even distinctly Christian – about this, and most of what Cobbett writes on the Church of England is disparaging in the extreme; nevertheless, he remained a member of that Church. Cobbett's reason was that the Church was by law established and so part of that English 'Constitution' to which he was always loyal, and which he always sought to restore, not destroy. He explained:[19]

A parson said to me, once, by letter: 'Your religion, Mr. Cobbett, seems to me to be altogether political.' 'Very much so indeed,' answered I, 'and well it may, since I have been furnished with a creed which makes part of an Act of Parliament.' And, the fact is, I am no Doctor of Divinity, and like a religion, any religion, that tends to make men innocent and benevolent and happy, by taking the best possible means of furnishing them with plenty to eat and drink and wear.

Believing that a full belly for the labourer was the only secure foundation for public morality, Cobbett issued alongside the later *Sermons* a complementary work, also in monthly parts, *Cottage Economy: containing information relative to the brewing of Beer, making of Bread, keeping of Cows, Pigs, Bees, Ewes, Goats, Poultry and Rabbits, and relative to other matters deemed useful in the conducting of the affairs of a Labourer's Family*. Cobbett hoped by this to teach the labourer and his wife how to establish a material basis for that independence of spirit which the *Sermons* had called for. It was difficult to be a militant Reformer on a diet of tea, sorrel and potatoes, but Cobbett would show that the labourer, if given a fair wage, could, with careful management and self-help, enjoy the full larder that he had enjoyed in that ideal Old England of his memories and dreams:[20]

The people of England have been famed, in all ages, for their *good living*; for the *abundance of their food* and *goodness of their attire.* The old sayings about English roast beef and plumb-pudding, and about English hospitality, had not their foundation in *nothing* . . . it is *abundant living* amongst the people at large, which is the great test of good government, and the surest basis of national greatness and security.

So Cobbett taught domestic management in such declining arts as home-brewing and home-baking to provide cheaper and far better substitutes for the products of commercial bakers and brewers, while, in passing, delivering his customary philippics against tea – 'a weaker kind of laudanum which . . . communicates no strength to the body' and wastes time and fuel – and 'Ireland's lazy root', the innutritious potato. A labouring family could live well if it constantly practised small economies; for instance, if, instead of buying candles, it made rushlights, as Cobbett's grandmother used to.

In a new collected edition of *Cottage Economy* in 1823 Cobbett added instructions 'to the wives and children of country labourers relative to the selecting, the cutting and the bleaching of the plants of English grass and grain, for the purpose of making hats and bonnets'. This was his attempt to create some new domestic industry in the villages to replace those handicrafts destroyed by the growth of factories. He assured his readers that he never would have published his scheme if he had thought that it might create a new class of factory owners and merchants, 'bonnet lords to rival the calico lords', but this could not be the case here, where the material – rye or wheat straw and certain grasses – 'in many cases can scarcely be denominated private property'.[21] He claimed great success for this, as for nearly all his schemes. Cobbett's own writings contain many references to widows, cripples or other poor villagers maintaining their families from straw-plaiting according to his instructions, but there are independent witnesses to his success. For instance, Carlyle in a letter of 1827 wrote of a cottager who four years earlier had procured a loan of *Cottage Economy* from a farmer, had learned to plait Leghorn bonnets, and thus was now able to support her husband, a sick, unemployed weaver, and daughter.[22] *Cottage Economy* sold well; Cobbett, with his customary self-satisfaction, reported a sale of 'pretty nearly' 50,000 by 1827, and reckoned 'it must be a real devil in human shape who does not applaud the man who could sit down to write this book, a copy of which every *parson* ought, upon pain of loss of ears, to give to every girl that he marries, rich or poor.'[23]

In preaching the doctrines of self-help, thrift, early-rising, orderliness and hard work to labouring people, Cobbett was not out of line with other popular educators of the day, and *Cottage Economy*, which had the rare distinction among Cobbett's publications of a favourable notice (by Brougham) in the *Edinburgh Review*, does in some respects anticipate the work of the Society for the Diffusion of Useful Knowledge founded by Brougham in 1825; but Cobbett was always scornful of everyone else's efforts in popular education, all of which he lumped together as part of that 'comforting' system by which the rulers 'amused' the working classes, and diverted their attention from the real cause of their poverty in order to make them easier to plunder. Cobbett was right when he claimed that working men needed to be taught their political rights, but wrong when he said they should be taught nothing else. In one of many open letters to Brougham he writes:[24]

> think of John Plodpole, with every finger as thick as your wrist,
> and chaps between the finger and thumb, a quarter of an inch
> deep, no more capable of running over the leaf of a book than
> you are of turning over with the spade, twenty rod of ground in
> a day; only think of poor John, coming home from hedging, with
> a nitch of wood upon his back, to which is appended a pair of
> gloves or cuffs, each as big as your brief-bag; only think of him,
> with a pair of shoes weighing half a score of pounds, and with
> jacket impenetrable by thorns; think of poor John; now pray
> think of him, pray do look at him, who, when he throws down
> his nitch is so tired that he is ready to follow it to the earth. . . .
> [Is this] the person who is to sit down over his handful of fire and
> his farthing or half-farthing rushlight, and meditate on 'the
> profound wisdom, sustained by unbounded learning, and
> embellished with the most brilliant fancy, which so richly furnishes
> every page of the Essays of Bacon'?

Poor John, said Cobbett, needed bacon to eat, not Bacon to read.

Cobbett, as usual, is taking a political opponent by the scruff of the neck and trying to make him *see* what he sees: 'pray do look at him'. The juxtaposition of the dialect 'nitch' (a Plodpole word) and the learned 'appended' (a Brougham word), the comparisons between John's fingers and Brougham's wrists and between John's gloves and Brougham's well-filled brief-bag, make it clear that Cobbett knows the labourer far better than Brougham and his class ever could, while at the same time they show that he can address Brougham as an intellectual equal. Cobbett is 'on the side' of Plodpole, but the effect of the tone and all the implications of this passage is that Plodpole is as different a creature from Cobbett as he is from Brougham. In using Plodpole as part of a sarcastic attack on Brougham, Cobbett seems to have forgotten the well-grown, broad-shouldered, and perhaps thick-fingered, gardener's boy who once had experienced a birth of intellect as he puzzled over the profound wisdom, unbounded learning and brilliant fancy of *A Tale of a Tub*, and the young soldier who had sat over his handful of fire – or share of it – to learn Lowth's *Grammar* by heart. Cobbett *knows* the facts of rural life and labour as Brougham never can; but this vital, affectionate, exaggerated little sketch of John Plodpole is patronizing in its gentlemanly assumption that there is an admirable innocence in semi-literacy. Cobbett is the last man who should have regarded Plodpole in this way.

It sometimes appears that for Cobbett education, like religion, was nothing more or less than a well-filled belly and innocence. There was 'true education' for instance when farm servants used to live with their masters:[25]

> In the farm-houses there used to be a long oak table, three inches through, at which the whole family sat. The breakfast was by candle-light in winter; and it consisted of beer, bread and bacon or other food, prepared by the dame and the maids, while the men and boys and masters went out to feed and clean their horses and cattle by lantern-light. It was not a mess consisting of *tea-water* and *potatoes*. When the men went out they had their bottles of beer and their luncheon bags. It was not *water* and cold *potatoes* to eat in the field. The return from plough was the signal for dinner, the horses having been fed first. At night all assembled again, and all were in bed four hours before midnight. This was *education*. This was *good-breeding*. From this arose the finest race of people that the world ever saw.

Admirable as this may have been, it had not been Cobbett's education, and it was not remotely like the kind of education that Cobbett's writings were imparting to labourers at that time. Cobbett in fact was helping to create a cohesive body of literate, self-reliant, politically alert and active industrial workers, though he was slow to realize this. So his writings on 'education' are largely this unreflective yearning for a lost past, which is always less complicated, less falsely-refined than the present. They resemble his writings on entertainment, where he laments the disappearance of the mountebank and Jack-pudding, and hates the rise of 'a playhouse: no, a *theatre*' in every provincial town:[26]

> The player-people have driven out these legitimate buffoons of the country, as the Hanover-Rats drove out black English-Rats which were poor harmless creatures that very seldom plundered either the mow or the dairy. . . . Oh let us have the out-a-doors vagrants back again! Let us have the Mountebanks and the Jack-puddings; let the country fellows and girls have their *two-penny hops*; and then let the tract distributors do their worst.

The success of the *Grammar*, *Sermons* and *Cottage Economy* made up for reduced sales of the *Political Register*, but Cobbett – determined to restore his fortunes fully – was writing furiously throughout the 1820s. In his *Poor Man's Friend* (1826–7) he produced what he regarded as his best work, and in the *History of the Protestant 'Reformation'* (1824) his best seller. For a little over a year in 1822–3 he had a large share in the old-established evening newspaper *The Statesman* and wrote for it daily political articles and summaries of parliamentary proceedings, which he gathered into a volume under the sarcastic title, *Cobbett's Collective Commentaries; or, Remarks on the Proceedings in the Collective Wisdom of the Nation*. He wrote much on husbandry. In 1822 he issued his 'new and improved' edition of Jethro Tull's *Horse Hoeing Husbandry*. The treatise on gardening he had written in America was published in 1821 as *The American Gardener* and republished in an enlarged edition as *The English Gardener* (1828). There was also a treatise on forestry, *The Woodlands*, published in numbers at irregular intervals (1825–8), and a *Treatise on Cobbett's Corn* (1828). 'Cobbett's Corn' was maize, which, at considerable cost, Cobbett attempted to popularize in England. The *Political Register*, too, offered advice on farming and gardening, and carried many advertisements for seeds and plants which Cobbett sold from his nursery at Kensington, and, later, from the larger one he set up on Barn-Elm Farm at Barnes in Surrey. His activities as a seedsman and his promotion of the English straw-plait earned him in 1823 the silver medal of the Society of Arts. Farming and horticulture were healthful and pleasurable, though never profitable, diversions, but the chief object was political: 'If I wrote grammars, if I wrote on agriculture; if I sowed, planted, or dealt in seeds; whatever I did had first in view the destruction of infamous tyrants.'[27]

Writing upon rural society Cobbett continued to harp on old

themes. Again and again in the *Political Register* he returned to the engrossing of farms and enclosure of wastes:[28]

> I do not believe that it would be going too far to say, that nine-tenths of the farmhouses of England have been destroyed since the day that the 'good old King' [George III] came to the throne. As if this were not enough, *large part of the commons have been enclosed.* Nothing that man could devise would be more injurious to the country than this.

Cobbett did more than write. In 1827, by a timely memorial to the Parliamentary Committee, he managed to foil an attempt to enclose Waltham Chase, near Botley.[29] The familiar motto from *Isaiah, v, 8,* 'Woe unto them that join house to house, that lay field to field', appeared in 1821 at the head of Cobbett's letter on large and small farms, addressed to the great Norfolk landowner Thomas William Coke of Holkham (cf. p. 17 above). Though his achievements were greatly exaggerated by contemporary panegyrists, Coke was a benevolent, enlightened (if despotic) landlord who encouraged his tenants to improve their farming methods, and who banished from the parishes where he reigned both the workhouse and the alehouse. In many respects he was close to the traditional ideal of the good landlord, and not unworthy of Cobbett's admiration – particularly as he had been an opponent of Pitt – but Cobbett was now beginning to take a disenchanted view of the whole class of landlords, so, although Coke was 'the best landlord and the best husbandman in England', he had made a grave error in organizing his estates into large farms only. As usual, Cobbett was able to trace back the trouble to the Debt and paper-money, so, in the great annual sheep-shearings at Holkham:[30]

> You saw assembled around what you thought the effect of *improvement in agriculture,* when it really was the effect of a false, fraudulent, amassing paper-money; that brought before your eyes the prosperous *tens,* and that kept the starving *hundreds* carefully hidden from your sight.

Soon afterwards, Cobbett confronted Coke, and addressed him less respectfully. On 3 January 1823, Coke and other leading Whigs called a meeting of county electors at Norwich to petition the government upon agricultural distress, but Cobbett forced his way on to the platform and, amid scenes of wild disorder, persuaded the meeting to adopt his own petition which called for:[31]

1. An appropriation of part of the property of the church to the liquidation of the debt: 2. A reduction of the standing army, including staff, barracks and colleges, to a scale of expense as low as that of the army before the last war: 3. A total abolition of all sinecures, pensions, grants, and emoluments, not merited by public services: 4. A sale of the crown lands, and an application of the money towards the liquidation of the debt: 5. An equitable adjustment with regard to the public debt, and also with regard to all contracts between man and man.

(In this last phrase Cobbett, and his fellow-petitioners, no doubt had in mind those leases drawn up in the wartime agricultural boom whose high rents had still to be paid in peacetime slump.) The Norfolk Petition was a flash in the pan, and Coke (henceforth to be known by Cobbett as 'Daddy Coke' or 'Dictator-General') was easily able to organize counter-petitions, but for a while Cobbett imagined that he had set in motion an invincible Reform movement among farmers.

In 1815 Cobbett had still believed that all ranks of rural society, landlords, farmers and labourers, had a common interest, but the Corn Law of that year showed the true situation: that the 'landed interest' in Parliament no more cared for the true interest of most men who lived on the land than it cared for the 'general welfare' of the whole nation. As Byron put it in *The Age of Bronze* (1823):

'For what were all these country patriots born?
To hunt, and vote, and raise the price of corn?

In the 1820s Cobbett writes with uncompromising hostility towards the whole class of country gentlemen. Thus when he sees them fall victim to the moneyed men, he finds an appropriately crude metaphor by which to represent the viewpoint of reformers and the unfranchised masses: 'If a robber have taken my purse; if I see him fallen upon by other robbers; shall I endeavour to rescue him that he may quietly keep my purse; or shall I assist them in rifling him with a *chance*, at any rate, of obtaining my own again?'[32] Cobbett looks forward grimly to their deserved extinction:[33]

These incomparable cowards; these wretched slaves; these dirty creatures who call themselves country gentlemen, deserve ten times as much as they have yet had to suffer. They are the makers of their own ruin. . . . Their shocking subserviency to men in power and their agents; their incomparable meanness; all these mark them out as worthy of that fate which awaits them.

One creature Cobbett still hated more than a squire was a wealthy, pluralist, non-resident parson. He knew 'of no more meritorious and ill-used men than the working clergy', but he found the wealth of the higher clergy objectionable and asked, as many had done before him:[34]

> Did Christ choose for his Apostles men with immense estates, scores of manors, scores of gamekeepers, and with apparel the most sumptuous that can be conceived? Did he ever say or insinuate, that the success of his saving word depended upon the teachers of it having palaces for their places of residence; having parks well stocked with deer; having retinues of servants?

So when the Church in 1818 applied successfully to Parliament for grants to supplement the stipends of the poorest clergy and to build new churches in growing towns, Cobbett protested that these expenses should have been met, not by the over-burdened taxpayer, but out of the already over-swollen revenues of the Established Church, and that, in any case, the clergy were quite incapable of filling the churches they already had.

Cobbett had the farmer's inbred dislike of tithes, though in his early Tory writings he had defended them. By 1819,[35] he was claiming that tithes had been instituted primarily for the relief of the poor, and only secondarily for the maintenance and ornament of churches and the support of the (unmarried) clergy. Since the Reformation the income from tithes had been wholly expended on the clergy and their families, or, in many cases, had fallen into the hands of laymen. The Church of England had betrayed its ancient trust, so that Parliament had every right, indeed had a moral duty, to take from it at least two-thirds of its tithes and use them for 'national' purposes, specifically to help liquidate the National Debt. This was the first demand of the Norfolk Petition of 1823. The matter of tithes would, no doubt, have figured prominently in the *Plough-Boy's History of the Church*, which Cobbett announced as 'forthcoming' in June 1818, but his Church-history when at last it did appear (in sixteen parts, 1824–6) was *A History of the Protestant 'Reformation', in England and Ireland, showing how that event has impoverished and degraded the main body of the People in those Countries*, and was a polemic in the struggle for Roman Catholic emancipation.

As early as 1804 Cobbett had urged the repeal of the Test Acts which imposed disabilities on Roman Catholics,[36] and, though as late as the *Sermons* (1821) he was writing in the old rousing Protestant manner of persecutions under Louis XIV, he had also written of the wrongs suffered by Irish Roman Catholics under English Protestant rule.[37] For some years the Irish Catholics had found allies among English Radicals, but Cobbett did not concern himself much with the question of Roman Catholic emancipation until the success, in 1823, of Daniel O'Connell's Catholic Association, which provided a brilliant pattern for widespread, peaceful political agitation and a strong body of potential allies against the corrupt boroughmongers. This was the occasion for Cobbett's *History of the Protestant 'Reformation'*; the facts came from John Lingard's *History of England* (eight volumes, 1819–30), which by 1823 had advanced to the end of the sixteenth century. Though Lingard, a priest, obviously wrote with a Romanist bias, his *History* had a temperate tone which Cobbett nowhere tries to imitate; on the contrary his tone is unremittingly shrill and he often shamelessly distorts the facts even as Lingard had presented them.

Cobbett's theme is that the 'Reformation' (which henceforth he habitually wrote thus, in inverted commas) was not an act of purification but one of bloody devastation, a fraud 'engendered in lust and brought forth in hypocrisy and perfidy', which had in its turn evilly engendered more and yet more monstrous 'reformations' in the shape of the Cromwellian Commonwealth and the 'Glorious Revolution' of 1688 which had brought the Debt (begotten by Bishop Burnet), the seeds of the 'Pitt System' and all our woe. All the French wars of the eighteenth century – so expensive to the present taxpayer – were kin to this unholy progeny in that they had been undertaken to keep an unpopular Protestant dynasty on the throne:[38]

> If you will follow me in this inquiry, I will first show you how this thing called the 'Reformation' began; what it arose out of; and then I will show you its progress, how it marched on, plundering, devastating, inflicting torments on the people, and shedding their innocent blood. I will trace it downward through all its stages, until I show you its natural result, in the schemes of Parson Malthus . . . in the present misery indescribable of the labouring classes in England and Ireland, and in that odious and detestable system, which has made Jews and paper-money makers the real owners of a large part of the estates in this kingdom.

Throughout this *History* runs the contrast between an ideal pre-Reformation England and a miserable present reality. The oft-cited passage from Fortescue reappears of course to show that the medieval labouring man was much better fed, better clothed and better housed, and had more real political freedom than his modern counterpart. When the medieval Church held its property in trust for the poor there were no paupers; only the spoliation of the Church by Tudor 'Reformers' had made a Poor Law necessary. The nation had declined since the days when Plantagenet kings with patriotic levies (not standing amies) had conquered France. Even population had declined. England must have been more populous in the Middle Ages; otherwise, Cobbett asked, how could men have raised and filled the many great churches now stranded in tiny, poverty-stricken villages, or even standing alone on the sites of vanished villages. Depopulation was an old eighteenth-century bogey and Cobbett was ridiculed in his own day, and later, for raising it. He was wrong about national population, but right in claiming that many villages had shrunk or disappeared since the Middle Ages.[39]

That other old countryman's bogey, the monopolizer of corn, appears in a passage comparing past and present:[40]

> Ah! Good God! what has the thing called the 'Reformation' produced at Norwich! Who is there at Norwich now to keep hospitality? 'St. Andrew's Hall', as it is now called, which was the church of this Priory, is now the Corn-market, and now hears, instead of the chantings of its benevolent monks, the chafferings and the cheapenings, the lyings and roguish cant, of sly Quaker corn-monopolizers. The questions here now are, not how and when malt and wheat shall be distributed to the poor and the stranger; but, how they shall be hoarded up, made dear, and kept from the thirsty and the hungry.

Cobbett goes on to point out that it was from the platform on which once stood the high-altar of this Priory, that he read out his Norfok Petition which, he is sure, will have a great effect. His sense of place, his historical imagination, and the deep-seated popular prejudices of the countryside all play together around this little self-portrait of Cobbett standing between past and present upon a market platform in Norwich.

Another lament for the loss of hospitality is coupled with Cobbett's dislike of modern landlords (of both kinds), but has, too, a touch of conventionally romantic 'Gothick' sentiment that is less often found in his writings.[41]

> Go to the site of some once-opulent Convent. Look at the cloister, now become, in the hands of a rack-renter, the receptacle for dung, fodder and fagot-wood: see the hall, where, for ages, the widow, the orphan, the aged and the stranger, found a table ready spread; see a bit of its walls now helping to make a cattle-shed, the rest having been hauled away to build a workhouse: recognize, in the side of a barn, a part of the once magnificent Chapel: and, if, chained to the spot by your melancholy musings, you be admonished of the approach of night by the voice of the screech-owl, issuing from those arches, which once, at the same hour, resounded with the vespers of the monk, and which have, for seven hundred years, been assailed by storms and tempests in vain; if thus admonished of the necessity of seeking food, shelter, and a bed, lift your eyes and look at the white-washed and dry-rotten shell on the hill, called the 'gentleman's house;' and, apprized of the 'board-wages' and the spring guns, suddenly turn your head; jog away from the scene of devastation; with 'old English Hospitality' in your mind, reach the nearest inn, and there, in room half-warmed and half-lighted, and with the reception precisely proportioned to the presumed length of your purse, sit down.

Where William of Wykeham spent his income on providing churches, hospitals and schools, the present Bishop of Winchester (Sir George Pretyman Tomline, once Pitt's tutor) has divided 'twenty-four livings, five prebends, one chancellorship, one archdeaconship, and one mastership, worth perhaps, altogether more than twenty thousand pounds a year' among ten of his relations, and is now supplementing his income by allowing 'small beer to be sold out of his episcopal palace at Farnham'.[42] In William of Wykeham's day:[43]

> the poor of the parish of Farnham, having [Waverley Abbey] to apply to, and having for their neighbour a Bishop of Winchester who did not sell small beer out of his palace, stood in no need of poor-rates, and had never heard the horrid word pauper pronounced. Come, my townsmen of Farnham, you, who, as well as I, have, when we were boys, climbed the ivy-covered ruins of this venerable abbey. . . . You know what poor-rates are and you

know what church-rates are. Very well, then, there were no poor-rates and no church-rates as long as Waverley Abbey existed and as long as Bishops had no wives. . . . The Church shared its property with the poor and the stranger, and left the people at large to possess their own earnings. And, as to matters of faith and worship, look at that immense heap of earth round the church, where your parents and my parents, and where our progenitors, for twelve hundred years, lie buried; then bear in mind, that, for nine hundred years out of the twelve, they were all of the faith and worship of the monks of Waverley; and, with that thought in your mind, find, if you can, the heart to say, that the monks of Waverley, by whose hospitality your fathers and my fathers were, for so many ages, preserved from bearing the hateful name of pauper, taught an idolatrous and damnable religion.

Again we feel the sense of place, of history and the constant pressure upon the reader of Cobbett's egotism, while an appeal to direct, particular, personal experience is coupled with the widest and wildest generalizations.

Cobbett's *History* duly made its contribution to the debate on Roman Catholic emancipation. He claimed that, good as Lingard's *History* was, it would never produce 'a thousandth part of the *effect* that mine will produce in the space of three years'; upon which a modern writer has justly observed, 'Unhappily, a Gresham's Law of journalism might support Cobbett'.[44] Certainly Cobbett's violent, racy, absurd, anguished, graphic polemic has been reprinted many times, even in the present century, in the interests of Catholic Truth.

While Cobbett was attacking the Protestant Establishment, he was also plunging happily into the internal disputes among supporters of Roman Catholic emancipation. Thus, when O'Connell accepted compromises in the Irish Catholic Emancipation Bill which came before Parliament in 1825, Cobbett promptly consigned him to the inferno which already contained Burdett (who had moved this weakened Bill). The immediate result was a special edition of the *Political Register* entitled 'Big O and Sir Glory: or Leisure to Laugh, a comedy in three acts' – not the first, or the last, or the least tedious of Cobbett's several ponderous efforts in comic dramatic dialogue.[45] About this item, he quarrelled also with two other leading Radicals, Henry Hunt (the 'Orator') and Richard Carlile.

From time to time during the 1820s, Cobbett announced the

imminence of Reform and the dissolution of the accursed 'System', and on 6 April 1826, during a financial crisis which involved the failure of several country banks and a run on the Bank of England, he held a great public dinner, his 'Feast of the Gridiron', to proclaim the fulfilment of all his prophecies concerning gold repayments. In the summer of that year Cobbett stood as Parliamentary candidate at Preston, his expenses being paid by a fund raised by Sir Thomas Beevor, a Norfolk squire; but at a rowdy election he was bottom of the poll. Cobbett's influence had declined from its peak of 1816–17; Heine, who saw him in 1827 wrote:[46]

> He is a chained house-dog who falls with equal fury on every one whom he does not know, often bites the best friend of the house, barks incessantly, and just because of this incessantness of his barking cannot get listened to, even when he barks at an actual thief. Therefore the distinguished thieves who plunder England do not think it necessary to throw the growling Cobbett a bone to stop his mouth. This makes the dog furiously savage, and he shows all his hungry teeth. Poor old Cobbett! England's watch-dog!

Cobbett, for his part, could manage without Heine's pity, or anyone else's, and wrote:[47]

> The caitiffs . . . now begin to comfort themselves with the thought that I am a 'Poor Old Man'; and that I cannot possibly last long. It is an 'old man', recollect, who can travel five hundred miles, make speeches of half an hour long twice a day for a month; put down the saucy, the rich, the tyrannical, make them hang their heads in his presence; an 'old man', recollect, that can be jostled out of his majority at an election; and that can return towards his home through forty miles of huzzas from the lips of a hundred and fifty thousand people.

It was for the benefit of these cheering but unenfranchised thousands that Cobbett wrote his *Poor Man's Friend* (1826–7), a set of five letters 'addressed to the Working Classes of Preston', sold in twopenny parts but distributed free in Preston itself. He later called it his 'most learned work' and his favourite work. In it he believed he had demonstrated that, according to all divine and human laws, no one should die of hunger amid abundance of food. According to the Law of Nature, indeed, there is no private property, and all belongs equally to all. Though men had joined together in civil society and established rights of private property on the basis of their labour in clearing and cultivating the land, it was never intended that all of the land should become the property of the few while the many should be impoverished. So the owners of land were charged with the care of the poor. In the Middle Ages the clergy owned land in trust for the maintenance of the poor, as Cobbett had already shown in the *History of the Protestant 'Reformation'*. Though the Poor Law of 1601 was an unsatisfactory substitute for medieval charity, it did confirm the legal *right* of the poor to be maintained by the landowners: 'Every inch of land, every brick and tile in a house . . . is pledged by the law to prevent the people from suffering from want.'[48]

The circulation of the *Political Register* in the mid-1820s was to be reckoned in hundreds, where once – in the twopenny *Pamphlet* form – it had been thousands, but the journal did remain in being when other Radical journals died. The famous *Black Dwarf*, for instance, had gone out of business in 1824. Fat profits from those best-sellers – the *Grammar* the *Sermons* and the *History of the Protestant 'Reformation'* – subsidized the *Political Register* and enabled Cobbett to substantiate the proud claim he made in his Preston election address that he was no place-hunter:[49]

> Then, it would be base and bootlessly base in me to participate in any shape or manner in the taxes squeezed out of the people. What do I want in this world but the things that I have? I have a house at Fleet Street, I have another at Kensington, I have another at Barn-Elm. . . . These are all good houses, too: they are furnished with every necessary. At Barn-Elm I have now a farm of nearly a hundred acres, the richest land I believe in this whole world, except those marshes which bring diseases along with their riches. What more than this can I want? I have horses at my will: always not less than half a dozen men to start at my call: I feed more hungry, meritorious people than any lord in the kingdom: God has blessed me with health and strength very rare at my age: I am enabled to set a great example of enterprize, industry, early rising, perseverance, to all around me.

At Barn-Elm Cobbett continued on a larger scale his expensive experiments in maize-growing, and it is in the *Treatise on Cobbett's Corn* that he gives a detailed account of the Barn-Elm household, where he boarded eight young men and a boy and gave them substantial meals off an old-fashioned thick oak table, and where he himself was in bed at nine and up at four in the morning, ready to take up the pen the moment the fire was lighted.[50] Like Botley House, this was a little corner of the old England of his youth saved from the general ruin.

Cobbett's recent idealization of the Middle Ages did not prevent him from continuing to idealize the 1760s and seventies, and while the *History of the Protestant 'Reformation'* was coming from the Press he wrote in the *Political Register* of those more recent 'Dark Ages':[51]

> I verily believe, that if I had been born in these days of slavery, of rags, and of hunger, I should never have been any more known in the world, than the chap I, at this very moment, see slinking by the side of a road-waggon, with scarcely a shoe on his foot, and with a smock-frock that none but actual beggars wore in the *'dark ages'* when I was a boy . . . in those *'dark ages'* that the impudent Scotch economists talk about, we had a great many holidays. There were all the fairs of our own place, and all the fairs of the places just round about. There were several days at Christmas, at Easter, at Whitsuntide; and we had a day or two at *Hollantide*, as we used to call it, which came in November, I believe, and at *Candlemass*. Besides these, there were cricket-matches, and single-stick matches; and all these were not thought too much. . . . I never knew a labouring man, in those *'dark ages'*, go out to his work in the morning without a bottle of beer and a satchel of victuals, containing cheese, if not bacon, hung upon his *crook*. A *bottle-crook* made as usual a part of the equipage of a labourer, as his smock-frock, or his hat did. Except in about five or six instances, in Sussex, I have not seen a *bottle-crook* these twenty years. Accordingly be it observed, that there wanted no schools, no Lancasterian or Bell work, no Tracts, no circulation of Bibles, to make the common people generally honest and obedient. I remember a little sort of fair that used to be held at a village in Surrey. I remember the white smock-frocks and red handkerchiefs, and nice clean clothes of the girls, that used to ornament that fair. By accident, I stumbled upon it in a Rural Ride two years ago. Not a tenth part of the people, and these, in general, ragged and dirty, with some few girls drawn off in tawdry cottons, looking more like town prostitutes than country girls; and this was a pretty fair sample of the whole country.

7

Rural Rides and Advice to Young Men: 1830

Towards the end of 1829 Cobbett announced the forthcoming publication of a collection of the 'Rural Rides' which had first appeared in the *Political Register*, but the book did not appear until October 1830. Though the confused pagination and unaccountable omission of parts of certain 'Rides' indicate some carelessness on the part of the compiler, the principle of selection for *Rural Rides* appears to have been to include only the tours made on horseback between September 1822 and October 1826 in the area south and east of a line from Norwich to Hereford– Cobbett's 'home-ground'. By omitting tours undertaken partly by coach in 1821–2 and the northern tours of 1828–9, he achieved a kind of unity of time, place and locomotion.[1] The 'Rides' are reprinted exactly as they appeared in the *Political Register*, so that Cobbett's narrative retains all the freshness and immediacy of its original form as a daybook written in snatches. He rode on horseback, rather than by coach, to see the country and to meet country people of his own choosing. For a man of sixty, Cobbett displayed (and boasted of) great hardiness, for he was often in the saddle fasting from daybreak to sunset in all weathers – on one occasion riding for two hours wet to the skin in order to rid himself of the 'hooping cough'.[2] He was usually accompanied by one of his sons or a friend, and, whenever he could, he stayed with a farmer or landowner friend.

The main object was to see the condition of the country folk and talk politics to them. So he delivered his formal 'Rustic Harangues' on tithes, taxes, corn laws, placemen, paper-money and the need for Reform, to meetings of farmers and freeholders in market towns, but he also spoke with the labourers in the fields as he passed. Thus as he rode towards that most 'rotten' of boroughs, the accursed hill of Old Sarum:[3]

I met a man going home from work. I asked how he *got on*. He said, very badly. I asked him what was the cause of it. He said the *hard times*. 'What *times*,' said I; 'was there ever a finer summer, a finer harvest, and is there not an *old* wheat-rick in every farm-yard?' 'Ah!' said he, '*they* make it bad for poor people, for all that.' '*They*?' said I, 'who is *they*?' He was silent. 'Oh, no no! my friend,' said I, 'it is not *they*; it is that Accursed Hill that has robbed you of the supper that you ought to find smoking on the table when you get home.' I gave him the price of a pot of beer, and on I went, leaving the poor dejected assemblage of skin and bone to wonder at my words.

Near the very hop-gardens at Farnham where Cobbett himself had worked as a boy he found an old playmate of his in a gang of labourers at parish-work, that is, 'at the expense of half-ruined farmers and tradesmen and landlords, to break stones into very small pieces to make nice smooth roads lest the jolting in going along them, should create bile in the stomachs of the overfed tax-eaters'. Better roads brought readier access to town markets and benefited all engaged in agriculture (not excluding labourers) – as Cobbett knew when he helped to project and build the new turnpike through Botley – but in his present state of mind the spectacle of labourers mending roads was 'a state of things, where all is out of order':

here are farmers *unable* to pay men for working for them, and yet compelled to pay them for working in doing that which is really of no use to any human being. There lie the hop-poles unstripped. You see a hundred things in the neighbouring fields that want doing. The fences are not nearly what they ought to be. The very meadows, to our right and our left in crossing this little valley, would occupy these men advantageously until the setting in of the frost.

So Cobbett spoke to them of the true causes of their misery: 'However, in speaking of their low wages, I told them, that the farmers and hop-planters were as much objects of compassion as themselves, which they acknowledge.'[4] Farmers could not afford to pay a living wage to their labourers, because they were so heavily taxed to support the 'dead-weight' of pensioners, sinecurists, fundholders and a thundering stand-ing army in time of peace. Loanmongers and stock-jobbers became rich and with their financial power propped up a corrupt government which ruled in their interest and retained perpetual power by its control of rotten boroughs. The once independent landed gentry had enough political power to check all this, but, in order to share the places and pensions, they had cravenly thrown in their lot with the moneyed men. However, they would find soon that the moneyed men had eaten them all up; the gentry would follow the farmers and the labourers in a total ruin of what had once been the 'landed interest'. So, riding with a sense of relief out of Tunbridge Wells, Cobbett reflected that this 'toad-stool' town is a product of the gambling system brought in by the moneyed men. The means for this gamble 'are *now* coming out of the farmer's capital and out of the landlord's estate; the labourers are stripped; they can give no more: the saddle is now fixing itself upon the right back'.[5]

So the farmworkers starved amid plenty. They were pauperized, while their share of food and raiment was taken off to support the Debt, the 'dead-weight' and the standing army. At Cricklade, Cobbett came to a farm near the new canal:[6]

> I saw in *one single farm-yard here* more food than enough for four times the inhabitants of the parish . . . but, while the poor creatures that raise the wheat and the barley and cheese and the mutton and the beef are living upon potatoes, an accursed *Canal* comes kindly through the parish to convey away the wheat and all the *good food* to the tax-eaters and their attendants in the Wen. . . . We have very nearly come to the system of Hindoostan, where the farmer is allowed by the Aumil, or tax-contractor, only *so much* of the produce of his farm to eat in the year! The thing is not done in so undisguised a manner here; here are *assessor, collector, exciseman, supervisor, informer, constable, justice, sheriff, jailor, judge, jury, jack-sketch, barrack-man.* Here is a great deal of *ceremony* about it.

The canal, like the road at Farnham, is an unlikely agent of villainy, but it is something new, and that is enough. Cobbett's fancy takes fire, generating a grotesque string of professional oppressors who constitute a kind of Asiatic despotism. The bizarre comparison and the list of assorted professions both have in them a hint of Swift.

According to Cobbett, this ceremonious process has beggared the countryside in order to enrich the towns, so urban growth is itself a sign of rural decay. Continually he denounces the Great Wen itself and its satellites: Sunning Hill near Windsor 'is a spot all made into "*grounds*" and gardens by *tax-eaters*. The inhabitants of it have beggared twenty agricultural villages and hamlets.' He denounces garrison towns, such as 'odious, hellish' Portsmouth, and even towns which have had industrial growth, such as Frome with its 'swaggering inns', but some of his bitterest invectives are reserved for Cheltenham:[7]

> which is what they call a *'watering place'*; that is to say, a place, to which East India plunderers, West India floggers, English tax-gorgers, together with gluttons, drunkards, and debauchees of all descriptions, *female* as well as male, resort, at the suggestion of silently laughing quacks, in the hope of getting rid of the bodily consequences of their manifold sins and iniquities. When I enter a place like this, I always feel disposed to squeeze up my nose with my fingers. It is nonsense, to be sure; but I conceit that every two-legged creature, that I see coming near me, is about to cover me with the poisonous proceeds of its impurities. To places like this come all that is knavish and all that is foolish and all that is base; gamesters, pick-pockets, and harlots; young wife-hunters in search of rich and ugly and old women, and young husband-hunters in search of rich and wrinkled or half-rotten men, the former resolutely bent, be the means what they may, to give the latter heirs to their lands and tenements.

Cobbett is attacking in the conventional way a common eighteenth-century satirical target; he is almost Smollett's Matthew Bramble to the life. But, more than this, the physical and moral infirmities of the watering place's visitors symbolize the diseased condition of the whole corrupt and corrupting carcase of the 'Thing', while indicating that the death of the 'Thing' cannot be long delayed.

At Cheltenham, Cobbett recalled a speech made twenty years earlier in the House of Commons '*in favour of the non-residence of the Clergy*' which 'expressly said, that they and their families ought to appear at *watering places*, and that this was amongst the means of *making them respected by their flocks*'. In every parish that he visited he looked at the parsonage and, as often as not, damned some fat absentee parson who has deserted his moral and legal duty to live with his flock, but who continued to sack the produce of tithe and glebe. Coming to one of the six parishes of which the highly-connected Reverend John Dampier was rector, he exclaimed:

> It is a part of our system to have certain *families*, who have no particular merit; but who are to be maintained, without why or

wherefore, at the public expense. . . . If you look through the old lists of pensioners, sinecurists, parsons, and the like, you will find the same names everlastingly recurring. They seem to be a sort of creatures that have an *inheritance in the public carcass*, like the maggots that some people have in their skins. The family of Dampier seems to be one of those.

The 'famous cock-parson, the "Honourable and Reverend" George Herbert' was another. Herbert was Lord Carnarvon's brother and rector of Burghclere where Cobbett frequently stayed with his farmer friend, William Budd. Herbert 'had grafted the *parson* upon the *soldier* and the *justice* upon the parson; for, he died, a little while ago, a *half-pay officer in the army, rector of two parishes,* and *chairman of the quarter sessions.*'[8] In fact, he had six ecclesiastical livings, worth three-thousand pounds a year in all.

Cobbett, as the writer of sermons, has much to say of the preaching. On a typical Sunday (31 August 1823), riding through Kent from Goudhurst to Tenterden, he hears four or five sermons. Three of them are from Methodists. One is 'shaking the brimstone bag most furiously' at a congregation of Sunday-school boys and girls; he is a sleek fellow who probably eats as much meat as any ten of his charges. Another ought to be put in the stocks. A third, worst of all, is preaching the doctrine of election: 'He distinctly told us, that a man *perfectly moral*, might be *damned*; and that "the *vilest of the vile,* and the *basest of the base*" (I quote his very words) "would be saved if they became *regenerate*".' This outrages all Cobbett's religious instincts. The Anglican parson at Goudhurst was inviting his congregation to give money to the Society for Promoting Christian Knowledge; Cobbett, while he was not computing the size of the church and reckoning to what extent population had declined since the Reformation, was wondering why 'all the deacons, priests, curates perpetual, vicars, rectors, prebends, doctors, deans, archdeacons and fathers in God, right reverend and most reverend' were not capable of promoting Christian knowledge themselves. At Tenterden Church, looking at the pews, he commented on the odious social distinctions brought into Christian worship as a result of the Reformation.[9]

Cobbett's rides took him to many medieval parish churches and all the cathedrals in his area. His comments are always those of a politician, not an antiquarian, but amid his invectives a sense of wonder is faintly discernible. In Salisbury Cathedral he marvels at the impudence of men who represent as ignorant and benighted their medieval forefathers who 'conceived the grand design, and who executed the scientific and costly work', who 'carried so far towards the skies that beautiful and matchless spire'. 'These fellows, in big white wigs, of the size of half a bushel, have the audacity, even within the walls of the Cathedrals themselves, to rail against those who founded them.' Among the few surviving ruins of Malmesbury Abbey[10]

> there is now a *door-way*, which is the most beautiful thing I ever saw, and which was nevertheless, built in Saxon times, in 'the *dark* ages', and was built by men, who were not begotten by Pitt nor by Jubilee-George. What *fools*, as well as ungrateful creatures, we have been and are! There is a broken arch, standing off from the sound part of the building, at which one cannot look up without feeling shame at the thought of ever having abused the men who made it. No one need *tell* any man of sense; he *feels* our inferiority to our fathers, upon merely beholding the remains of their efforts to ornament their country and elevate the minds of the people.

Everywhere, of course, he finds huge and magnificent parish churches in poor villages with only a handful of inhabitants, and asks whence came the means and the hands to build these churches if there has not been considerable rural depopulation since the Middle Ages.

Cobbett's imaginary medieval world fulfilled completely his ideal of a society of well-fed, well-clothed husbandmen living on the land and enjoying the best from it, but – compared with the miserable present – the England of his own youth, we are not surprised to learn, was close to the ideal. He writes a great deal in familiar and traditional vein about the engrossing of farms and rural depopulation. At Burgh-clere, for instance:[11]

> one single farmer holds by lease, under Lord Carnarvon, as one farm, the lands that men, now living, can remember to have formed *fourteen farms*, bringing up, in a respectable way, *fourteen families*. In some instances these small farm-houses and homesteads are completely gone; in others the buildings remain, but in a tumble-down state; in others the house is gone, leaving the barn for use as a barn or as a cattle-shed; in others, the out-buildings are gone, and the house, with rotten thatch, broken windows, rotten door-sills, and all threatening to fall, remains as the

dwelling of a half-starved and ragged family of labourers, the grand-children, perhaps, of the decent family of small farmers that formerly lived happily in this very house. This, with few exceptions, is the case all over England; and, if we duly consider the nature and tendency of the hellish system of taxing, of funding and of paper-money *it must be so.*

Where much engrossing had occurred the farmers, needless to say, had acquired luxurious habits and sought to ape the manners of the gentry. Cobbett came to a farm-sale near Reigate where there was a parlour, a carpet, a mahogany table, decanters and a bell-pull, and where the farmer had evidently found it cheaper and more gentleman-like to pay his labourers starvation wages and let them look after themselves, than to board and feed them in the old-fashioned way. This farmer's father, 'I dare say' (an habitual phrase with Cobbett), used 'to sit at the head of the oak-table [in the kitchen] along with his men, say grace to them, and cut up the meat and the pudding'; so Cobbett, reflecting 'on the thousands of scores of bacon and thousands of bushels of bread' that had been eaten from the table, vowed to buy it 'for all the good it has done in the world'. This was a very proper resolution for the man who boasted that 'I have bought and have roasted more whole sirloins of beef than any man in England.'[12] The oak table where master and men used to sit down together was a favourite symbol in the myth of happy old rural England; among contemporary poets it appeared for instance in Bloomfield's *The Farmer's Boy* and Clare's *The Parish.*

The richer the land, the more likelihood there was of engrossing and enclosure and of the impoverishing of the labourer; conversely on poorer lands where there were still unenclosed wastes the labourer fared better. Cobbett came to a hamlet in the rich corn-land of the Isle of Thanet:[13]

The labourers' houses, all along through this island, beggarly in extreme. The people dirty, poor-looking; ragged, but particularly *dirty.* The men and boys with dirty faces, and dirty smock-frocks, and dirty shirts; and, good God! what a difference between the wife of a labouring man here, and the wife of a labouring man in the forests and woodlands of Hampshire and Sussex! Invariably have I observed, that the richer the soil, and the more destitute of woods; that is to say, the more purely a corn country, the more miserable the labourers. The cause is this, the great, the big bull

frog grasps all. In this beautiful island every inch of land is
appropriated by the rich. No hedges, no ditches, no commons, no
grassy lanes: a country divided into great farms; a few trees
surround the great farm-house. All the rest is bare of trees; and
the wretched labourer has not a stick of wood, and has no place
for a pig or cow to graze, or even to lie down upon. The rabbit
countries are the countries for labouring men. There the ground is
not so valuable. There it is not so easily appropriated by the few.

Writers who before Cobbett's birth had commented on the greater
independence and insubordination of woodland and heath men, as
compared with men living in open lowland, were observing the same
difference.

According to Cobbett engrossing was operating higher in the social
scale. Between Warminster and Devizes, 'All the way along, the
mansion-houses are nearly all gone. There is now and then a *great place*,
belonging to a *borough-monger*, or some one connected with boroughmongers; but all the *little gentlemen* are gone.' Time and time again he
notes where old estates have fallen into the clutches of Jews and jobbers.
In Herefordshire and Worcestershire he observes that the great family
of financiers and boroughmongers, the Barings, are 'adding field to
field and tract to tract . . . depositing their eggs about, like cunning old
guinea-hens, in sly places, besides the great open, showy nests that they
have'. One of their larger estates in Hampshire had been bought from
the Russells, but the Russells had received it as part of the loot disbursed
by the old wife-killer, Henry VIII, so that there is a kind of justice in
the long working-out of the 'System'. Looking at the great estates
of new moneyed men or placemen, Cobbett has a physical sense of
the weight of corruption and of the 'Thing'. Thus, passing through
Kent,[14]

> I asked a man whose fine woods those were that I pointed to, and
> I fairly gave *a start*, when he said, the Marquis Camden's. Milton
> talks of the *Leviathan* in a way to make one draw in one's
> shoulders with fear; and I appeal to any one, who has been at sea
> when a whale has come near the ship, whether he has not, at the
> first sight of the monster, made a sort of involuntary movement,
> as if to *get out of the way*. Such was the movement that I now
> made. . . . It is Bayham Abbey that this great and awful sinecure
> placeman owns in this part of the county. Another great estate he
> owns near *Sevenoaks*. But here alone he spreads his length and

breadth over more, they say, that *ten or twelve thousand acres of land.*

Landowners new and old have betrayed their trust in allying themselves with the wealthy against the poor:[15]

> the foul, the stinking, the carrion baseness, of the fellows that call themselves '*country gentlemen*', is, that the wretches, while railing against the poor and the poor-rates; while affecting to believe, that the poor are wicked and lazy . . . they never even whisper a word against pensioners, placemen, soldiers, parsons, fundholders, tax-gatherers, or tax-eaters.

They support a system of taxation which benefits the 'dead-weight', they bring in Corn Laws to keep prices high and they conduct a little one-sided rural war of their own in enforcing the Game Laws. Riding through Kent, Cobbett's attention is caught by a notice-board 'standing in a garden near a neat little box of a house. The words were these. "Paradise Place. *Spring guns and steel traps are set here.*"' One case in particular under the Game Laws horrified him, and he refers to it several times in *Rural Rides*. At the Lent Assizes at Winchester in 1822, James Turner was accused of helping to kill a gamekeeper employed by the famous sportsman Thomas Assheton Smith, and Charles Smith was accused of shooting, but not killing, one of Lord Palmerston's gamekeepers. Both were sentenced to death and they were hanged on the same gallows. At the same Assizes sixteen other prisoners were condemned to death but the two poachers were the only ones hanged. Cobbett had presented a petition to Parliament referring to these cases, urging that the severity of the Game Laws made it inevitable that poachers should attempt to defend themselves against gamekeepers, and that the remedy lay in amending the laws.[16]

Against these monstrosities Cobbett can set the activities of good landlords who have kept up the labourers' wages, who know their tenants and mix with them on the hunting field – rather than indulge in the selfish, solitary sport of shooting. Plenty of these appear in *Rural Rides*, and even where Cobbett has no direct evidence of a landowner's virtues he can readily infer them from the appearance of the labourers. Thus, of the Duke of Buckingham's turnip-hoers at Avington in Hampshire:[17]

> These girls were all tall, straight, fair, round-faced, excellent complexion, and uncommonly gay. They were well dressed, too,

and I observed the same of all the men that I saw down at Avington. This could not be the case if the Duke were a cruel or hard master.

There is plenty of denunciation in *Rural Rides* but no despair. Nature may be perverted where, for the present, labourers starve amid plenty, stock-jobbers build their 'suburban boxes on spewy gravel', or the waters of a lovely stream drive a mill that manufactures banknotes, but the heart of the land is sound, and in many places man and nature are what they should be. At Bishopstrow in Wiltshire, land, houses and girls are neat and pretty, as they all should be:[18]

> The arable land goes down before the house, and spreads along the edge of the down, going, with a gentle slope, down to the meadows. So that, going along the turnpike road, which runs between the lower fields of the arable land, you see the large and beautiful flocks of sheep upon the sides of the down, while the horn-cattle are up to their eyes in grass in the meadows. Just when I was coming along here, the sun was about half an hour high; it shined through the trees most brilliantly; and, to crown the whole, I met, just as I was entering the village, a very pretty girl, who was apparently, going a gleaning in the fields.

In West Sussex:

> I called to me a young man, who, along with other turnip-hoers, was sitting under the shelter of a hedge at breakfast. He came running to me with his victuals in his hand; and, I was glad to see, that his food consisted of a good lump of household *bread* and not a very small piece of *bacon*. . . . In parting with him, I said, 'You do get some *bacon* then?' 'Oh, yes! Sir,' said he, and with an emphasis and a swag of the head which seemed to say, 'We *must* and *will* have *that*.' I saw, and with great delight, a pig at almost every labourer's house. The houses are good and warm; and the gardens some of the very best that I have seen in England.

In the same area Cobbett saw a woman bleaching her home-spun and home-woven linen, and elsewhere he found cottagers making gloves, and, of course, the famous straw-plait, using the methods publicized in *Cottage Economy*. In all the little corners of England where domestic industry survived, where women and girls could be put to their 'natural employment', labourers' families would always rise above pauperism; in these places the 'Lords of the Loom' were being successfully defied, and their system which drew wealth into great masses.

Everywhere Cobbett rides as a farmer, with an eye to the lie of the land, the soil, the drainage, the condition of the crops and livestock. Good husbandry is his first concern, and whenever he comes to a new scene he first describes the nature of the soil and says what it will best grow. Thus, between Selborne and Thursley, 'I am here got into some of the very best barley-land in the kingdom; a fine, buttery, stoneless loam, upon a bottom of sand or sand-stone. Finer barley and turnip-land it is impossible to see.' In the Vale of Pewsey he is not indulging in anthropomorphic fancy when he says that the trees, 'generally *elms*, with some *ashes* . . . delight in the soil that they find here'. He feels the wholeness of nature, and of man in nature, because he is constantly alive to the physical character of the land and the manner in which it shapes, and is shaped by, the working lives of husbandmen. For instance, every one of his journeys took him at some point or other into the downland; so we find him frequently discussing the merits of a well-draining chalk bottom. Near Winchester:[19]

The country where the soil is stiff loam upon chalk, is never bad for corn. Not rich, but never poor. There is at no time any thing deserving to be called dirt in the roads. The buildings last a long time, from the absence of fogs and also the absence of humidity in the ground. The absence of dirt makes the people habitually cleanly; and all along through this country the people appear in general to be very neat. It is a country for sheep, which are always sound and good upon this iron soil.

Near Andover the surface of the land:

presents, in the size and form of the fields, in the woods, the hedge-rows, the sainfoin, the young wheat, the turnips, the tares, the fallows, the sheep-folds and the flocks . . . that which I, at any rate, could look at with pleasure for ever . . . there are no ditches, no water-furrows, no dirt, and *never any drought* to cause inconvenience. The *chalk* is at bottom and it takes care of all.

This is down to earth in every way, but Cobbett also senses the strangeness and wonder of the land itself. Looking at the three hills called 'The Devil's Jumps' near Farnham, he asks:[20]

How could waters rolling about have formed such hills? How could such hills have bubbled up from beneath? But, in short, it is all wonderful alike: the stripes of loam running down through the chalk-hills; the circular parcels of loam in the midst of chalk-hills; the lines of flint running parallel with each other horizontally along the chalk-hills; the flints placed in circles as true as a hair in the chalk-hills; the layers of stone at the bottom of the hills of loam; the chalk first soft, then some miles farther on, becoming chalk-stone; then, after another distance, becoming burr-stone, as they call it; and at last, becoming hard, white stone, fit for any buildings.

Then, Cobbett finds the formulations of his own mind as unexpected, wonderful and natural as the flint formations in the chalk hills. Sitting in a comfortable Wiltshire inn he is amazed to discover himself suddenly thinking about Grimshaw, the mayor of Preston, who had rigged the election against Cobbett in several ways, one of which was in the construction of restricted approaches (called 'ditches') to the polling-booths:[21]

> I am now sitting at one of the southern windows of this inn, looking across the garden towards the rookery. It is nearly sun-setting; the rooks are skimming and curving over the tops of the trees; while, under the branches, I see a flock of several hundred sheep, coming nibbling their way in from the Down, and going to their fold.
>
> Now, what ill-natured devil could bring Old Nic Grimshaw into my head in company with these innocent sheep? Why, the truth is this: nothing is *so swift as thought*: it runs over a life-time in a moment; and, while I was writing the last sentence of the foregoing paragraph, *thought* took me up at the time when I used to wear a smock-frock and to carry a wooden bottle like that shepherd's boy; and, in an instant, it hurried me along through my no very short life of adventure, of toil, of peril, of pleasure, of ardent friendship and not less ardent enmity; and after filling me with wonder, that a heart and mind so wrapped up in every thing belonging to the gardens, the fields and the woods, should have been condemned to waste themselves away amidst the stench, the noise and the strife of cities, it brought me *to the present moment*, and sent my mind back to what I have yet to perform about Nicholas Grimshaw and his *ditches*.

Cobbett has several audiences. He is reviewing the state of the country-side, reporting back to readers of the *Political Register* and proposing his usual remedies for social, economic and political ills; he is addressing his farmer and freeholder audiences with 'Rustic Harangues', and cottagers and labourers by the wayside; he is conversing with his companion, usually one of his sons, about what they see as they ride; but, significantly he is often, as here, simply talking to himself.

There is no kind of formal unity in *Rural Rides*, but all is connected within Cobbett's consciousness, and this is nowhere clearer than in those places where the landscape is a landscape of memory. Thus he shows his son, James, one of the haunts of his youth at Farnham:[22]

> There is a little hop-garden in which I used to work when from eight to ten years' old; from which I have scores of times run to follow the hounds, leaving the hoe to do the best that it could to destroy the weeds; but the most interesting thing was, a *sand-hill*, which goes from a part of the heath down to the rivulet. As a due mixture of pleasure with toil, I, with two brothers, used occasionally to *desport* ourselves, as the lawyers call it, at this sand-hill. Our diversion was this: we used to go to the top of the hill, which was steeper than the roof of a house; one used to draw his arms out of the sleeves of his smock-frock, and lay himself down with his arms by his sides; and then the others, one at head and the other at feet, sent him rolling down the hill like a barrel or a log of wood. By the time he got to the bottom, his hair, eyes, ears, nose and mouth, were all full of this loose sand; then the others took their turn, and at every roll, there was a monstrous spell of laughter. . . . This was the spot where I was receiving my *education*; and this was the sort of education; and I am perfectly satisfied that if I had not received such an education, or something very much like it; that, if I had been brought up a milksop, with a nursery-maid everlastingly at my heels; I should have been at this day as great a fool, as inefficient a mortal, as any of those frivolous idiots that are turned out from Winchester and Westminster School, or from any of those dens of dunces called Colleges and Universities.

Of course this passage has the raucousness that tends to appear whenever Cobbett admits himself 'perfectly satisfied that . . .', but as his memory sets to work the sandhill becomes a concrete symbol of his own sturdy self-reliance, of permanent characteristics which unite the child and the man, and which, it is implied, have been transmitted to the man's child, who also is to be spared school and university.

Three years later, with his youngest son, Richard, Cobbett is back at Farnham, again showing that his life is all of a piece and that the child is father of the man:[23]

> I showed him the spot where the strawberry garden was, and where I, when sent to gather *hautboys*, used to eat every *remarkably fine one*, instead of letting it go to be eaten by Sir Robert Rich. I showed him a tree, close by the ruins of the Abbey, from a limb of which I once fell into the river, in an attempt to take the nest of a *crow*, which had artfully placed it upon a branch so far from the trunk as not to be able to bear the weight of a boy eight years old. I showed him an old elm tree, which was hollow even then, into which I, when a very little boy, once saw *a cat go*, that was *as big as a middle-sized spaniel dog*, for relating which I got a great scolding, for standing to which I, at last, got a beating; but, stand to which I still did.

He is still standing to it.

Rural Rides is Cobbett himself – cantankerous, naïve, unfair, preposterously conceited, but innocently and splendidly responsive to the life of man in nature. The only work that contains as much of his personality is his *Advice to Young Men* (published in fourteen sixpenny parts between July 1829 and September 1830). This work is addressed to men (and women) 'in the Middle and Higher Ranks of Life' and is not primarily political in intention; nevertheless it is something of a Radical's *apologia pro vita sua*. For years, government supporters and churchmen had denounced the Reformers as examples of every vice, but here Cobbett replied with a self-portrait of all the benefits of industry, sobriety, independence and thrift. He quoted, approvingly, Rousseau's observation that 'men are happy, first, in proportion to their virtue, and next, in proportion to their *independence*',[24] and illustrated it from his own life.

Cobbett's first piece of advice is that men must work, not only because this is their duty to their dependants and fellow men, but because useful work is the clue to happiness. He was in no doubt that his public success and private happiness were triumphs of will, effort and character-training, and he saw that others could achieve similar happiness if they would develop their own powers as fully and strenuously as he had. Entirely by his own exertions, Cobbett has raised himself from common ploughboy to one of the most powerful political writers in the land. He was fortunate in enjoying good health, of course, but even this was self-made, for it was attributable to self-imposed habits of early-rising, sobriety and frugality, and love of exercise and fresh air. His physical regimen and love of hard work even gave him a moral advantage over other political writers, for, as he had never been debased by luxury, he had never become a drone or slave. How different from Dr Johnson, says Cobbett – a man of great genius, and, for a time, of great industry, who accepted a pension merely in order to indulge in the pleasures of the table, even though he had, in his *Dictionary*, correctly defined 'Pensioner' as 'A slave of state', but 'When this celebrated author wrote his Dictionary, he had not been debased by luxurious enjoyments.' As a dastardly state-pensioner, Johnson wrote *Taxation no Tyranny* which 'defended, and greatly assisted to produce, that unjust and bloody war' which severed the United States from England. William Gifford's was an even worse case, but:[25]

> Endless are the instances of men of bright parts and high spirit having been, by degrees, rendered powerless and despicable, by their imaginary wants. . . . Dryden, Parnell, Gay, Thomson, in short, what poet have we had, or have we, Pope only excepted, who was not, or is not, a pensioner, or a sinecure placeman, or the wretched dependent of some sort of the Aristocracy?

Cobbett scatters his literary judgments, or prejudices, freely through the *Advice*. Addison, Blair, Johnson and 'the punning and smutty Shakespeare' come under his lash as usual, but he seems to distrust most literature, since most poets, playwrights and romancers teach bad morality. Thus *Cymbeline* and the once-popular *Douglas* by John Home (a 'base parasite', like Shakespeare) perpetrate the pernicious falsehood 'that there is in *high birth*, something of *superior nature*, instinctive courage, honour, and talent'. This is how Cobbett describes *Tom Jones*:[26]

> Here are two young men put before us, both sons of the same mother; the one a *bastard* (and by a parson too), the other a *legitimate child*; the former wild, disobedient, and squandering; the latter steady, sober, obedient, and frugal; the former every thing that is frank and generous in his nature, the latter a greedy hypocrite; the former rewarded with the most beautiful and

virtuous of women and a double estate, the latter punished by
being made an outcast. How is it possible for young people to
read such a book, and to look upon orderliness, sobriety,
obedience, and frugality, as *virtues*? And this is the tenor of almost
every romance, and of almost every play, in our language. In the
'School for Scandal,' for instance, we see, two brothers; the one a
prudent and frugal man, and, to all appearance, a moral man, the
other a hair-brained squanderer, laughing at the morality of his
brother; the former turns out to be a base hypocrite and seducer,
and is brought to shame and disgrace; while the latter is found to
be full of generous sentiment, and Heaven itself seems to interfere
to give him fortune and fame. In short, the direct tendency of the
far greater part of these books, is, to cause young people to despise
all those virtues, without the practice of which they must be a
curse to their parents, a burden to the community, and must,
except by mere accident, lead wretched lives.

More than he cared to admit, Cobbett shared the views of the contemporary Evangelicals he despised so much.

The *Advice*, like the *Grammar* and everything else that Cobbett wrote,
is full of political asides, but its last paragraphs make an excursion,
unusual for him, into general political theory, when he takes, and
greatly simplifies, the notions of Locke and Rousseau concerning the
'social contract', and adapts them to the aims of the Parliamentary
reformers, just as in the *Poor Man's Friend* (1826-7) he had adapted
them to a defence of the existing Poor Law. So, in the *Advice*, he again
tells how civil society arose when, in order to secure mutual protection, men divided the land over which, according to the Law of Nature,
they had all formerly ranged freely, and established a law of property
based upon labour. In time inequalities of property arose:[27]

but these truths are written on the heart of man: that all men are,
by nature, *equal*; that civil society can never have arisen from any
motive other than that of the *benefit of the whole*; that, whenever
civil society makes the greater part of the people *worse off* than
they were under the Law of Nature, the civil compact is, in
conscience, dissolved, and all the rights of nature return.

These rights include

the right of enjoying life and property; the right of exerting our
physical and mental powers in an innocent manner; but, the great

right of all, and without which there is, in fact, *no right*, is, the right of *taking a part in the making of* the laws by *which we are governed.*

The purpose of government is to secure the well-being of the common people, that is, to restore the labourer's life to what it was when Cobbett was a boy. Denunciation and retrospective idyll play in counterpoint, as they do in so much of his political writing, but, refreshingly, in the *Advice* the idyllic tones are dominant:[28]

> Those who have, as I so many hundreds of times have, seen the labourers in the woodland parts of Hampshire and Sussex, coming, at night-fall, towards their cottage-wickets, laden with fuel for a day or two; whoever has seen three or four little creatures looking out for the father's approach, running in to announce the glad tidings, and then scampering out to meet him, clinging round his knees, or hanging on his skirts; whoever has witnessed scenes like this, to witness which has formed one of the greatest delights of my life, will hesitate long before he prefer a life of ease to a life of labour. . . . This used to be the way of life amongst the labouring people; and from this way of life arose the most able and most moral people that the world ever saw, until grinding taxation took from them the means of obtaining a sufficiency of food and of raiment; plunged the whole, good and bad, into one indiscriminate mass, under the degrading and hateful name of paupers.

The sentimentalized, retrospective Arcadia is a world of domestic virtues, but it is not an utterly lost world, for these virtues survive, he implies, in Cobbett himself, who, in this as in much else, sees himself as a living image of Old England.

The dominant theme of the *Advice* is Cobbett's domestic happiness. All his public success he attributes to the fact that he is happily married, and in unaffectedly idyllic terms he writes of a courtship and married life marked throughout by mutual consideration, loyalty, trust and respect. Cobbett writes with his usual unashamed egotism, but upon subjects more likely than usual to engage his readers' sympathies. Thus, of an episode of his early married life in Philadelphia:

> that famous Grammar for teaching French people English, which has been for thirty years, and still is, the great work of this

kind, throughout all America, and in every nation in Europe, was written by me, in hours not employed in business, and, in great part, during my share in the night-watchings over a sick, and then only child, who, after lingering many months, died in my arms.

Or, at Botley, writing those powerful *Political Registers*, 'many a score papers have I written amidst the noise of children, and in my whole life never bade them be still. . . . That which you are *pleased with*, however noisy, does not disturb you.'[29] Cobbett's tender domestic relations are the obverse of his violent public controversies, and his hatred of his enemies is all the more extreme when they seem to threaten his family. As he will never forget the tears of his young children when he was torn from his family and thrown into prison on that unhappy day in 1810, so he rejoices in the deaths of many of the men then ranged against him – Gibbs, Ellenborough, Perceval, Liverpool and Canning. He hated Malthus because that audacious and merciless parson has declared war on the poor labourer's family.

Malthus is hateful on another score, for Cobbett detests the 'filthiness' of birth-control. Running through the entire *Advice*, indeed, is a prudery which, though some might call it 'Victorian', is in fact very characteristic of Cobbett's age – Mrs Grundy was invented in the eighteenth century and Bowdler was born before Cobbett. So Cobbett condemns the indelicacy of women who employ man-midwives, or use 'hireling breasts' to feed their children. The woman who hires a wet-nurse does so from the worst of motives, that is, 'to *hasten back*, unbridled and undisfigured, to those enjoyments, to have an eagerness for which, a really delicate woman will shudder at the thought of being suspected'. His sense of delicacy is offended even by the thought of a widow remarrying, for she 'has *a second time* undergone that surrender, to which nothing but the most ardent affection, could ever reconcile a chaste and delicate woman'.[30]

If Cobbett was as strict as the most prudish Evangelical in sexual matters, his notions of child-rearing were very free. Hannah More had written that it was a 'fundamental error to consider children as innocent beings', rather they were creatures of 'a corrupt nature and evil dispositions.'[31] John Wesley agreed:[32]

Break their wills betimes. Begin this work before they can run alone, before they can speak plain, perhaps before they can speak at all. . . . Let a child from a year old be taught to fear the rod and to cry softly; from that age make him do as he is bid, if you whip him ten times running to effect it. . . . Break his will now, and his soul shall live, and he will probably bless you to all eternity.

Cobbett, by contrast, boasted that he had never struck any of his children, and had always enjoyed their respect, love and obedience. In the passages of the *Advice* dealing with education he is the avowed disciple of Rousseau, whose *Émile* he had read in those early years as a language tutor in Philadelphia:[33]

> I have always admired the sentiment of Rousseau upon this subject. 'The boy dies, perhaps, at the age of ten or twelve. Of what *use*, then, all the restraints, all the privations, all the pain, that you have inflicted upon him? He falls, and leaves your mind to brood over the possibility of your having abridged a life so dear to you.' I do not recollect the very words; but the passage made a deep impression upon my mind, just at the time, too, when I was about to become a father; and I was resolved never to bring upon myself remorse from a such a cause. . . . I was resolved that, as long as I could cause them to do it, my children should lead happy lives.

Cobbett shared Rousseau's notions concerning the spontaneous development of the child, and carried them into effect in the education of his own children. Rousseau had said that the child's natural teachers are his parents, and his best environment the countryside; Cobbett's children secured both advantages when the family settled at Botley, and some of the most delightful passages of the *Advice* are Cobbett's fresh, easy accounts of the way he reared his children there:

> The mind as well as the body, requires time to come to its strength; the way to have it possess, at last, its natural strength, is not to attempt to load it too soon; and to favour it in its progress by giving to the body good and plentiful food, sweet air, and abundant exercise, accompanied with as little discontent or uneasiness as possible.

So the Cobbett children were first introduced to useful, innocent, practical pursuits:

> Each his flower-bed, little garden, plantation of trees; rabbits, dogs, asses, horses, pheasants and hares; hoes, spades, whips, guns;

always some object of lively interest, and as much *earnestness* and *bustle* about the various objects as if our living had solely depended upon them.

Young children cannot understand ideas or mere words, but *things* will educate them; the child must come to book-learning only when he is ready and eager for it. Then:[34]

> A large, strong table, in the middle of the room, their mother sitting at her work, used to be surrounded with [the children], the baby, if big enough, set up in a high chair. Here were ink-stands, pens, pencils, India rubber, and paper, all in abundance, and every one scrabbled about as he or she pleased. There were prints of animals of all sorts; books treating of them: others treating of gardening, of flowers, of husbandry, of hunting, coursing, shooting, fishing, planting, and, in short, of every thing, with regard to which *we had something to do*. One would be trying to imitate a bit of my writing, another *drawing* the pictures of some of our dogs or horses, a third poking over *Bewick's Quadrupeds*, and picking out what he said about them; but our book of never-failing resource was the French *Maison Rustique*, or *Farm-House*. . . . I never have been without a copy of this book for forty years, except during the time that I was fleeing from the dungeons of Castlereagh and Sidmouth in 1817; and, when I got to Long Island, the *first book I bought* was another *Maison Rustique*.
>
> What need had we of *schools*? What need of *teachers*? What need of *scolding* and *force*, to induce children to read, write, and love books?

The reference to Castlereagh and Sidmouth reminds Cobbett's reader of the threatening presences which lay, and in new embodiments still lie, beyond the charmed family circle of health and virtue.

Formal 'education' might be as much of a threat to domestic virtue and happiness as those 'dungeons' were. It was wrong to gather any human beings into large, systemized masses, and doubly wrong so to gather children. Large schools are like gaols, barracks and factories, which corrupt not 'by their walls, but by their condensed numbers'. Worse, any scheme of national public education would place in the hands of the government of the day a new tool for indoctrination and intimidation. It already seemed that the principal aim of Sunday schools (which had spread widely since the foundation of the Sunday

School Society in 1785) was to extend work-discipline into the seventh day, and thus make poor children more orderly, tractable, submissive and dutiful in the factories workshops or fields on the other six days of the week. All men could not be Cobbetts, but given decent living conditions and freedom from the 'comforting' interference of his so-called betters, any man could establish a happy, virtuous home in which he could create the physical conditions, and set the parental example, by which his children could healthfully and happily educate themselves.

The Advice to Young Men is Cobbett's happiest book:[35]

> Born and bred up in the sweet air myself, I was resolved that they should be bred up in it too. Enjoying rural scenes and sports, as I had done, when a boy, as much as any one that ever was born, I was resolved, that they should have the same enjoyments tendered to them. When I was a very little boy, I was, in the barley-sowing season, going along by the side of a field, near Waverley Abbey; the primroses and blue-bells bespangling the banks on both sides of me; a thousand linnets singing in a spreading oak over my head; while the jingling of the traces and the whistling of the ploughboys saluted my ear from over the hedge; and, as it were to snatch me from the enchantment, the hounds, at that instant, having started a hare in the hanger on the other side of the field, came up scampering over it in full cry, taking me after them many a mile. I was not more than eight years old; but this particular scene has presented itself to my mind many times every year from that day to this. I always enjoy it over again; and I was resolved to give, if possible, the same enjoyments to my children.

It is characteristic of Cobbett that he should still enjoy this childhood experience, unclouded by the sense of mortality and mutability with which many a man would have recalled an event in his own life sixty years earlier. Thanks to the power of memory, Cobbett's sensuous joy in life at sixty-six is as fresh and whole-hearted as a child's. He recreates a childhood experience in its time, place and circumstance, giving us a sense of the wholesomeness of work and play in the countryside; and the leaping delight that runs through his recollection is more than sufficient warrant for the rightness of his views on child-rearing. There is a no less beautiful, though more self-consciously idyllic, passage in the Advice[36] where he describes his flirtation with a New Brunswick girl, and where, again, the emotions of his youth rush back into his heart and pen at the moment of writing. As in some of the freshest parts of *Rural Rides*, the landscape that Cobbett sees best and loves best of all is the landscape of memory.

8

The Anti-climax
of Reform: 1830-35

Rural Rides, as published in 1830, contained no rides later than 1826. Cobbett did not ride in 1827, and made only one short excursion in 1828 to visit his friend Joseph Blount at Hurstbourne Tarrant. In 1829 he made short rides into East Sussex and Hertfordshire, and then in mid-December set out for a 600-mile-long political lecture tour through Birmingham, Derby, Liverpool, Manchester, Rochdale, Halifax, Leeds, Sheffield, Nottingham and Leicester. This tour was the beginning of his belated attempt to understand the new manufacturing industries, and the social changes arising from industrialism which, did he but know it, were making impossible any return to the old England of his youth.

Cobbett had written much about factories earlier, of course. In the 'Letter to Luddites' (p. 87 above), he had claimed that the introduction of power-machinery was not responsible for unemployment, but elsewhere he wrote of the harm done to rural society by the decay of handicrafts and domestic industry. Thus on a ride in the valley of the Wiltshire Avon, he saw miserable families who were all the poorer because the women and children could no longer card and spin wool at home for the broad-cloth weavers. Like a good physiocrat Cobbett sees that agriculture is the primary occupation and must engage a great part of the nation's population. The women and girls who live in country districts cannot, like the men and boys, find employment all the year round upon the land. So:[1]

In the '*dark ages*', when I was a boy, country labourers' wives used to spin the wool, and knit the stockings and gloves that were wanted in the family. My grandmother knit stockings for me after she was blind. In those '*dark ages*', the farmers' wives and daughters and servant maids, were spinning, reeling, carding, knitting, or at

something or other of that sort, whenever the work of the farmhouse did not demand them.

But now the factory owners, the 'Lords of the Loom, Seigneurs of the
Twist, Sovereigns of the Spinning-Jenny and Great Yeomen of the
Yarn', enabled by the funding system and encouraged and assisted by
the foolish government, have drawn away from the land all this
profitable employment for women and girls, and have concentrated it
in factories where:

> you can see the poor children pining away their lives in these hells
> upon earth; you can see them actually gasping for breath,
> swallowing the hot and foul air, and sucking the deadly *cotton-fuz*
> into their lungs.

What Cobbett says here was true of many factories, but he wrote
from hearsay. When at last he visited a textile factory for the first
time in his life, in 1830, he was favourably impressed.[2] His only
recorded close personal involvement in the social problems of mech-
anization had an unsavoury outcome. In 1831 a deputation of unemployed hand-printers asked him to discontinue the printing of the
Political Register by power-machinery, but Cobbett replied that
machine-printing saved time and money and that he left technical
matters to his printer, who had assured him that he could find no
employment for hand-printers. The unpleasantness of the episode lies
in the fact that Cobbett went on to tell the hand-workers how little he
ate himself, that they could not expect to live off the labour of others,
and that they had no business to be walking the streets when, in the
fields outside London, harvest-time was beginning. Cobbett's mis-
understanding of the situation is less reprehensible than his sancti-
moniousness.[3]

The Northern Tour of 1829–30 was a kind of revelation. Unex-
pectedly, Cobbett warmed to the industrial scene:[4]

> All the way along from Leeds to Sheffield, it is coal and iron, and
> iron and coal. It was dark before we reached Sheffield; so that we
> saw the iron furnaces in all the horrible splendour of their
> everlasting blaze. Nothing can be conceived more grand or more
> terrific than the yellow waves of fire that incessantly issue from the
> top of these furnaces. . . . The combustibles are put into the top of
> the furnace, which stands thirty, forty, or fifty feet up in the air,

and the ever-blazing mouth of which is kept supplied with coal and coke and iron-stone, from little iron wagons forced up by steam, and brought down again to be re-filled. It is a surprising thing to behold; and it is impossible to behold it without being convinced that, whatever other nations may do with cotton and with wool, they will never equal England with regard to things made of iron and steel.

This is virtually the stock response of eighteenth-century travellers from the South – a combination of awe in the face of fearful grandeur, or 'sublimity', and of patriotic pride in the face of inventiveness and patent wealth. The land hereabouts was beggarly, with hardly a stack of wheat to be seen anywhere:

But this is all very proper: these coal-diggers, and iron-melters, and knife-makers, compel us to send the food to them, which indeed, we do very cheerfully, in exchange for the produce of their rocks, and the wondrous works of their hands.

Cobbett announces this, the simplest fact, as if it were a personal discovery, and perhaps it was for him. He had discovered the true harmony of town and country. Whatever one might continue to think concerning stock-exchanges and watering-places, these industrial towns were vital parts of the organism that was England, not 'wens' upon its skin.

After his Northern Tour, Cobbett spent a month in London, giving several lectures, and then set out on an even longer tour, lasting ten weeks and taking him through East Anglia, the Fens, Lincolnshire and Yorkshire, and then, by way of the great Midland industrial towns, from the Humber to the Severn. Cobbett was making a bid for national leadership of the Reform agitation sweeping the country in 1830, but he was not to be as dominant as he had been in the winter of 1816–17. Though he began in 1830 to publish cheap reprints of *Political Register* articles in a legitimate monthly form, as *Twopenny Trash, or, Politics for the Poor*, the real struggle for the freedom of the Press, was still being conducted by the indomitable Carlile and by others, such as Henry Hetherington whose cheap, unstamped *Poor Man's Guardian* carried the heading, 'Published contrary to "Law" to try the power of "Might" against "Right"'. Many local societies of working men disregarded Cobbett and constitutionalism and dreamed of new forms of society, and if such men were followers of Robert Owen they drew down

Cobbett's anathemas. Cobbett had nothing to do with the National Union of Working Classes which after 1830 became the rallying point for many groups of very radical reformers. He had respectful, even enthusiastic, audiences for his lectures all over the country, but he had no widespread following. As he travelled he became more and more convinced that there were few people, even among the labourers, who did not clearly understand the cause of their misery and the need for parliamentary reform, but what action, other than petitioning, they could take in the light of this understanding was not at all clear. Though Cobbett muttered darkly and extravagantly that conditions in the English countryside exactly paralleled those in France on the eve of the Revolution, he continued to oppose any form of violence, and it was difficult to see just what other effective action the labouring classes could take if their masters, who still electorally constituted 'the people', were not inclined to act.

The initiative for reform had to lie with the Whig Opposition in Parliament. Most of the propertied 'public' and their Parliamentary representatives, Whig and Tory, landed, moneyed, trading and manu-facturing, had been united in opposition to reform as long as there remained any threat of violent revolution, but as this threat receded in the 1820s the real economic and political differences between the various 'interests' emerged more clearly. The rising classes of merchants and industrial employers in the North and Midlands voiced ever more loudly their objections to economic policies, such as the Corn Laws and taxes on industrial raw materials, designed to suit the landowners but calculated to obstruct the growth of trade and industry, and they looked to some measure of parliamentary reform to achieve changes in economic policy. Though some Tory ministers, such as Peel, Huskisson and Canning, were more prepared than others to meet the wishes of merchants and manufacturers, the Tory party remained set against Reform, but the Whigs saw the possible advantage to themselves of widening the franchise sufficiently to capture the future electoral sup-port of the middle classes. Cobbett still detested the Whigs, and at the beginning of that eventful year, 1830, he reprinted as a *Political Register* motto a passage from a *Register* of 1807:[5]

The great enemies of real liberty have always been the Whigs. The Riot Act, the Septennial Bill, the infernal Excise, are all the works of the Whigs. The Tories, as they are called, will find at last, that they have no security but by joining with the people. The people have never hated them as they have hated, and do hate the Whigs, who are false, designing hypocrites, with liberty on their lips, and tyranny in their hearts.

This was not the first, or last, time that Cobbett's views would anticipate Disraeli's, or that he would file a bill of complaints that could have come from Bolingbroke's pen, but his present, and quite justified, fear was that the Whigs would capture the Reform movement by offering just enough 'moderate' reform to gain the support of the middle classes, drive a wedge between them and the lower orders, and so neutralize true Radicalism.

At the beginning of July 1830 the news of George IV's death caused Cobbett hastily to cut short a lecturing tour he had just begun in the West, and to hurry back to London. In the *Political Register* he announced his plans for a *History of the Regency and Reign of George IV* and uttered his funeral oration over the unlamented monarch:

> As a son, as a husband, as a father, and especially as an *adviser of young men*, I deem it my duty to say that, on a review of his whole life, I can find no one good thing to speak of, in either the conduct or character of this king; and, as an Englishman, I should be ashamed to show my head, if I were not to declare that I deem his reign (including his regency), to have been the most unhappy, for the people, that England has ever known.

The gusto of this, as of so many other of his diatribes, reminds us that Cobbett, like Gwendolen Fairfax, found speaking his mind to be more than a moral duty. Cobbett lost no time, now, in addressing a series of admonitory letters to the new King: 'Happy would it have been for this nation, and for your family, if your brother, the late King, had listened to my advice, instead of suffering his authority to be used in the various measures intended to crush me';[6] and much more in the same style.

In July 1830, too, revolution had begun in France, followed shortly by a successful nationalist rising in Belgium and an unsuccessful one in Poland. While none of these was the work of a Radical or working-class movement, the happy coincidence of George IV's death and revolution in Europe gave Cobbett renewed hope for speedy reform in England. On 16 August he presided over a great dinner in honour of the French people, and between August and October gave a series of lectures in London on 'The French and Belgian Revolutions and

English Borough-mongers'. In Cobbett's mistaken view this latest French revolution was effected:[7]

> not by the aristocracy – not by military gentlemen – not by gentlemen with whiskers or long spurs – not by gentlemen of any description in fact – not even by the middle classes, but by the working people alone; by men who quitted their shops, who laid down their needles, and their awls, and their saws, and rushing out into the streets of Paris, said 'If there be no alternative but slavery, let us put an end to the tyrants'.

'I am pleased at the Revolution,' he added, 'particularly on this account, that it makes the working classes see their real importance, and those who despise them see it too.'

After his unhappy and expensive experiences at Coventry and Preston, Cobbett decided that he could not afford to put himself up again as a Parliamentary candidate. When asked early in 1830 to stand, he said that he would not, unless his supporters raised ten thousand pounds, first to secure his election, and then to maintain him, so that he could buy land, give up the *Political Register*, and attend full-time to business in the House of Commons. A fund was opened, but, of course, nothing approaching the sum demanded by Cobbett was raised. So Cobbett stood back from the general elections of July and November 1830 and May 1831, even though in the second of these Henry Hunt was returned at Preston to become the first truly Radical voice in Parliament. This was the election that followed the Prime Minister Wellington's unequivocal declaration against Reform of any kind whatsoever. While it was taking place Cobbett helpfully offered himself to the King as Prime Minister, but, in the event, it was the Whig leader, Earl Grey, who was called upon to form the new government. Some measure of reform now seemed inevitable.

Cobbett, in his usual vein, blasted both the 'factions' of Whig and Tory as fellows fighting for public money – 'some dogs in possession of the carcase, and some growling and barking because they cannot get a share'. He was equally contemptuous of the few professed 'Radical' Members of Parliament, 'to whom I have always given the name of *Shoy-Hoys*' (or scarecrows). Such sham-Reformers not only fail to achieve parliamentary reform but do positive mischief by gulling the people into believing that the Reform cause is gaining ground when it is not, and when the two great factions are continuing to enjoy their plunder. Cobbett drives home his point with an apt illustration:[8]

The birds were committing great ravages upon some turnip-seed that I had at Botley. 'Stick up a shoy-hoy,' said I to my bailiff. 'That will do *no good sir*;' 'It can do *no harm*, and therefore, stick one up.' He replied by telling me, that he had, that morning, in the garden of his neighbour Morell, who had stuck up a shoy-hoy to to keep the sparrows from his peas, actually seen a sparrow settled, with a *pod*, upon the *shoy-hoy's hat*, and there, as upon a dining table, actually pecking out the peas and eating them, which he could do with greater security there where he could look about him and see the approach of an enemy, than he could have done upon the ground, where he might have been taken *by surprise*. Just exactly such are the functions of our political shoy-hoys.

This was written in September 1830. In the following month Cobbett published his 'Plan of Parliamentary Reform addressed to the Young Men of England',[9] offering an uncompromising Radical programme based broadly upon Major Cartwright's proposals of fifty years earlier; it called for annual parliaments, the ballot, universal manhood suffrage (excluding felons and lunatics) and a residential, non-property qualification for Members. But the Whigs when they came to power at the end of the year had no intention of transferring political power to the 'mob'. In so far as they wanted reform, they wished firstly to redress the balance of representation so that populous counties and new large towns would gain members at the expense of the obviously rotten boroughs, and secondly to extend the franchise to embrace the property of the middle classes.

Meanwhile the state of the unpropertied agricultural labourers remained miserable. Cobbett wrote of men found in May 1830 dead under a hedge:[10]

and when opened by the surgeons nothing but sour sorrel was found in their stomachs. . . . Besides suffering from want, the working people have been made to endure insults and indignities such as even Negroes were never exposed to. They have been harnessed like horses or asses and made to draw carts and wagons; they have been shut up in the pounds made to hold stray cattle; they have been made to work with bells round their necks like cows put out to graze; they have been made to carry heavy stones backward and forward in fields or on the roads; and have, in these cases, had drivers set over them, just as if they had been galley

slaves; they have been *sold by auction* for certain times, as the
Negroes are sold in the West Indies; the married men have been
kept separated from their wives, by force, to prevent them from
breeding; and, in short, no human beings were ever before treated
so unjustly, with so much insolence, and with such damnable
barbarity, as the working people of England have been within the
sixteen, and particularly, within the last ten years.

He wrote this against the background of the 'Captain Swing' disturbances in the autumn and winter of 1830,[11] when the agricultural
labourers of the southern counties from Kent to Wiltshire rose to
demand secure employment and a living wage. They travelled about in
bands, burning ricks and breaking threshing-machines; they called on
parsons to reduce tithes and landowners to reduce rents so that farmers
could pay higher wages; they trundled the most oppressive Poor Law
overseers out of villages in the very carts to which paupers had been
harnessed; they destroyed workhouses at Selborne and Headley (near
Farnham) and extorted money from wealthy men (including the
Bishop of Winchester); they sometimes sent letters signed 'Captain
Swing' to parsons, overseers, farmers or landowners, but, although
these letters contained bloody threats, there was hardly any violence
against persons. 'Wiltshire Bennett', Member of Parliament, an advocate of a harsher Poor Law and notorious oppressor of the poor in his
own parish, was pelted with stones, and Bingham Baring, of the
Hampshire banking family, had his hat knocked off by a hammer; but
these were rare and isolated incidents. Mostly the labourers acted with a
restraint which earned them sympathy not only from farmers, many of
whom were prepared to support agitation to reduce rents, tithes and
taxes, but even from some local magistrates who agreed that their wage
demands were reasonable. However, as a class, the gentry took fright.
The government sent soldiers to the affected counties, and when the
Whigs came to office in November 1830 the Home Secretary, Lord
Melbourne, suppressed the labourers' rioting with even more vigour
than his Tory predecessor had done. The Whigs were determined to
show that, though they were committed to Reform, they were strong
enough to maintain public order. The labourers melted away before the
soldiers, the ringleaders were caught and tried by special commissioners sent from London to those districts where the local magistrates
could not be trusted to impose sufficiently harsh, exemplary punishments. As a result of the trials 400 men were imprisoned, 450

transported, and 9 hanged – which 9 included the nineteen-year-old ploughboy, Henry Cook, who had damaged Bingham Baring's hat.

Cobbett reported the whole affair of what he called the 'rural War' very fully in the *Political Register*. While condemning the arson he painted very graphically the misery which had prompted the risings; at the same time he scoffed at the Government's contention that the rioting labourers were the dupes of political agitators:[12]

> It is no new feeling of discontent that is at work: it is a deep sense of grievious wrongs; it is long-harboured resentment; it is an accumulation of revenge for unmerited punishment; it has long been smothered in the bosoms of these our injured and suffering countrymen, and it has now *bursted forth*.

But Cobbett had been lecturing on Reform in Sussex only two weeks before the Captain Swing disturbances there, and some of the rioters around Winchester and Micheldever in Hampshire were known to be readers of the *Political Register*; the Whigs determined to prosecute him. A young Sussex labourer under sentence of death for rick-burning was induced to confess that he never should have thought of 'douing aney sutch thing if Mr. Cobet had never given aney lactures', so Cobbett was thereupon indicted for a libel published in the *Political Register* of 11 December 1830 'with the intent to raise discontent in the minds of the labourers in husbandry, and to incite them to acts of violence'. At the trial Cobbett was able to demonstrate that the indictment contained only garbled extracts from an article which, as a whole, had a tendency opposed to the one imputed to it, but he went on to turn the proceedings into a trial of the government for its callous indifference to the sufferings of the labourers. Cobbett had subpoenaed several Cabinet ministers, and, after compelling them to listen to his long, blistering denunciation, he called Brougham, the Lord Chancellor, to the witness-box and forced him to admit that he, in his capacity of President of the Society for the Diffusion of Useful Knowledge, had, only a few days after the publication of the alleged libel, asked Cobbett for leave to reprint the 'Letter to Luddites' of 1816, as a dissuasive against this most recent wave of machine-breaking. 'What times are these', declared Cobbett, 'when the Lord Chancellor comes to Cobbett's sedition-shop to get something wherewith to quieten the labourers!' Then he tendentiously questioned Lord Melbourne about the pardon granted to his accuser. His success was complete when the jury failed to agree on a verdict and the judge discharged him. Cobbett's triumph at this trial was as great as his humiliation had been in 1810.

During the trial the Attorney-General, prosecuting, had said that, although the price was a shilling, the *Political Register* was read by the labouring classes all over the country: 'It is taken in many places where the poor are in the habit constantly of resorting.' They clubbed together and sat 'in great societies' to read it, and it had 'a prodigious effect' – upon which Cobbett retorted, 'I hope in God it has'. Cobbett's writings at this time show even more confidence than ever. He writes of Brougham's Society for the Diffusion of Useful Knowledge tracts having to be 'pushed about' to reach the working classes, whereas his own *Twopenny Trash* 'will contain a spring, in its inside, to set it and keep it in motion'.[13] He dashed off a high-spirited anti-Malthusian tract in the form of a stage-comedy, *Surplus Population* (1831, enlarged 1835). Cobbett had cleared all the debts he intended to clear, and was beginning to reap the financial rewards of a busy decade of popular writing, so he started large-scale farming once again. The properties at Kensington and Barn-Elm were given up, and late in 1831 he acquired a long lease of Normandy Farm at Ash, close to his birthplace at Farnham. 'I took a farm', he said,[14]

> for several purposes: 1. To please myself, and to live at the end of my days, in those scenes in which I began them; 2. To make the life as long as nature, unthwarted by smoke and confinement, would let it be; 3. To make a complete Tullian farm; 4. To make a Locust coppice; 5. To raise garden seeds in the best possible manner.

Cobbett could not devote much time and attention to farming because the final struggle for Reform was on. The Whigs had introduced their Reform Bill into Parliament on 1 March 1831, and all the nation was discussing 'the Bill, the whole Bill, and nothing but the Bill'. Defeated in the Commons, the Whig government resigned, appealed to the country, and returned after the general election in May with a greatly increased majority. The second Reform Bill introduced at the end of June, differed only in detail from the first, and, despite Tory obstruction in Committee, passed the Commons in September, only to be promptly rejected by the Lords. This provoked rioting in the provinces; Nottingham Castle was burned down, Derby gaol was sacked, and in Bristol three gaols, the Mansion House and the Bishop's Palace were all destroyed. Cobbett, again, warned that the situation was exactly like that at the beginning of the French Revolution. The third Bill, little different from its predecessors, passed the Commons in March 1832 and went to the Lords, who, after obstruction, threw it out in May. When the King refused to create enough new peers to pass the Bill, the Whig government resigned. Now the Duke of Wellington, the most determined enemy of Reform, sought to scrape together a Tory ministry which might command a sufficient majority to pass an emasculated reform bill, for, at this stage, no government could have taken office and refused reform altogether. Cobbett, claiming to be a reporter rather than a promulgator of sedition, wrote:[15]

> To describe the agitation in London, and the anger of the people against the Lords, the Bishops, Wellington, and particularly against the King, is a task that no tongue or pen can perform. Every man you met seemed to be convulsed with rage: to refuse to pay taxes was amongst the mildest of the measures that were proposed. . . . A cry for a republic was pretty nearly general; and an emigration to Hanover formed the subject of a popular and widely-circulated caricature. Resistance in every shape and form was publicly proposed; and amongst the means intended to defeat the King and the new Minister, was that most effectual of all means, *a run upon the Bank for gold.*

Wellington's efforts were vain; the King recalled Grey, and, in order to avoid the creation of peers, asked Wellington and his followers to absent themselves from the Lords and allow the Bill to pass, which at last it did in June 1832.

Cobbett believed that 'we owe the Reform Bill more to the Country Labourers than to all the rest of the nation put together', because the labourers in the winter of 1830–1 had shown that they would not remain quiet under their sufferings. Everyone should be grateful to these labourers: 'I feel this gratitude in a peculiar degree; because, taking England throughout, I know more of their toils, their sufferings, and their virtues, than any other man.' So, when the Royal Assent was given to the Reform Bill on 7 July and Reform festivals were held all over the country, Cobbett chose to celebrate among the Hampshire farm-workers at Sutton Scotney. Cobbett chose this spot because it was here that an assembly of labourers had signed a petition for reform in October 1830, and where the labourers of ten parishes met peaceably in November 1830 'to remonstrate with the farmers, the parsons, and the landowners, with regard to the wages that had reduced them to a state of half-starvation', and where near by, in Micheldever churchyard, lay the body of Henry Cook who had been hanged for damaging Bingham Baring's hat which had followed as a consequence of that meeting.[16]

In his *Grammar* Cobbett had written, 'Moderate reform – an expression which has been well criticized by asking the gentlemen who use it how they would like to meet *moderate chastity* in a wife', and his own *Plan of Parliamentary Reform* in October 1830 had insisted on the full Radical programme, including annual parliaments, universal male suffrage and secret ballot. Yet in the event he welcomed the Whig's moderate Reform Bill. Though this Bill broke the power of the boroughmongers by sweeping away the rotten boroughs completely and giving representation to the growing industrial towns, it made no provision for shortening the duration of parliaments or for the secret ballot; it extended the franchise only to ten-pound householders in towns, and leaseholders and tenant-farmers in the country – that is, it enfranchised the propertied middle classes. Nevertheless, Cobbett agreed with many other Radical leaders that their own movement was not strong or united enough to force Radical reform through by constitutional agitation (or, indeed, by armed insurrection), and therefore that it would be expedient to support the bill on the principle that half a loaf is better than no bread. So Cobbett, while still expressing distrust of the Whigs, now sought to enrol the working classes in support of the Bill, even though he realized that they might be resentful:[17]

> I am aware that, to ensure the cheers of men, justly angry with what is done, I ought to foster their discontent; but I am also aware that a short time will convince them that I am best consulting their good as well as the preservation of my own character, by giving all the support in my power to this measure of the Government.

Like most public men, Cobbett had always believed that the public good and the characters of public men were closely involved with each other, so that when Henry Hunt, the only out-and-out Radical in Parliament, stuck to his guns and spoke out strongly against the Bill, Cobbett attacked both his opinions and his character. For Cobbett, who had fared so badly when he had stood as candidate in Preston, Henry Hunt, Member of Parliament for Preston, was now the 'Preston cock on the Preston dunghill', crowing loud out of vanity and opposing the Bill merely in order to attract public attention.[18] Hunt retorted by claiming that Cobbett had betrayed the labouring classes and was selling them to the Whigs for his own advancement.

It was the old story of Radical disunity. The protest against corruption in high places united all reformers, while the devising and carrying through of specific plans for reform divided them. Hunt and Cobbett were both wrong in assigning to each other wholly self-interested motives, but Hunt's attitude was less confused, if less realistic, than Cobbett's; and Cobbett, from time to time during the Reform Bill agitation, seems to have had doubts over the way in which he had not sold, but given, the working-class Reform movement to the Whigs:[19]

> According to our laws and usages, a man by whom a woman is
> *in the family way (enceinte)* is, in certain cases, *compelled to marry her,*
> and then he is said *to be led to the church in a halter.* Yet he, when in
> the church, promises and vows that he will *love* and *cherish the*
> *bride* to the end of their days! Just such a marriage is now taking
> place between the Whig-Ministry and Reform; I have very kindly
> furnished the *halter* for the happy occasion.

In August 1831 Cobbett was adopted as parliamentary candidate for Manchester, so in a series of lectures there and in *Political Register* articles he announced what he would attempt to do if elected. He promised, among many other things, to relieve the nation of the burden of sinecures, a standing army and tithes, and to wipe out the National Debt by the sale of ecclesiastical estates, Crown lands and the 'misapplied property of corporate bodies'. In July of the following year, when the Reform Bill was passed, Cobbett was adopted by Oldham, and he held on to both adoptions until the general election took place in December 1832. Before that, in the autumn, he undertook his longest lecture-tour of all, through the Midlands, the North and Scotland, with election campaigns in Manchester and Oldham on the outward and the return journeys. Cobbett's new audiences in Scotland found, as George Gilfillan wrote, not a 'rude, truculent barbarian' but:[20]

> a tall, stout, mild-faced, broad-shouldered, farmer-looking man,
> with a spice of humour lurking in his eye, but without one vestige
> of fierceness or malignity either in his look or demeanour. His
> private manners were simple, unaffected – almost gentlemanly. His
> mode of addressing an audience was quiet, clear, distinct, and
> conversational; and the fury and the fervour of the demagogue

alike were wanting. The most sarcastic and provoking things oozed out at his lips like milk or honey.

The people of Edinburgh 'welcomed him as a curiosity, and went to see and hear him as a raree show. . . . He came, tickled their midriff – they laughed, applauded, and forgot him as soon as his back was turned.' Cobbett's impact was perhaps greater than Gilfillan allowed, but it was certainly less than Cobbett himself imagined.

The election in December was, as usual, spread over several days, but on the second day Cobbett and his popular Radical ally, the mill-owner, John Fielden, were so far ahead in the poll at Oldham that their opponents withdrew. Cobbett at once withdrew from the Manchester contest, and so, a few months short of seventy years old, he became a Member of Parliament.

Cobbett had always had an exaggerated notion of what one man of principle could do in an assembly of rogues and vagabonds; in 1824 he wrote:

> If I had been in Parliament at the close of the war against Bona-parte in the year 1814; or, in 1816; or, in 1819; or, in 1822; if I had been in Parliament at either of these epochs, things could not have been as they are now. The *cash-measures* never could have been taken; the land and labour could not have been oppressed as they now are; the debt could not have been what it is now.

In 1827 Cobbett claimed to be more fit for the office of Prime Minister than any other person in the kingdom.[21] Cobbett's supporters spent a great deal of time, trouble and money in trying to get him into Parliament, but when at last he arrived there he was not very effective. He detested and never mastered the rules of the House of Commons, and was never able to accustom himself to be polite towards his enemies during debates. Above all he hated the parliamentary practice of beginning business after the hour when most honest men had finished a day's work, and of bringing vital matters up for discussion after midnight. Cobbett spent much of his time in carping criticism of the Speaker, whose election he had opposed, and in such vain projects as an attempt to remove Sir Robert Peel from the Privy Council because of his views on paper-money and gold. Once, after an unusually long harangue against Peel, he was met with groans, hootings and yells when he rose to speak again.[22] Cobbett spoke against foreign trade in his old 'Perish Commerce' vein, against national schools and 'Heddukashion' for labourers, and against any civic improvements of London which might encourage residence in the hated 'Wen'; he continued to preach his doctrine of an 'equitable adjustment' of the Debt; he aired all his old ideas and prejudices, but the House would not listen. When divisions were taken on motions introduced by Cobbett, he rarely had more than sixteen or eighteen supporters. Members who did not detest him displayed an amused tolerance; for instance, there is young E. L. Bulwer's affectionate, wondering mockery:[23]

> he seeth not why the Speaker of the House of Commons should have more than a hundred a-year; he knoweth many an honest man among his constituents who would be Speaker for less. He accuses the aristocracy of an absolute and understood combination to cheat the good citizens of his borough. He thinketh that Lord Grey and Sir Robert Peel meet in private, to consult how they may most tax the working-classes. He hateth the Jews because they don't plough. He has no desire that the poor man should be instructed.

Cobbett's audience remained outside Parliament in the readers of the *Political Register*, which he continued to his death.

Cobbett's best speech in the Commons was a brief, ironic contribution to the debate on Lord Shaftesbury's Factory Bill in July 1833. Representatives of the textile interest had argued that to reduce from twelve to ten the hours worked by children in the mills would destroy the profitability of manufacture and deliver a great blow to the wealth and power of the nation. Cobbett thereupon congratulated the House on a discovery:

> we have this night discovered, that the shipping, the land, and the Bank and its credit, are all nothing worth compared with the labour of three hundred thousand little girls in Lancashire! Aye, when compared with only an eighth part of the labour of those three hundred thousand little girls, from whose labour, if we only deduct two hours a day, away goes the wealth, away goes the capital, away go the resources, the power, and the glory of England!

Cobbett's sarcasm on this particular point was unavailing in the House, but outside he joined John Fielden, his fellow-member for Oldham, and Robert Owen, his one-time enemy, in agitation to reduce the working hours for all labourers. 'Rousseau', he wrote in the *Political*

Register, 'has very justly observed, that the man who is compelled to work all the hours that he is awake, is . . . to all intents and purposes a *slave.*'[24]

The labouring classes for whom Cobbett spoke had, like him, expected parliamentary reform to better their condition, but, like him, they were disappointed: 'Therefore, casting aside all disquisitions relative to forms of government, and political and constitutional rights, they have betaken themselves to what they deem the best method of insuring them sufficiency of food and of raiment in return for their labour.' So they were throwing their energies into the formation and strengthening of Trade Unions: 'The Government newspapers have been recommending the Parliament to pass a *law* to put an end to these unions. Better call for a law to prevent those inconvenient things called *spring-tides.*'[25] Cobbett wrote occasionally in support of the unions and on the right to strike, he joined the agitation on behalf of the Tolpuddle Martyrs, and he performed a useful service in calling for a House of Commons Select Committee to expose the infiltration of trades unions by officers of Peel's new, hated, police-force, but, of course, he had nothing to do with the infant proto-socialist movements of the 1830s.

Cobbett's worthiest action in Parliament was his long and bitter fight against the New Poor Law. The Old Poor Law, particularly as modified in the agricultural counties by the 'Speenhamland System' worked badly. For the labourers the Speenhamland System destroyed incentives for effort and ambition, proscribed independence, and placed a premium upon indolence. For the farmers, it was the strongest possible incentive to reduce wages below even the level of subsistence. For the landowners, haunted by the Malthusian spectre of over-population and an ever-increasing poor-rate, it was an equally strong motive to pull down cottages on their estates and, by their power in Select Vestries, to cut down scales of parish relief and compel overseers to make more deterrent the conditions for relief. The system created ill-will in both the donors and the recipients of relief. It remained in being simply because the various Tory governments since the 1790s had been unable to devise a new scheme of relief more acceptable to the landed interest, and because revolution was feared if the Old Poor Law were abolished.

When the Whigs came to power, a Royal Commission was set up under the chairmanship of the Bishop of London to report to Parliament on the Poor Law. Cobbett, who shared the popular suspicion that this Commission would advocate the abolition of the Old Poor Law in favour of some scheme along Malthusian lines, denounced it as 'one amongst the memorable fooleries of this Whig-Ministry', declaring that it could not possibly be effective: 'I know they can do nothing to the Poor Laws: the chopsticks [agricultural labourers] will see to that.'[26] Cobbett confidently predicted that the reformed Parliament which would meet within the year would dismiss the Commission. He was wrong. The reformed House of Commons kept the Commission in being and energetically acted upon its recommendations. The New Poor Law, 1834, was a triumph of Malthusian principles and of the bureaucratic energy of a new age. Under it the existing powers of Justices of the Peace and parish vestries were set aside, and in their place three Poor Law Commissioners in London were empowered to establish 'Union' workhouses by means of a compulsory union of parishes. The Commissioners laid down the three main conditions under which the local Guardians who managed the workhouses might grant relief, which stipulated that there should be no relief to the able-bodied except inside a workhouse, that such relief had to be 'less eligible' than the most unpleasant means of earning a living outside, and that men must be separated from their wives in order to prevent the possibility of pauper-breeding. The object of the New Poor Law was to shock the labouring classes into self-reliance.

Cobbett fought this cold Act at every stage. He believed that the Old Poor Law should be left as it was, that government taxation should be lightened by cutting sinecures, pensions and so forth, and the Debt repudiated, so that employers could find work for everyone at increased wages, and thus make poor relief necessary only for the unfortunate few who might from time to time, even in the best of societies, be un-employed or incapacitated. As usual Cobbett took his stand on ancient rights and liberties, for in his writings over a period of thirty years he had asserted the *right* of relief. In the *History of the Protestant 'Reformation'*, in *The Poor Man's Friend* and more briefly elsewhere Cobbett had offered an historical proof that the poor had a right to a decent main-tenance out of the land. There had been a social contract between the men who owned land and those who did not – this contract was effectively re-enacted in the Middle Ages when the poor were sup-ported out of the tithes, and again by the Elizabethan Poor Law under which the poor were to be supported out of the produce of all land. While the social contract may be historically unsound, it is morally sure: the rights which 'agreeably to the laws of our country, we all inherit from our forefathers' include:[27]

the right to live in the country of our birth; the right to have a living out of the land of our birth in exchange for our labour duly and honestly performed; the right, in case we fall into distress, to have our wants sufficiently relieved out of the produce of the land, whether that distress arise from sickness, from decrepitude, from old age, or from the inability to find employment; because there are laws, and those laws are just, to punish us if we be idle or dissolute.

Cobbett's arguments, such as they were, cut little ice in the hearts of Whig or Tory Members of Parliament, though he spoke on every possible occasion against the Commission's report and the ensuing Bill. 'The object of the Bill,' Cobbett said, 'was to rob the poor man to enrich the landowner. . . . They were now about to dissolve the bonds of society; they were going to break faith with the poor man.' This, then, was 'war upon the cottage'. In Cobbett's attacks on the powers of the three Poor Law Commissioners ('the three Bashaws of Somerset House') lurked his traditional suspicion of 'Court' and 'Ministry', and still, perhaps, some faint gleams of hope that the landed gentry might again be what once they were in his ideal Old England. The New Poor Law, he said, was:[28]

a scheme for bringing every thing and every body within the control, the immediate control, of the kingly part of the Government. This bill will totally abrogate all the local government of the kingdom: the gentlemen and the magistrates will be totally divested of all power, tending to uphold their character, and to secure their property and their personal safety in the country.

The Bill was revolutionary; it sought to destroy part of the Constitution, and it could only provoke a counter-revolution from the poor:

Pass this bill and you destroy the constitution as far as relates to the necessitous . . . you dissolve the social compact, as far as relates to the working people. There must be two parties to an obligation: without protection on the one side there can be no right to demand obedience on the other. Read the 28. chapter of *Deuteronomy*. You will there find, and in the next chapter, what is to be the fate of those who are the oppressors of the poor.

The very last article that Cobbett wrote for the *Political Register* reviewed the outbreak of rioting in the country against the New Poor

Law and reasserted those traditional popular rights of which he had always seen himself the guardian:

> here is the country disturbed; here are the jails filling; here are wives and children screaming after their fathers; here are these undeniable facts; and what is the cause? Not a desire to overturn the Government on the part of the people; not a desire to disobey the settled laws of the country; not any revolutionary desire; not any desire to touch any one of the institutions of the country. What is it then? Why a desire and a resolution, as far as they are able to adhere to it, to maintain the laws of their country.

Cobbett had often claimed that English landlords were attempting to reduce agricultural labourers to the brute misery of the potato-fed Irish, but it was not until the autumn of 1834 that he had the opportunity to travel in Ireland himself; and when he went there it was with the Old Poor Law – which had never applied to Ireland – and the new one very much in the forefront of his mind. Cobbett published in the *Political Register* an account of his Irish tour in the form of a series of ten letters addressed to Charles Marshall, one of the labourers on Normandy Farm, which letters movingly describe the sufferings of Irish small farmers and labourers under absentee landlords, such as that 'great swaggering fellow in Sussex, that they call the Earl of Egremont',[29] who drain away all the produce of a fertile land. Cobbett's blunt allusiveness is as much that of a private letter as it is that of the political lampoon, when, for instance, he introduces his indictment of Viscount Middleton, whose Irish rental was twenty-five or thirty thousand pounds but whose tenants lived in conditions worse than those enjoyed by animals in England: 'You know, that, at Pepperharrow (only about four miles from your cottage) there lives Lord Middleton. You know that he was a long while Lord-Lieutenant of our county. Now, Marshall . . . [on Middleton's Irish estates are hovels] none of them so good as the place where you keep your little horse.' Marshall would have known Lord Middleton only as the grand and respectable Lord-Lieutenant of Surrey, but Cobbett will expose the rags, dirt and hunger that follow the sordid and cruel extortion which supplies economic support for respectability and grandeur in Surrey. The indignant and piteous description of the Irish hovel forces upon Cobbett's readers the acute contrast between Viscount Middleton's grandeur and the poverty that supplies his riches, but the placing of this description in the course of a farmer's letter to his labourer points up another contrast. It is made abundantly clear that the relationship between Cobbett and Marshall is very different from that between Middleton and his Irish peasants:[30]

> Lord Middleton may say, that He is not the *landlord* of these wretched people. Ah! but his *tenant*, his *middleman*, is their landlord, and Lord Middleton gets the *more rent from him*, by enabling him to let these holes in this manner. If I were to give Mr. Dean [cf. p. 65 above] a shilling a week to squeeze you down to twelve shillings a week, who would you think was most to blame, me or Mr. Dean?

Throughout the series the intimate, allusive form of the private letter itself effortlessly conveys Cobbett's ideal of the master–man relationship. Cobbett represents himself as a fair, just and generous employer who, because he respects and understands his men, commands respect from such good fellows as the manly, sober, hard-working, well-fed and sensible Marshall. By employing the letter-form deliberately to establish a sympathetic *persona* at the same time as he attacks an enemy – and to use this *persona* as a moral norm against which to judge and condemn the enemy – Cobbett parallels Pope's technique in his letters and verse-epistles, except of course in the important circumstance that Cobbett's technique is so artless.

Declaring that the struggle for the rights of the poor must go on after his death, he issued *Cobbett's Legacy to Labourers* (1835), a statement of these rights, in a 'waistcoat pocket' format with a durable limp leather binding which gave the book a close, and doubtless intentional, resemblance to a prayer-book. The same format was used for two companion works, *Cobbett's Legacy to Parsons* (1835) and the posthumously published *Cobbett's Legacy to Peel*; but despite these testamentary dispositions, he regarded himself as still very much alive and active. Cobbett planned to write his autobiography under the title 'The Progress of a Plough-boy to a seat in Parliament'. He would start a newspaper (*Cobbett's Evening Journal*) when, perhaps, the *Political Register* could be dropped. Cobbett's last memorandum book[31] lists titles and chapter-headings for the books on which he was at work – 'The Poor Man's Bible, or Selections from the Two Testaments, preceded by an Essay on Infidelity', 'Cobbett's Legacy to Dissenters' and the 'Legacy to Lords'.

As busy and hopeful as ever, Cobbett wrote in the *Political Register* of 18 April 1835, from Normandy Farm, to the People of Oldham:[32]

My Friends,
This morning long before four o'clock, I heard the blackbirds
making the fields echo with their whistle; and a few minutes after
four I, for the first time this year, heard the *cuckoo*, which I never
before heard earlier than *May-day*. And now, this cuckoo will, on
Midsummer day, cease to call us up in the morning, and cease its
work of sucking the hedge-sparrow's eggs, depositing its own in
the nest, making the poor hedge-sparrow bring it up, until it be
big enough and strong enough to kill and eat the hedge-sparrow;
in all which respects it so exactly resembles the at once lazy and
greedy and ungrateful and cruel vagabonds, who devour the fruit
of our labour. . . . But, my friends, I do verily believe that, before
we shall hear this harbinger of summer again, the vagabonds, of
whom it is the type, will have received a *souse*, such as they never
received before.

Cobbett returned to the 'Wen' for another tiring session of a House
whose late hours and tobacco smoke he detested so much, but he was
on his farm again when he died on 18 June 1835 at the age of seventy-
two. A few hours before his death he asked to be carried around the
farm to see how the work was going in the fields. The last entry in his
diary was on 12 June, and read: 'Ploughing home field'.

9

Epilogue

In the years between Cobbett's first employment as a bird-scarer in the fields at Farnham and his last as the Radical Member of Parliament for a Lancashire industrial town, the old England and the new mingled strangely. The most recent editor of *Rural Rides* writes that Cobbett's life 'reads as if a character from Fielding had adventured his way through a world created by Dickens,'[1] and up to a point this is true – if we ignore the complication introduced by the fact that Cobbett's condemnation of Fielding and Fielding's characters (p. 157 above) would not have been altogether out of place in the mouth of Mr Podsnap or even Mr Chadband. The old England had cottage industries, mountebanks, fairs, singlestick matches, all-powerful Justices of the Peace, borderers on the wastes and children playing and working in the fields. The new England had factories, provincial theatres, railways, Poor Law Commissioners in London and schools for the poor. In the old world news had travelled in country districts no quicker than pedlars moved from hamlet to hamlet: as Cobbett himself recalled, 'The shouts of victory or the murmurs at a defeat, would now-and-then break in upon our tranquillity for a moment; but I do not remember ever having seen a newspaper in the house.'[2] In the new world, fast coaches could bring to thousands of literate working men a cheap *Political Register* printed on steam-powered presses. By the very act of becoming a powerful and popular political journalist, Cobbett had helped to create that new world, even though the constant message of his writing was that he desired no innovation and merely wished 'to see the poor men of England what the poor men of England were when I was born'.

Control of the new world lay, as it still lies, with the Benthamites. The spirit of Bentham codified, organized, tightened and centralized government, and in Cobbett's view whether it brought into being an

186

all-compassing system of oppression such as the New Poor Law, or whether it irritatingly dictated 'the exact depth proper for a shop-window',[3] it was to be opposed as tending to bring everything and everybody under the immediate control of the 'kingly part of government' (cf. p. 182 above). That Cobbett, in attacking the New Poor Law of 1834, used phrases which would not have been out of place in the pages of John Almon's *Political Register* in the 1760s, or of the *Craftsman* in the 1720s, or even in the mouths of members of Charles I's parliaments, is yet one more indication that his politics have, on the one hand, much in common with Swift and Bolingbroke's landed Toryism, and, on the other, with the more tenuous political tradition represented by eighteenth-century 'Real Whigs' and 'Commonwealthmen'. Cobbett founded no party, for he hated the idea of party; and he neither toppled any government nor persuaded it to adopt any of the measures that he so passionately advocated. In attempting to further his stated, and often self-contradictory, political aims, he persistently beat his head against a brick wall, with little damage to the wall and none to his head. Despite the extraordinary mobility of a career that took him through all three of the great ranks of society, and despite the egalitarian implications of such notions as universal suffrage, Cobbett believed to the end of his life that a relatively static, hierarchical, 'master and man' society was according to Nature.[4] In a later age a man of his character, tastes, opinions and abilities might well have become a Fascist leader. Certainly it would be misleading to call Cobbett a 'left-wing' Radical, for he was in fact a reactionary, always looking backwards and shouting the slogans of the past. Like so very many 'patriots' before him, he detested placemen, sinecurists, undeserving pensioners, luxury, effeminacy, tea, the East India Company, Methodists, standing armies, Jews, the Italian opera, faction, bureaucracy, Cabinet government, loan-jobbers, fund-holders, paper-money, evil communications that corrupted good manners, and anything that tended (as most of these things apparently did) to depopulate rural areas. But if Cobbett was a crank he was in good company. In so far as his political attitudes were an instinctive and absolute rejection of all the notions of Bentham – the man who, in Hazlitt's words, 'turns wooden utensils in a lathe for exercise, and fancies he can turn men in the same manner'[5] – Cobbett was at one with most of the great romantic poets and critics of his day (of whom only Shelley may be reckoned a Benthamite), while his specific denunciations of abuses may be easily paralleled in the imaginative writing of his notable contemporaries, many of whom were, as it happens, personal and political enemies.

Radical Byron joined Major Cartwright's Hampden Club, spoke in favour of Roman Catholic emancipation and in defence of the Luddites, and found room in the verse-satires written between 1811 and his death for denunciations of English oppression in Ireland and the East, of taxes levied to support royal mistresses or to pension Wellington, of Game laws, Corn laws, tithes and the 'land self-interest', of paper-money and Jewish financiers, and of George III, his sons and his ministers. At the same time he censured his friend John Cam Hobhouse, the Radical candidate, for speaking and dining with the 'low, designing, dirty levellers', Cobbett and Henry Hunt.[6]

Shelley's idealism removed him as far from Cobbett as his aristocratic Whig background did, but when in *The Mask of Anarchy* he sees freedom in terms of the labourer's bread (stanzas *liii–lvi*) he is speaking the language that Cobbett understood; so, too, in the *Hymn to Intellectual Beauty* when he claims that the true virtues of free men are 'Love, Hope, and Self-esteem', for if anyone preached and practised the virtues of self-esteem in the sense that Shelley means, it was Cobbett. In *Swellfoot the Tyrant*, Shelley wote his satire on the Queen's Case (an affair which prompted Keats's *Cap and Bells* and many digressive stanzas in Byron's *Don Juan*), but, like Hazlitt, he regarded the Radicals' concern in this matter as mostly cant. The targets of much of his political prose and verse – Eldon, Ellenborough, Castlereagh, Sidmouth, Malthus and the Prince Regent – are those of Cobbett and all Radicals; he was deeply shocked by the activities of Oliver the Spy and by Peterloo; but he recognized that the problems of injustice and its solution are more complex than Cobbett allowed:

> The rich are damned, beyond all cure,
> To taunt, and starve, and trample on
> The weak and wretched; and the poor
> Damn their broken hearts to endure
> Stripe on stripe, with groan on groan.
>
> Sometimes the poor are damned indeed
> To take, – not means for being blest, –
> But Cobbett's snuff, revenge; that weed
> From which the worms that it doth feed
> Squeeze less than they before possessed.
> (*Peter Bell the Third*, III, 86–95)

Shelley deplored Cobbett's divisiveness in the Radical movement,[7] but accepted his views upon paper-credit and public finance, and used them in 1820 in his own *A Philosophical View of Reform*. Shelley's friend Peacock, that most urbane of Parliamentary reformers wrote satires against paper-money (as did Tom Moore), and damned in traditional terms such pests as Scotch economists, common-enclosing, game-bagging, poacher-persecuting landlords, Utilitarian philosophers, tyrannical factory owners, and the 'Steam Intellect Society'; but, of course, at the heart of his work is an irony that sets him apart from Cobbett and, for that matter, Shelley.

The older generation of Romantic poets (except for the republican Landor and Blake) had lost most of their revolutionary ardour by the time Cobbett joined the Radicals – though as late as 1809 Southey and Wordsworth were still supporters of Burdett on the issue of Reform, and, like Blake and Cobbett, were inclined to take an unholy delight in the scandalous revelations concerning Mrs Clarke and the Duke of York.[8] The Tory Southey in his *Quarterly Review* articles and in *Sir Thomas More* (1829) continued to analyse the social ills that he had written of in *Letters from England* (1807): the widening gap between rich and poor, the game laws, Malthusianism, the growth of cities, the social and physical effects of industrialism, monopolies of farms, and many other matters that had also aroused Cobbett's anger. The century-old complaints flow from Southey's pen as freely as from Cobbett's: 'As the greedy spirit of trade has destroyed the small farmers, and is in like manner destroying the small tradesman, so has the class of inferior gentry almost disappeared.'[9] Except in his belief that the suppression of the monasteries had contributed to the growth of pauperism, Southey differed absolutely from Cobbett over the causes (and the remedies) of all the social ills of the day. In 1834 he backed Cobbett's activities in Factory Reform, but for the previous quarter-of-a-century he had been Cobbett's fiercest and most persistent literary opponent, and in the savage years between Waterloo and Peterloo had even advocated more draconian measures of oppression than the ones actually adopted by the government.

The other Lake Poets shared a general nostalgia for cottage industry and admiration for the small farmer. We need not take seriously Coleridge's attempts in 1796 to cultivate the acre or two behind his cottage and his claim that 'I would rather be an expert self-maintaining gardener than a Milton if I could not unite both',[10] or pay much attention to his and Wordsworth's cultivation of the 'yeoman' Thomas

Poole whose letters on 'Monopolists and Farmers' were inserted by Coleridge in the *Morning Post* in 1800. Yet Wordsworth's sensitive portrayal of the moral life of the independent small landholder in *Michael* is quite another matter. Wordsworth's commentary upon this poem in a letter to Charles James Fox could well speak for Cobbett, who so strongly believed that the country man's, and his own, moral identity was closely and equally bound to land and family:[11]

> The domestic affections will always be strong amongst men who live in a country not crowded with population, if these men are placed above poverty. But if they are proprietors of small estates, which have descended to them from their ancestors, the power which these affections will acquire amongst such men is inconceivable by those who have only had an opportunity of observing hired labourers, farmers, and the manufacturing Poor. Their little tract of land serves as a kind of permanent rallying point for their domestic feelings, as a tablet upon which they are written which makes them objects of memory in a thousand instances when they otherwise would be forgotten. It is a fountain fitted to the nature of social man from which supplies of affection, as pure as his heart was intended for, are daily drawn.

All three Lake Poets joined in the general denunciation of the Convention of Cintra and distrusted Wellington ever after, but Wordsworth's famous tract on the Convention seems particularly close in spirit to Cobbett. Like Cobbett, he avoids all political complexities; he is moved by simple enthusiasm for the Spanish insurrection and simple indignation against the Convention. As he declares that the Convention is denounced by the universal voice of the people 'with that unanimity which nothing but the light of truth spread over the inmost concerns of human nature can create',[12] the reader is impressed by a sense of great power; Wordsworth makes us aware that he, and we, are participating in a general swell of popular feeling. This, too, is Cobbett's mood at the height of the success of the *Political Register* when he expresses democratic emotion – not the democratic idea based upon some theory of popular rights – but the response to, and articulation of, a current of popular feeling which may be interpreted as the popular will. It is a demagogy that is by no means ignoble.

Among the Radical or quondam Radical Romantic writers only Hazlitt and Leigh Hunt ever bestowed much praise on Cobbett. Hazlitt's

fine essay in *Table Talk* (1821) remains far and away the best characterization of Cobbett as a man and a writer, perhaps because admiration
falls well short of idolatry. Hazlitt has caught perfectly Cobbett's
political temper, and the vitality which can thrive only on opposition:[13]

> wherever power is, there is he against it; he naturally butts at all
> obstacles, as unicorns are attracted to oak-trees, and feels his own
> strength only by resistance to the opinions and wishes of the rest
> of the world. To sail with the stream, to agree with the company,
> is not his humour. If he could bring about a Reform in Parliament,
> the odds are that he would instantly fall foul of and try to mar his
> own handy-work; and he quarrels with his own creatures as soon
> as he has written them into a little vogue – and a prison. I do not
> think this is vanity or fickleness so much as a pugnacious
> disposition, that must have an antagonist power to contend with,
> and only finds itself at ease in systematic opposition.

It is possible that the quarrelsome Hazlitt, so given to retrospection and
so full of truculent honesty himself, understood Cobbett so well because
he resembled him. Nevertheless, the celebrated contemporary artist
who was closest to Cobbett in political opinions, prose style, back
ground and temperament was surely Thomas Bewick. Bewick was the
son of a small farmer and was bred up to work with his hands in
sturdy independence at a useful trade. A large, athletic, powerful old
man in the 1820s, he set down the reminiscences of a long life, and
intermingled denunciations of placemen, pensioners, Pitt, Game Laws,
boroughmongers and absentee landlords with advice on the need for
fresh air, physical exercise, temperate habits and rural pursuits and his
recollections of youth's sunshine days.[14] Some of Bewick's engraved
tailpieces might be regarded as visual counterparts to Cobbett's anec-
dotes of his own youth.

In this generation Cobbett, Bewick and Wordsworth (and in the
next, one might add, Clare) belong together in that the democratic
tendencies of their thought and art harmonize with a fundamental
conservatism, and in that their own integrity as men and artists is
closely bound up in a feeling for the land itself. For Cobbett, 'The
order of the world demands that nine-tenths of the people should be
employed on, and in the affairs of *the land*.'[15] This was not a realistic
reckoning when Cobbett made it in 1832, but it was in keeping with
the age-old agricultural philosophy which located all true wealth, all
national prosperity, and all private and public health and virtue upon

the land. A tradition of poets running from Virgil to Wordsworth would have assented to Cobbett's claim, made in 1821:[16]

> if the cultivators of the land be not, generally speaking, the most virtuous and most *happy* of mankind, there must be something at work in the community to counteract the operations of nature. This way of life gives the best security for health and strength of body. It does not *teach*, it necessarily produces *early rising*; constant *forethought*; constant *attention*; and constant *care of dumb animals*. The nature and qualities of all living things are known to country boys better than to philosophers.

Cobbett's understanding and love of the land and the men who worked upon it is perhaps the only continuous, unbroken thread in the strange tangle of his political opinions during forty years of journalism.

Cobbett's views were never adapted to, or shaped by, modern industrialism, yet most of his readers at the height of his influence were members of the nascent working class in the new industrial towns. Despite – or perhaps because of – his industrial readership, Cobbett's effectiveness lay less in his theories about paper-money, electoral reform, or whatever, than in his creation of a mythical but not insubstantial lost Eden of old rural England. Cobbett, like countless generations of georgical writers before him, glorified agricultural labour in its hardihood, innocence and usefulness, and by its associations with patriotism, morality and the beauties of nature. Like Goldsmith, he mourned the destruction of a legendary England of happy husbandmen, but his forms, purposes and experiences are so different from Goldsmith's that the sweet Auburn he creates, whether it is in the Farnham of his own childhood or in the untidy woodlands of Hampshire and Sussex where independent cottagers still lived, is altogether less wistful, more workaday and more substantial than the rural idealizations of any poet. Cobbett exaggerated the material comforts of labourers in old England, but he did not exaggerate the beauty of the man-made (yet natural) landscape where they worked, and the decency of a life regulated by the cycle of the seasons, not that of the steam-engine. Cobbett's readers were mostly in the industrial towns, but many of them had only recently left the land, and it was Cobbett, perhaps more than anyone else, who kept alive in the consciousness of urban workers a folk-memory of rural beauty and seemliness, and, allied with this, a sense of lost rights in the land. The effect of Cobbett's writings was felt in the Chartist Land Colonies of the 1840s, in Ruskin's

St George's Farm in the 1870s, and in many other schemes to recreate a bold, hardy, independent race of husbandmen.

Considered apart from his politics, Cobbett stands alongside such contemporaries of his as Gilbert White, Constable, Bewick, John Crome, William and Dorothy Wordsworth and Clare, as a teacher who taught Englishmen how to see and know their land. He engages the reader in his own delight:[17]

> The custom is in this part of Hertfordshire . . . to leave a *border* round the ploughed part of the fields to bear grass and to make hay from, so that, the grass being now made into hay, every cornfield has a closely mowed grass walk about ten feet wide all round it, between the corn and the hedge. This is most beautiful! The hedges are now full of the shepherd's rose, honeysuckles, and all sorts of wild flowers; so that you are upon a grass walk, with this most beautiful of all flower gardens and shrubberies on your one hand, and with the corn on the other. And thus you go from field to field (on foot or on horseback), the sort of corn, the sort of underwood and timber, the shape and size of the fields, the height of the hedge-rows, the height of the trees, all continually varying. Talk of *pleasure-grounds* indeed! What, that man ever invented, under the name of pleasure-grounds, can equal these fields in Hertfordshire?

In Herefordshire:

> As I came along I saw one of the prettiest sights in the *flower* way that I ever saw in my life. It was a little orchard; the grass in it had just taken a start, and was beautifully fresh; and, very thickly growing amongst the grass, was the purple flowered *Colchicum*, in full bloom. . . . The flower, if standing by itself, would be no great beauty; but, contrasted thus, with the fresh grass, which was a little shorter than itself, it was very beautiful.

Regretting the lack of birdsong in Lincolnshire:

> Oh! the thousands of linnets all singing together on one tree, in the sand-hills of Surrey! Oh! the carolling in the coppices and the dingles of Hampshire and Sussex and Kent! At this moment (5 o'clock in the morning) the groves at Barn-Elm are echoing with the warblings of thousands upon thousands of birds. The *thrush* begins a little before it is light; next the *black-bird*; next the *larks*

begin to rise; all the rest begin the moment the sun gives the
signal; and, from the hedges, the bushes, from the middle and
topmost twigs of the trees, come the singing of endless variety;
from the long dead grass comes the sound of the sweet and soft
voice of the *white-throat*, or *nettle-tom*, while the loud and merry
song of the *lark* (the songster himself out of sight) seems to
descend from the skies.

However blind he might be to new ideas, Cobbett has a corporeal eye
that cannot choose but see, and fortunately his eye is often caught by
some natural or man-made beauty, so that these little, fresh, unpreme-
ditated georgics, and those idyllic 'born and bred in the sweet air'
recollections, are continually springing up out of his polemics like wild
flowers among rocks.

Whether he is gathering together the impressions of a day's rural
riding or whether he is confidently producing what he claims to be a
definitive history of paper-money or Protestantism, Cobbett always
writes rapidly and spontaneously, without reflection or plan. His
advice in his *Grammar* 'on putting sentences together' was:[18]

> Use the first words that occur to you, and never attempt to *alter a
> thought*; for, that which has come of itself into your mind is likely
> to pass into that of another more readily and with more effect than
> anything which you can, by reflection, invent.
>
> Never stop to *make a choice of words*. Put down your thoughts in
> words just as they come. Follow the order which your thought
> will point out; and it will push you on to get it upon the paper as
> quickly and as clearly as possible.

Many ideas – puerile or barbarous, sensible or compassionate – came of
themselves into Cobbett's mind, and if any red herring – or living
shark – should float by as he is writing, his pen will follow it with a
twist and a flicker 'as quick as thought'. So old Nic Grimshaw suddenly
swims into the description of a view from a Wiltshire inn window and
the smock-frocked shepherd's boy who carries a wooden bottle as
Cobbett once did (cf. p. 154 above). Whether the theme is paper-
money or Reform, we are likely to find Cobbett talking, *inter alia*,
about Methodism, the plunder of the East, engrossing, tea, Wilberforce, Shakespeare, pianos in farmers' parlours, standing armies,
Milton, Cobbett's corn, Malthus, sentimental plays, rural depopulation, Swift, gin, the Italian opera, Pope, blue smock-frocks, potatoes,

old English hospitality, the Wen, Sunday schools, thick oak tables, fundholding widows, tree-planting or Quaker corn-factors. Cobbett was unable to follow Johnson's injunction to 'clear your *mind* of cant'. Typically, nearly half of his 4,000-word letter to the editor of the *Agricultural Magazine* in 1815 on the subject of potatoes was devoted to attacking the 'barbarous trash' of *Paradise Lost*, and Shakespeare's bombast, puns and obscenities.[19] Such literary opinions, not to speak of the whole style of his political life, would justify the label 'Philistine' which Arnold attached to him (cf. p. 209 below, note 46), were it not for Cobbett's enlightened view of Swift and Pope – particularly of Pope's often mistakenly judged character – and his feeling for the natural scene, which is quite as sensitive as Arnold's.

Sometimes Cobbett's thoughts push so hard that syntax is forgotten:[20]

> [Puddings] must have been of Saxon or British origin; for we not only do not meet with them in France; but Frenchmen, who, instead of being the most polite, are, when cookery is talked off, the most rude people in the world; and, while sitting within the smell of one of their own kitchens (for not to smell it, you must get out of the house, be it big as it may); while sitting within the smell of one of these, which is a sort of mixture, between fragrance and a stink; and, while I think of it, there is a place of this sort in Cockspur-street, where the kitchen is under the causeway, having some little gratings in the causeway, for the escape of the fumes; I am sure, that, to fifty different persons, or, at least, fifty different times, in walking over those gratings, I have said to some one or more that were with me, 'which of two things that one could name does that smell most like?'

In fairness, we should remember that Cobbett can write more crisply on the topic of food: in *A Year's Residence in the U.S.A.*, for instance, he says, 'you are here disgusted with none of those *eaters* by *reputation* that are found, especially *among the Parsons*, in England; fellows that *unbutton* at it.'

The sentence on (or off) puddings is of unusual length and slackness for Cobbett. His syntax and punctuation usually achieve a more staccato effect, to suggest a finger digging insistently in the ribs of an auditor. This is so in the 'Pray look at hims' when he addresses Brougham on the matter of John Plodpole's education (p. 130 above), or in the sharp, main-verbless phrases that open an attack on Wilberforce for alleged indifference to the lot of English labourers: 'A very large portion of the labourers of England. A very large portion of those who raise all the food, who make all the buildings, who prepare all the fuel, who, in short, by their labour, sustain the community. A very large part of these exist in a state of almost incessant hunger.' Cobbett often writes as if he is making a physical assault upon his enemies. For instance, he declares that he will enjoy dealing with the Edinburgh Reviewers exactly as a poacher 'wires' a rabbit. First, he describes in accurate detail how the poacher makes the wire noose and sets it. Then:[21]

> By and by, in the dark, comes the rabbit dancing along, anticipating the clover, as the Edinburgh Reviewers are now anticipating the sweets of the taxes [when the Whigs win the general election in 1830]; his head goes through the noose, down drops the toiler [the stick holding up the noose], he finds himself entangled, pulls to disentangle himself, the harder he pulls the tighter becomes the noose, he dances and pulls in every direction, and, at last, down he falls, choked by his own efforts, and in the morning you find him with head doubled in size by his fatal efforts, with eyes forced from their sockets, and, if in a corn or grass field, lying on a circular spot, about four feet in diameter, the grass or corn trampled down as smooth as the turnpike-road. Just in this way I will deal with the Edinburgh Reviewers.

It is with the demeanour of a poacher picking up a live rabbit and preparing to knock it on the head that Cobbett begins an open letter: 'Wilberforce, I have you before me in a canting pamphlet. . . .' Cobbett has no intention, with Jack Ketch and Dryden, of making a malefactor die sweetly: 'Swift has told us not to chop *blocks* with *razors*. Any *edge*-tool is too fine for work like this: a pick-axe, that perforates with one end and drags about with the other, is the tool for this sort of business.'[22] Cobbett joyfully welcomed and embraced the charge of 'coarseness' often levelled at him by his enemies. He was always a rough fighter and sometimes a dirty fighter, but, like his idol, Pope, he received knocks as hard as those he gave. Cobbett's habitual disregard for the feelings of others and his frequent unfairness are perhaps less reprehensible than his occasional shabby evasions (for instance, in the libel action of 1820) and his desertions of friends and supporters – though these may, at least, be comprehended as the effects of panic. Cobbett's impetuosity in both advance and retreat made him as much of a danger to his friends as to his enemies, particularly as he had a disconcerting habit of confusing and exchanging these two classes of people.

Whether Cobbett is brutally tearing apart an enemy in print, or shouting down interrupters at a rowdy county meeting, or describing his farm, he projects himself as a rough-and-ready Englishman. Carlyle[23] was not the only admirer who likened him to John Bull; a visitor to Barn-Elm wrote, 'I never saw a finer baron of beef at any nobleman's country hall at Christmas time than I have seen at Cobbett's table, and the old man seemed to have a peculiar pleasure and pride in standing up before it, a large carving-knife and fork in hand, ready to give his friends a prime cut.'[24] Cobbett himself described in a 'Rural Ride' how carefully he chose and bought a sixty-one-pound sirloin in Nottingham market; he boasted that he had bought and roasted more whole sirloins of beef than any man in England, and once confided to his readers. 'I am the weight of a four bushel sack of good wheat.'[25] There must be no doubt that it is *good* wheat. All contemporary reports agree in saying that Cobbett dressed in London and in the country like a gentleman-farmer of the eighteenth century, with knee-breeches, shining top-boots, a grey broadcloth coat and a distinctive scarlet broadcloth waistcoat with the flaps of the pockets hanging down in the old fashion. Cobbett's paternalism, too, was of the old fashion (cf. pp. 64–5, 141, 149 above). When he advertised for ploughboys he announced that none would be hired who did not come in smock-frocks, and for a farm-apprentice he demanded that the boy should be the son of a farmer and have lived all his life on a farm distant from certain named cities and watering-places.[26]

Like other Radical leaders, Cobbett made a great virtue of self-dependence, and elevated his own principles, prejudices and tastes into moral absolutes. Unaffectedly he sees himself as personifying the old rural values, or the ideal family affections, or the spirit of Reform; and so he dramatizes himself as the tiny child clambering over stiles with difficulty, the infantryman in his great, high, coarse, hairy cap, the father writing unruffled amid the noise of children, the journalist-hero in his American tent, the farmer talking with happy labourers at Botley and unhappy ones out on his 'Rides', and in countless other roles. When he plans to write his autobiography, Cobbett sees himself as personifying natural rights:[27]

> my chief object in writing it, or, at least, one of my chief objects, being to assert the natural rights of the working people; to assert

the superiority which nature frequently gives them over birth, title, and wealth. I shall entitle my book 'The Progress of a Plough-boy to a seat in Parliament, as exemplified in the History of the Life of William Cobbett, Member for Oldham'; and, I intend that the frontispiece to the book shall represent me, first in a smock-frock, driving the rooks from the corn; and, in the lower compartment of the picture, standing in the House of Commons, addressing the Speaker.

Cobbett painted himself better than he was, of course; he was sometimes a bully, a liar and a coward, though perhaps not more of a bully, a liar and a coward than most men. Again, his financial mismanagement at times verged upon dishonesty, but in many respects he justified the admiration which he lavished upon himself. He was manly, shrewd, hard-working and naïvely sincere in whatever cause he was, for the moment, embracing, and the enormous self-esteem that enabled him to face and overcome repeated misfortunes was surely itself a kind of rectitude. Cobbett's unashamed egotism and constant aggressiveness are those of the ambitious, self-made man who is obstinate, wilful and perhaps at bottom insecure. A man who feels so eagerly that he has his own way to make in the world will rarely act generously to others.

Cobbett's egotism is not unlike that of Rousseau, whose notions of education he admired so much. Cobbett, too, makes his own private and personal life the measure of all value, and asserts his selfhood against the present ills of society. In his eyes the whole operation of the 'System' and much of the legislation brought in by nine Prime Ministers were attacks upon him personally; Rousseau also believed he was persecuted by highly placed enemies. Like Rousseau's, Cobbett's

life was one long war with self-sought foes,
Or friends by him self-banish'd;[28]

and in the cases of both men these friends included benefactors. Cobbett played to the gallery, and if Irving Babbitt was correct when he called Rousseau 'the father of yellow journalists',[29] then Cobbett was the eldest son. What F. J. C. Hearnshaw wrote of Rousseau might with more truth be said of Cobbett: 'He was an unsystematic thinker, untrained in formal logic. He was an omnivorous reader with undeveloped powers of assimilation. He was an emotional enthusiast who spoke without due reflection.'[30] Cobbett was highly opinionated and often changed his opinions, so that, like Rousseau's, his writings taken in bulk betray many self-contradictions. Of course, the differences between the two men are quite as significant as the similarities. Cobbett resembled Rousseau as little in the range, power and originality of the Frenchman's thinking as he did in the indiscipline and undutifulness of his private life. Rousseau fulfilled the duties of a father less satisfactorily than did Cobbett, but both men held firmly to a vision of childhood that might sustain and shape the adult. In both, nostalgic reverie was, paradoxically, an active power to drive them forward. Cobbett's nostalgia gave him understanding and faith at the same time as it shaped his views on the future, so that his golden age was at once retrospective and prospective.

Cobbett's recollections of oaken tables, bacon, roast beef, plumpudding, pewter plates, sports and holidays in the 1770s may have helped to form his political blueprints for the 1830s, but the power and urgency of his writing about his own childhood suggests that retrospection mattered most to him because it satisfied emotional needs. With Hazlitt he agreed that the past is a 'real and substantial part of our being', and 'it is the past that gives me most delight and most assurance of reality'.[31] The child that Cobbett was is always vividly before him, perhaps trudging afield on his little legs with his bag of bread and cheese and wooden bottle of small beer swung over his shoulders on a little crook, or sitting in his blue smock-frock under a haystack at Kew reading *A Tale of a Tub* and experiencing the birth of intellect. When one of his own sons is present, too, the feeling runs strongest of all, because the continuity of affectionate memory is projected forward into urgent and loving hopes. In those little respective idylls in *Rural Rides*, and especially in *Advice to Young Men* (e.g. pp. 155–6, 163 above), Cobbett conveys a sense of personal wholeness within a landscape of memory and expectation that is not dissimilar in effect to Coleridge's lovely *Frost at Midnight*. Memory illuminates past, present and future, and strengthens self-awareness. When Cobbett shows one son the sandhill where he received the education that made him the man he is, or tells another how he 'stood to' his story about the cat, he asserts the continuity of his own personality. Like Rousseau – as Hazlitt described – he had 'the most intense consciousness of his own existence',[32] and time and again his retrospection gives body to Wordsworth's aphorism that the child is father of the man. As he hopes that his sons will enjoy what he once enjoyed when he saw the primroses and bluebells by Waverley Abbey, or heard the linnets' song and the ploughboy's whistle and the jingling traces, or was caught up in the excitement of the hunt, Cobbett recreates the emotion of that far-off childhood moment. The power, vigour and beauty of Cobbett's best work, like Wordsworth's, arise from recollected emotion.

Cobbett may find a permanent place in political histories as a champion of the freedom of the Press, and his forthright expression of certain opinions may still be of service to interested groups – Guild Socialists, Roman Catholics, or whoever – but most people who read Cobbett today will read him in *Rural Rides* and *Advice to Young Men*, and will read him as a sensuous egotist who never forgot that his first knowledge grew out of the visible world, who continued to wind his own being around all that he met, and who continually looked over the map of his own existence to suffuse it with 'The spirit of pleasure and youth's golden gleam'.[33]

Notes

Chapter 1 Merry England?

1 King's and Colquhoun's population estimates are edited, with commentary, in Dorothy George, *England in Transition* (1931, revised 1953), and Harold Perkin, *The Origins of Modern English Society, 1780–1880* (1969); Massie's estimate is in Peter Mathias, 'The Social Structure in the Eighteenth Century', *Economic History Review*, series 2, X (1957–8), pp. 30–45.

2 Walter Harte, *Essays on Husbandry* (1764), p. 205.

3 *The Origins of Modern English Society, 1780–1880*, p. 23.

4 Arthur Young, *The Farmer's Letters to the People of England* (1767), pp. 263, 279.

5 Quoted in *The Origins of Modern English Society, 1780–1880*, p. 22.

6 *Annual Register for 1766*, pp. 138–9.

7 *Letters on a Regicide Peace* (1796), Letter I, in *Works* (Bohn's Standard Library), vol. V, p. 199.

8 *The Example of France . . . a Warning to Britain* (1794), p. 106.

9 *The Wealth of Nations* (5th edn, 1789), Book I, chap. xi, 'Conclusion'.

10 *Ibid.*

11 William Blackstone, *Commentaries on the Laws of England* (2nd edn, 1766–9), Book I, chap. i.

12 Henry St John, Viscount Bolingbroke, *Remarks on the History of England* (1730), Letter VII, in *Works* (1777), vol. I, p. 338.

13 Letter to Pope, 10 January 1721, in *Correspondence of Alexander Pope*, ed. G. Sherburn (1956), vol. II, p. 70.

14 Lewis Namier, *The Structure of Politics at the Accession of George III* (1929, rev. 1957). See also: Namier, *England in the Age of the American Revolution* (1930, rev. 1961); John Brooke, *The Chatham Administration, 1766–1768* (1956); J. B. Owen, *The Rise of the Pelhams* (1957).

15 Quoted in J. B. Owen, 'The Survival of Country Attitudes in the Eighteenth-Century House of Commons', in *Britain and the Netherlands*, vol. IV, ed. J. S. Bromley and E. H. Kossman (1971), pp. 68–9.

16 *Gentleman's Magazine* (January 1768), 17.

17 *Political Register*, II (March, April 1768), 218–43.
18 *Parliamentary History* (1806–20), vol. XVIII, pp. 1288–98.
19 John Cartwright, *The Legislative Rights of the Commonalty Vindicated; or Take Your Choice* (1776).
20 *Works* (1787), vol. X, pp. 25–7.
21 *Prose Works*, ed. H. Davis, vol. III (1940), pp. 6–7; cf. Defoe, *The Villainy of Stock-Jobbers Detected* (1701). The best modern account of public finance in the years before Cobbett's birth is P. G. M. Dickson, *The Financial Revolution in England* (1967), which records and accounts for eighteenth-century prejudice against the moneyed interest as well as giving the fullest and fairest description of the development of public credit in the period 1688–1756.
22 *Cato's Letters* (1724), vol. IV, pp. 297–8.
23 *Correspondence of Alexander Pope*, vol. II, p. 70.
24 *Art of Governing* (1701), pp. 165–6.
25 *Political Register*, II (January 1768), 42.
26 Letter of 19 December 1767, in *Letters of Lord Chesterfield*, ed. B. Dobrée (1932), vol. VI, p. 2832.
27 *Correspondence of the Earl of Chatham*, eds. W. S. Taylor and J. H. Pringle (1838–40), vol. III, p. 405.
28 'Some Thoughts on Agriculture, both Ancient and Modern; with an account of the Honour due to an English Farmer', and 'Further Thoughts on Agriculture', in *The Universal Visitor*, February and March 1756; repr. in *Works*, vol. X, pp. 299–312.
29 *Works*, vol. X, p. 303.
30 *Essay on the Principle of Population* (new edn, 1803), pp. 437–8.
31 *Tatler*, 31, 37, 96, 202.
32 C. Chenevix Trench, *The Poacher and the Squire* (1967), p. 117.
33 *Harcourt Papers*, ed. E. W. Harcourt (1880–1905), vol. III, p. 101.
34 L. C. Knights, *Drama and Society in the Age of Jonson* (1937), *passim*.
35 *Torrington Diaries*, ed. C. B. Andrews (1934), vol. II, p. 238.
36 *Annals of Agriculture*, vol. II (1784), pp. 381–2.
37 *Enquiry into Reasons for and against Enclosure of Open Fields* (1767), p. 22.
38 *Harcourt Papers*, vol. III, p. 135.
39 *Enquiry into the Causes of the Present High Price of Provisions* (1767), pp. 112, 115.
40 Chapter iii. A Gillray cartoon featuring the farmer's harpsichord is reproduced in Dorothy George, *England in Transition*, plate 9.
41 G. E. Mingay, 'The Size of Farms in the Eighteenth Century', *Economic History Review*, series 2, XIV (1961–2), 469–88.
42 *Hints to Gentlemen of Landed Property* (1775), pp. 230–1.
43 *The Farmer's Letters to the People of England* (1767), pp. 353–4.
44 Joyce Godber, *History of Bedfordshire* (1969), p. 365. There is general information on the eighteenth-century agricultural labourer's diet in J. C. Drum-

mond and Anne Wilbraham, *The Englishman's Food*, revised Dorothy Hollingsworth (1957), pp. 206–10; and G. E. Fussell, *The English Rural Labourer* (1949), pp. 82–91.

45 *Arthur Young's Tour in Ireland* (1776–1779), ed. A. W. Hutton (1892), vol. II, p. 45.

46 *A Plan of the English Commerce* (1728), pp. 91–2.

47 *Letters on the English Nation* (1755), vol. I, 102–3.

48 Quoted in Paul Mantoux, *The Industrial Revolution*, revised T. S. Ashton (1964), p. 433.

49 *Thoughts and Details on Scarcity* (1795); quoted in A. Cobban, *The Debate on the French Revolution* (1950), pp. 409–10.

50 Edward Chamberlayne, *Anglia Notitia, or the Present State of England* (1755).

51 G. E. Mingay, *English Landed Society in the Eighteenth Century* (1963), p. 250; E. W. Martin, *The Secret People* (1954), p. 65. Addison described a grinning match in *Spectator* 173.

52 Quoted in E. L. Jones, *Seasons and Prices* (1964), p. 78.

53 *The Wealth of Nations* (5th edn, 1789), Book I, chap. x, part ii.

54 *Travels through France and Italy* (1766), letter xxxvi, 23 March 1765.

55 *A Six Months Tour through the North of England* (2nd edn, 1771), vol. IV, p. 420.

56 *Travels in France during the years 1787, 1788 and 1789*, ed. C. Maxwell (1929), p. 279.

57 Mons. L'Abbé Le Blanc, *Letters on the English and French Nations* (1747), vol. I, p. 177.

58 Pehr Kalm, *Visit to England*, transl. J. Lucas (1892), pp. 326, 208.

Chapter 2   Ploughboy, Soldier and 'Peter Porcupine': 1763–1800

1 *Tour through the Whole Island of Great Britain*, ed. G. D. H. Cole (1927), vol. I, p. 142.

2 *Journal of Gilbert White*, 10 September 1770.

3 *Rural Rides*, eds G. D. H. Cole and M. Cole (1930), vol. III, p. 740.

4 *Torrington Diaries*, ed. C. B. Andrews (1934), vol. I, p. 76.

5 *The English Gardener* (1833), para. 15.

6 *Torrington Diaries*, vol. I, p. 77.

7 *Six Weeks Tour through the Southern Counties of England and Wales* (2nd edn, 1769), pp. 216–19.

8 J. Malcolm, *et al.*, *General View of the Agriculture of Surrey* (1794).

9 *Rural Rides*, eds G. D. H. Cole and M. Cole, vol. II, p. 638.

10 *Natural History of Selborne* (1789), letters vii and ix.

11 W. Gilpin, *Observations on the Western Parts of England* (1798), p. 39.

12 *Natural History of Selborne*, letter v.

13 *Six Weeks Tour through the Southern Counties of England*, p. 218. On the

cultivation of hops at Farnham see also: R. Bradley, *The Riches of a Hop-Garden Displayed* (1729), pp. 11–12; W. Marshall, *Rural Economy of the Southern Counties* (1791), p. 47.

14 *A Year's Residence in the United States* (1818), para. 8.

15 *Life and Adventures of Peter Porcupine*, in *Porcupine's Works* (1801), vol. IV, pp. 31–3.

16 *Ibid.*, p. 34.

17 *Political Register*, 19 February 1820, 23–4.

18 Unpublished 'Memoir of William Cobbett' by J. P. Cobbett (Nuffield College Library).

19 *Porcupine's Works*, vol. IV, pp. 37–40.

20 *Ibid.*, pp. 40–3.

21 *Treatise on Cobbett's Corn* (1828), para. 159.

22 *Advice to Young Men* (1829–30), para. 44.

23 *Political Register*, 17 June 1809, 901.

24 *Advice to Young Men*, para. 39.

25 *Political Register*, 17 June 1809, 901.

26 *Advice to Young Men*, paras 95–6.

27 *Political Register*, 23 June 1832, 758.

28 *Porcupine's Works*, vol. I, pp. 153, 219. The second passage refers to Priestley's notable discovery of oxygen, but Priestley was known to have experimented lengthily on 'vitriolic acid air' or sulphur dioxide, while his first chemical publication had described a method of making 'mephitic julep' or soda-water.

29 *Ibid.*, vol. I, pp. 216–17.

30 *Ibid.*, vol. XII, p. 109.

31 *Ibid.*, vol. I, p. 97.

32 *Ibid.*, vol. II, pp. 8–9.

33 *Ibid.*, vol. IV, p. 114.

Chapter 3   A One-man Country Party: 1800–10

1 *The Porcupine*, 10 November 1800.

2 *Collection of Facts and Observations relative to the Peace with Bonaparte* (1801), p. 76.

3 *Political Register*, 30 July 1803, 141.

4 *Ibid.*, 30 June 1802, 796.

5 *Ibid.*, 17 July 1802, 56.

6 *Ibid.*, 18 February 1804, 254.

7 *Ibid.*, 1 September 1804, 298.

8 *Ibid.*, 20 April 1805, 597.

9 *Ibid.*, 6 December 1806, 872.

10 *Ibid.*, 22 February 1812, 242. By 'formerly', Cobbett does not mean the

seventeenth century, but the period in the 1780s just before Pitt was able to take office.

11 William Reitzel, *Autobiography of William Cobbett* (1967), p. 258; Edward Smith, *William Cobbett* (1878), vol. II, p. 2.
12 Cobbett to Lieutenant F. Reid, 22 May 1810 (Nuffield College Library).
13 Cobbett's Farm Accounts (Nuffield College Library).
14 *Political Register*, 27 February 1802, 176.
15 *The Windham Papers* (1913), vol. II, pp. 233–4.
16 *Political Register*, 10 August 1804, 173.
17 Charles Vancouver, *General View of the Agriculture of Hampshire* (1810), pp. 306–7.
18 R. S. Surtees, *Hawbuck Grange* (1847), chap. xii.
19 *Political Register*, 31 July 1813.
20 *Ibid.*, 26 May 1821, 518–21.
21 *Ibid.*, 2 October 1830, 421.
22 *Ibid.*, 15 March 1806, 361–2.
23 *Ibid.*, 364.
24 *Ibid.*, 29 July 1809, 116.
25 *Windham Papers*, vol. II, p. 238. When the Cobbetts went to Botley they had three sons, aged six, four and one year old, and a nine-year-old daughter; three more living children were born there – two girls and a boy.
26 *The Woodlands* (1825), Preface.
27 *Political Register*, 28 February 1807, 325.
28 *Ibid.*, 11 February 1804, 181.
29 *Ibid.*, 7, 21, 28 November 1807; 5, 12 December 1807; 16 April 1808.
30 *Ibid.*, 1 September 1810, 258.
31 *Ibid.*, 3 August 1811, 131.
32 *Ibid.*, 21 April 1810, 599.
33 *Ibid.*, 28 June 1806, 972.
34 *Ibid.*, 21 April 1810, 600.
35 *Ibid.*, 4 February 1809, 190.
36 *Edinburgh Review*, X (July 1807), 386–7.
37 *Political Register*, 4 February 1809, 183.
38 *Ibid.*, 10 September 1808, 400.
39 *Advice to Young Men*, paras 311, 313; *A Year's Residence in the United States*, paras 354–5.
40 *Political Register*, 4 February 1809, 185, 189.

Chapter 4   The Botley Demagogue: 1810–17

1 *Political Register*, 10, 17, 24, 31 October 1812, 449, 481, 513–25, 545–53.
2 *Ibid.*, 4 July 1812, 6.
3 *Ibid.*, 8 June 1816, 720–1.
4 *Ibid.*, 25 March 1815, 354.

5 *Ibid.*, 21, 28 May; 4 June; 22 October 1804; 28 January 1815.
6 *Ibid.*, 16 December 1815, 330; cf. p. 20 above.
7 *Ibid.*, 24 September 1803, 434.
8 *Ibid.*, 11 January 1812, 58–9.
9 *Ibid.*, 8 June 1816, 712.
10 *Ibid.*, 20 June 1818, 721–4; 9 May 1818, 509.
11 *De Laudibus Legem Angliae*, English transl. (1775), p. 129. Cobbett quotes this passage at length in *History of the Protestant 'Reformation'* (1824), paras 457–9, and often, in part, elsewhere in his writings.
12 *Political Register*, 2 August 1817, 557.
13 *Ibid.*, 27 February 1817, 234–5.
14 *Ibid.*, 3 October 1818, 206.
15 *Ibid.*, 2 August 1817, 529.
16 *Ibid.*, 16 November 1816, 611–12.
17 Quoted in A. Aspinall, *Politics and the Press, c. 1780–1850* (1949), p. 31, n. 2.
18 Quoted in R. K. Webb, *The British Working Class Reader, 1790–1848* (1955), p. 50.
19 *Political Register*, 2 August 1817.
20 Samuel Bamford, *Passages in the Life of a Radical* (1859), pp. 6–7.
21 *Table Talk* (1821), in *Complete Works*, ed. P. P. Howe (1930), vol. VIII, p. 50.
22 *Political Register*, 15 February 1817.
23 R. J. White, *Waterloo to Peterloo* (1957), p. 135.
24 *Political Register*, 8 March 1817, 309.
25 *Politics and the Press, c. 1780–1850*, p. 51.
26 *Ibid.*, p. 43.
27 Lord Holland, *Further Memoirs of the Whig Party, 1807–1821* (1905), pp. 253–4.
28 *Political Register*, 12 July 1817, 462–3.
29 *Political Register*, 4 October 1817, 804–5.
30 *Quarterly Review*, XXI (January 1819), 135.
31 *The Republican* (1826), p. 604.
32 *Political Register*, 12 July 1817, 480.

Chapter 5   American Farmer and English Grammarian: 1817–19

1 *Political Register*, 12 July 1817, 467.
2 William Reitzel, *Autobiography of William Cobbett* (1967), p. 262.
3 *A Year's Residence in the U.S.A.* (1818), para. 18.
4 *Political Register*, 26 July 1817, 517–18.
5 The Rising is described in R. J. White, *Waterloo to Peterloo* (1957), chap. XIV.
6 *Political Register*, 23 May 1818, 589; 26 December 1818, 605.
7 E. P. Thompson, *The Making of the English Working Class* (1963), p. 626.

8 *Letters of Percy Bysshe Shelley*, ed. F. L. Jones (1964), vol. II, p. 94.

9 T. L. Peacock, *Nightmare Abbey* (1818), chap. x.

10 Journal for 28 July 1817; 1, 17 August 1817; in *A Year's Residence in the U.S.A.*, para. 20.

11 *A Year's Residence in the U.S.A.*, paras 3–10. Cobbett was, in fact, aged fifty-five when he wrote this.

12 *Journals of Gilbert White*, ed. Walter Johnson (1931), p. 168.

13 E.g. *The Woodlands* (1825–9); *A Treatise on Cobbett's Corn* (1828).

14 Journal for 16 February 1818 in *A Year's Residence in the U.S.A.*, para. 20.

15 *A Year's Residence in the U.S.A.*, paras 349–53.

16 *Political Register*, 6 December 1817, 1089–90.

17 *Grammar of the English Language* (1818), para. 3.

18 *Ibid.*, paras 119, 127.

19 *Ibid.*, para. 173.

20 *Political Register*, 10 January 1807, 36.

21 *Ibid.*, 23 February 1811, 450–2. Cf. 14 November 1807, 750–1; 17 June 1809, 911; 7 March 1812, 299.

22 *Grammar of the English Language*, paras 240–6.

23 *Political Register*, 21 November 1818, 403.

24 The emergence of this class is the subject of E. P. Thompson, *The Making of the English Working Class* (1963).

25 *Essay on the Principle of Population* (new edn, 1803), pp. 531, 538. (Malthus omitted the 'table of nature' image from later editions of the *Essay*.)

26 E.g. *Political Register*, 16 February 1805, 230–1; 18 January 1806, 89.

27 *Complete Works*, ed. P. P. Howe (1930), vol. I, pp. 179–206.

28 *Political Register*, 8 May 1819, 983.

29 *Ibid.*, 9 April 1831, 79.

30 *Ibid.*, 29 August 1818, 221.

31 *Letters of Percy Bysshe Shelley*, ed. F. L. Jones (1964), vol. II, p. 70; see also vol. II, pp. 99, 177, 212–13.

32 *Political Register*, 4 September 1819, 80.

33 *Ibid.*, 17 February 1821, 469.

34 *Ibid.*, 22 June 1822, 728–9.

35 *Ibid.*, 13 November 1819, 364.

36 *Ibid.*, 17 February 1821, 434–5.

37 *Letters and Journals*, ed. R. E. Prothero (1904), vol. IV, p. 395.

38 *Political Register*, 24 December 1819, 503.

Chapter 6   Candidate, Courtier, Preacher, Teacher and Historian: 1819–29

1 A. Aspinall, *Politics and the Press, c. 1780–1850* (1949), p. 58.

2 *Political Register*, 6 November 1819; 5 December 1819; 6 January 1820; 6, 25 February 1820.

3 *Examiner*, 622 (12 March 1820), 162.

4 Susan Cobbett's notes (Nuffield College Library).

5 *Political Register*, 28 November 1818; 5, 26 December 1818; 6 March 1819.

6 *Henry Crabb Robinson on Books and their Writers*, ed. E. J. Morley (1938), vol. I, pp. 258–9.

7 Letter to Samuel Clarke, 30 April 1821 (Nuffield College Library).

8 *Common Places* (September–December 1823) in *Complete Works*, ed. P. P. Howe (1930), vol. XX, pp. 136–7.

9 *Selections from Cobbett's Political Works*, ed. J. M. and J. P. Cobbett (1835–7), vol. VI, p. 38.

10 *Rural Rides*, eds G. D. H. Cole and M. Cole (1930), vol. I, pp. 1–2.

11 *Ibid.*, vol. I, pp. 9, 61, 16, 61, 68, 10, 3, 33, 24.

12 *Ibid.*, vol. I, pp. 13–14.

13 *Ibid.*, vol. I, p. 37.

14 *Political Register*, 24 February 1821, 568.

15 *Ibid.*, 22 March 1822, 748.

16 William Wilberforce, *A Practical View of the Prevailing Religious System of Professed Christians* (1797), pp. 405–6.

17 *Cobbett's Sermons* (1822), p. 30.

18 *Ibid.*, pp. 287–9. Strictly speaking this is not the last Sermon, for in 1830 Cobbett brought the series up to the Judas-number of thirteen with a violently anti-Semitic *Sermon* under the title 'Good Friday; or, the Murder of Jesus Christ by the Jews'.

19 *Rural Rides*, ed. G. Woodcock (1967), p. 387.

20 *Cottage Economy* (1822), para. 8.

21 *Political Register*, 31 May 1823, 502.

22 *Collected Letters of Thomas and Jane Welsh Carlyle*, eds C. R. Sanders and K. J. Fielding (1970), vol. IV, p. 286.

23 *List of Mr. Cobbett's Books* (c. 1835).

24 *Political Register*, 5 February 1825, 348–9.

25 *Ibid.*, 7 April 1821, 11–12.

26 *Ibid.*, 28 April 1821, 245–6.

27 *Ibid.*, 14 August 1819, 8.

28 *Ibid.*, 16 October 1824, 132.

29 *Ibid.*, 2 October 1830, 488.

30 *Ibid.*, 26 May 1821, 506, 513.

31 *Annual Register for 1823*, 'History', p. 2.

32 *Political Register*, 20 October 1821, 905.

33 *Ibid.*, 24 May 1823, 477–8.

34 *Ibid.*, 14 July 1822, 654.

35 *Ibid.*, 23 January 1819, 549–61; cf. *Cobbett's Sermons* (1822), Sermon XII.

36 *Political Register*, 29 December 1804, 1061–2.

37 *Cobbett's Sermons* (1822), 16; *Political Register*, 18 April, 1 August 1807; 24 December 1808; 12 October 1811.

38 *History of the Protestant 'Reformation'* (1824–6), para. 6.
39 See Maurice Beresford, *The Lost Villages of England* (1954).
40 *History of the Protestant 'Reformation': Part Second* (1827), para. 15.
41 *History of the Protestant 'Reformation'* (1824–6), para. 155.
42 *Ibid.*, para. 124.
43 *Ibid.*, para. 184.
44 J. W. Osborne, *William Cobbett, his Thought and his Times* (1964), 216–17 (note).
45 Cobbett's other three-act comedies in the *Political Register* were 'Mexico, or the Patriot Bondholders' (1830) and 'Surplus Population, and Poor Law Bill' (1831, and separately printed 1835), but into his articles he often introduced little dialogues between the ministers of the day, between himself and his servants or friends, and between imaginary characters such as Giles Jolterhead the squire, Farmer Grub and Discount the moneylender (e.g. *Political Register*, 24 November 1814; 11 November 1815; 15 April 1820; 31 March 1821).
46 Quoted in Matthew Arnold, 'Heinrich Heine', *Cornhill*, VIII (1863), 237–8, where Arnold defines 'Philistine' with specific reference to Cobbett.
47 *Political Register*, 8 July 1826, 110.
48 *Ibid.*, 12 August 1826, 394.
49 *Ibid.*, 20 October 1827, 397.
50 *Treatise on Cobbett's Corn* (1828), para. 155.
51 *Political Register*, 16 October 1824, 143–4.

Chapter 7   *Rural Rides* and *Advice to Young Men*: 1830

1 The 1830 edition is conveniently reprinted by Penguin Books Ltd, ed. George Woodcock (1967). Some 'Rides' omitted from the 1830 edition are included in *Rural Rides*, ed. J. P. Cobbett (1853, reprinted by Everyman's Library, 1912 and in other modern editions); more were included in *Rural Rides*, eds G. H. D. Cole and M. Cole (1930).
2 *Rural Rides*, ed. G. Woodcock (1967), pp. 121–4.
3 *Ibid.*, pp. 321–2.
4 *Ibid.*, p. 42.
5 *Ibid.*, p. 176.
6 *Ibid.*, p. 363.
7 *Ibid.*, pp. 67, 339, 401.
8 *Ibid.*, pp. 402, 327, 436.
9 *Ibid.*, pp. 179, 187–8, 181, 186.
10 *Ibid.*, 324, 369.
11 *Ibid.*, p. 436.
12 *Ibid.*, pp. 227–8, 345.
13 *Ibid.*, p. 206.

14 *Ibid.*, pp. 348, 388, 384, 176.
15 *Ibid.*, p. 320.
16 *Ibid.*, pp. 207, 426–35 (cf. *Political Register*, 6 April 1822, 2–3; 29 March 1823, p. 796.)
17 *Ibid.*, pp. 140–1.
18 *Ibid.*, pp. 334–5, 126.
19 *Ibid.*, pp. 156, 304, 43, 438–9.
20 *Ibid.*, pp. 155–6.
21 *Ibid.*, p. 294.
22 *Ibid.*, pp. 40–1.
23 *Ibid.*, 249–50.
24 *Advice to Young Men* (1829–30), para. 326.
25 *Ibid.*, paras 18, 56, 19, 313.
26 *Ibid.*, paras 311–12.
27 *Ibid.*, paras 332–6.
28 *Ibid.*, paras 251–2.
29 *Ibid.*, paras 215–17, 161, 258.
30 *Ibid.*, paras 233, 221.
31 *Strictures on the Modern System of Female Education* (1799), p. 44.
32 Robert Southey, *Life of Wesley* (1890), p. 561.
33 *Advice to Young Men*, paras 281–2.
34 *Ibid.*, paras 286, 283, 291.
35 *Ibid.*, para. 288.
36 *Ibid.*, paras 141–51.

Chapter 8   The Anti-climax of Reform: 1830–35

1 *Political Register*, 30 November 1816, 562–92; *Rural Rides*, ed. G. Woodcock (1967), pp. 317–19; *Political Register*, 20 November 1824, 451–4; 10 July 1824, 110.
2 *Rural Rides*, eds G. D. H. Cole and M. Cole (1930), vol. II, 598.
3 *Political Register*, 27 August 1831, 567–8.
4 *Rural Rides*, eds G. D. H. Cole and M. Cole, vol. II, pp. 607–8.
5 *Political Register*, 9 January 1830.
6 *Ibid.*, 3 July 1830, 6; 17 July 1830, 66.
7 *Lectures on the French and Belgian Revolutions* (1830), lecture I, p. 1.
8 *Twopenny Trash*, 1 September 1830, 65.
9 *Political Register*, 30 October 1830, 545–72.
10 *Ibid.*, 4 December 1830, 871–2.
11 They are described in E. J. Hobsbawm and George Rudé, *Captain Swing* (1968).
12 *Twopenny Trash*, 27 November 1830, 810.
13 *Political Register*, 5 June 1830, 740.

14 Quoted in Edward Smith, *William Cobbett* (1878), vol. II, p. 302.
15 *Political Register*, 19 May 1832, 331.
16 *Ibid.*, 16 June 1832, 652–4.
17 *Ibid.*, 17 December 1831, 754.
18 *Ibid.*, 12, 19 February 1831; 12 March 1831.
19 *Ibid.*, 7 May 1831, 301.
20 George Gilfillan, *Galleries of Literary Portraits* (1856), vol. II, p. 29.
21 *Political Register*, 10 January 1824, 67; 22 December 1827, 774.
22 *Fraser's Magazine* (February 1862), 178.
23 E. L. Bulwer, *England and the English* (1833), p. 92.
24 *Political Register*, 20 July 1833, 180; 14 December 1833, 642.
25 *Ibid.*, 7 December 1833, 624.
26 *Ibid.*, 21 April 1832, 143.
27 *Rural Rides*, eds G. D. H. Cole and M. Cole (1930), vol. III, p. 761.
28 *Hansard's Parliamentary Debates*, series 3, XXIV, 929, 1050–2.
29 *Rural Rides*, eds G. D. H. Cole and M. Cole (1930), vol. III, p. 903.
30 *Ibid.*, vol. III, pp. 898–9.
31 Nuffield College Library.
32 *Political Register*, 18 April 1835, 146.

Chapter 9   Epilogue

1 *Rural Rides*, ed. G. Woodcock (1967), pp. 8–9.
2 *Porcupine's Works* (1801), vol. IV, p. 35.
3 *Treatise on Cobbett's Corn* (1828), para. 160.
4 *Political Register*, 23 June 1832, 754. See also: *Cottage Economy* (1821), para. 6.
5 *The Spirit of the Age* (1825), in *Complete Works*, ed. P. P. Howe (1930), vol. XI, p. 16.
6 *Lord Byron's Correspondence*, ed. John Murray (1922), vol. II, p. 143.
7 Letter to T. L. Peacock, 6 April 1819, in *Letters of Percy Bysshe Shelley*, ed. F. L. Jones (1964), vol. II, p. 94.
8 Geoffrey Carnall, *Robert Southey and his Age* (1960), p. 90; *The Poems of William Blake*, ed. W. H. Stevenson (1971), p. 611.
9 *Sir Thomas More: or Colloquies on the Progress and Prospects of Society* (1829), vol. II, pp. 255–6.
10 *Collected Letters of Samuel Taylor Coleridge*, ed. E. L. Griggs, vol. I (1956), p. 275.
11 *Letters of William and Dorothy Wordsworth*, ed. E. de Selincourt, revised C. L. Shaver (1967), pp. 314–15.
12 *Prose Works of William Wordsworth*, ed. W. Knight (1896), vol. I, p. 145.
13 *Complete Works*, ed. P. P. Howe (1930), vol. VIII, p. 54.

14 *Memoir of Thomas Bewick written by himself*, introduction by Edmund Blunden (1961). See e.g. pp. 152–5, 170, 173, 182–8.
15 *Rural Rides*, eds G. D. H. Cole and M. Cole (1930), vol. III, p. 841.
16 *Political Register*, 17 March 1821, 731.
17 *Rural Rides*, eds G. D. H. Cole and M. Cole, vol. I, p. 80; vol. II, pp. 426, 642–3.
18 *Grammar of the English Language* (1823), p. 180.
19 *A Year's Residence in the U.S.A.* (1818), paras 269–84.
20 *Treatise on Cobbett's Corn* (1828), para. 159.
21 *Political Register*, 18 September 1830, p. 355.
22 *Ibid.*, 24 May 1828, 670.
23 Thomas Carlyle, *Critical and Miscellaneous Essays* (1899), vol. IV, 39–40; E. L. Bulwer, *England and the English* (1833), p. 93; George Gilfillan, *Galleries of Literary Portraits* (1856), II, 32.
24 *Fraser's Magazine*, February 1862, 177.
25 *Rural Rides*, eds G. D. H. and M. Cole (1930), vol. II, p. 617, 399; vol. I, 28.
26 *Political Register*, 18 October 1828, 509.
27 *Ibid.*, 15 February 1834, 409.
28 Lord Byron, *Childe Harold's Pilgrimage*, canto iii, stanza 80.
29 Irving Babbitt, *Rousseau and Romanticism* (1919), p. 63.
30 *The Social and Political Ideas of some Great French Thinkers of the Age of Reason*, ed. F. J. C. Hearnshaw (1930), pp. 185–6.
31 *Complete Works*, ed. P. P. Howe (1930), vol. VIII, pp. 22, 24.
32 *Ibid.*, vol. VIII, p. 92.
33 William Wordsworth, *The Prelude* (1805), XI, 323.

Bibliography

Cobbett's Writings

The Soldier's Friend, 1792. Probably by Cobbett, see pp. 43–5 above.
Observations on the Emigration of Dr. Joseph Priestley, 1794.
Le Tuteur Anglais, 1795.
A Prospect from the Congress Gallery, continued as *The Political Censor*, 1796–7. Monthly reports of and commentaries upon debates in the American Congress.
The Life and Adventures of Peter Porcupine, 1796. Reprinted with introduction and notes by G. D. H. Cole, London, 1927.
Porcupine's Gazette, 4 March 1797 – 26 October 1799. A daily, and latterly a weekly, newspaper.
Porcupine's Works, 12 vols, 1801. Between 1794 and 1800 Cobbett wrote, edited or translated some forty anti-French or anti-Democrat pamphlets, most of which were reprinted here.
The Porcupine, 30 October 1800 – 31 December 1801. Daily periodical.
A Collection of Facts and Observations relative to the Peace with Buonaparte, 1801.
Letters on the Peace with Buonaparte, 1802.
Cobbett's Political Register, 1802–35. This fortnightly, weekly or twice-weekly periodical also appeared under the titles *Cobbett's Annual Register*, *Cobbett's Weekly Register* and *Cobbett's Weekly Political Register*. There was a French translation as *Le Mercure Anglois*, February–May 1803. Cheap reprints of *Political Register* articles appeared as:
Cobbett's Weekly Political Pamphlet, 2 November 1816 – 6 January 1820; and as
Cobbett's Two-penny Trash, or Politics for the Poor, July 1830–July 1832. Monthly.
Modern selections from the *Political Register* are:
A History of the Last Hundred Days of English Freedom, edited with an introduction by J. L. Hammond, London, 1921; and

The Opinions of William Cobbett, edited with an introduction by G. D. H. and M. Cole, London, 1944.

Over fifty of Cobbett's books and pamphlets between 1803 and 1835 were reprints of articles in the *Political Register,* but only the most important are listed separately in their chronological places below.

Important Considerations for the People of this Kingdom, 1803. Reprinted from the *Political Register.*

Cobbett's Parliamentary Debates, 27 vols, 1804–14. A compilation still in progress as *Hansard.*

Cobbett's Parliamentary History from 1066 to 1803, 36 vols, 1806–20. A compilation.

Cobbett's Complete Collection of State Trials, 33 vols, 1809–26. Cobbett was the initiator, but no more than nominal editor, of this work and of the two preceding ones. He lost control over all three in 1812.

Paper against Gold, 1815. Reprinted from the *Political Register,* 1810–15.

Cobbett's American Political Register, January–June 1816; May 1817–January 1818. Weekly periodical.

A Year's Residence in the United States of America, 1818. Reprinted with an introduction by J. E. Morpurgo, Arundel, 1964.

A Grammar of the English Language, 1818. Reprinted with an introduction by H. L. Stephen, London, 1906.

Cobbett's Evening Post, 29 January–1 April 1820. Daily newspaper.

A Letter from the Queen to the King, 1820. Signed by '*Caroline, R*', but written by Cobbett, see p. 120 above.

Cobbett's Sermons, monthly parts, 1821–2.

Preliminary Part of Paper against Gold, 1821. Reprinted from the *Political Register,* 1803–6.

The American Gardener, 1821. Revised as *The English Gardener,* 1828.

Cottage Economy, monthly parts, 1821–2.

Cobbett's Collective Commentaries, 1822. Reprinted Parliamentary articles from a newspaper, *The Statesman.*

A French Grammar, 1824.

A History of the Protestant 'Reformation', monthly parts, 1824–6. Reprinted with notes and preface by Abbot Gasquet, n.d.

Cobbett's Poor Man's Friend, 5 parts, 1826–7.

The Woodlands, 7 parts, 1825–8.

A Treatise on Cobbett's Corn, 1828.

The Emigrant's Guide, 1829.

Good Friday, or the Murder of Jesus Christ by the Jews, 1830.

Rural Rides, 1830. Reprinted from the *Political Register,* 1822–6. Reprinted with introduction and notes by George Woodcock, Harmondsworth, 1967. An enlarged edition drawing more material from the *Political Register* was edited, with notes, by J. P. Cobbett, 1853, and reprinted with introduction by

Edward Thomas, London, 1912, and introduction by Asa Briggs, London, 1957. A further enlarged edition was edited with introduction and notes by G. D. H. and M. Cole, London, 1930.

Advice to Young Men, 14 monthly parts, 1829–30; reprinted with preface by Philip Snowden, London, 1926.

Eleven Lectures on the French and Belgian Revolutions, 1830.

History of the Regency and Reign of George IV, monthly parts, 1830–4.

Cobbett's Plan of Parliamentary Reform, 1830. Reprinted from the *Political Register*.

Cobbett's Manchester Lectures, 1832.

A Geographical Dictionary of England and Wales, 1832.

Cobbett's Tour in Scotland, 1832. Reprinted from the *Political Register*.

Cobbett's Legacy to Labourers, 1835.

Cobbett's Legacy to Parsons, 1835.

Cobbett's Legacy to Peel, 1836. Reprinted from the *Political Register*, 1835.

Selections from Cobbett's Political Works, eds J. M. and J. P. Cobbett, 6 vols, 1835–7. Selections from *Porcupine's Works* and the *Political Register*.

Works on Cobbett

Clark, M. E., *Peter Porcupine in America* (Philadelphia, 1939).

Cole, G. D. H., *The Life of William Cobbett* (London, 1924; 3rd edn rev., 1947). The best 'Life' of Cobbett by anyone other than Cobbett.

Cole, G. D. H., ed., *Letters from William Cobbett to Edward Thornton, 1797–1800* (London, 1937).

Hazlitt, W., 'William Cobbett', *Table Talk*, vol. I (1821); reprinted in *The Spirit of the Age* (2nd edn, 1825) and in *Complete Works of William Hazlitt*, ed. P. P. Howe, vol. VIII (London, 1930). Still the best short critical account.

Osborne, J. W., *William Cobbett: his Thought and his Times* (New Brunswick, N.J., 1966). The most useful body of comment on Cobbett's ideas.

Pearl, M. L., *William Cobbett, a Bibliographical Account of his Life and Times* (Oxford, 1953). The fullest bibliography; its annotations provide a useful guide to Cobbett's life.

Reitzel, W., (ed.), *The Progress of a Plough-boy to a seat in Parliament* (London, 1933); reprinted as *The Autobiography of William Cobbett* (London, 1967). This strings together autobiographical parts of Cobbett's writings to form the best available 'Life'.

Biographies

The following 'lives' of Cobbett are of some interest, but all are inferior to G. D. H. Cole's.

Bowen, Marjorie, *Peter Porcupine* (London, 1935).

Briggs, A., *William Cobbett* (London, 1967).

Bibliography

Carlyle, E. I., *William Cobbett* (London, 1904).

Chesterton, G. K., *William Cobbett* (London, n.d.).

Melville, L., *Life and Letters of William Cobbett*, 2 vols (London, 1913).

Pemberton, W. Baring, *William Cobbett* (Harmondsworth, 1949).

Smith, E., *William Cobbett*, 2 vols (London, 1878).

Index

Index

Index